The Dakota Prisoner of War Letters

Dakota Kaŝkapi Okicize Wowapi

THE DAKOTA PRISONER OF WAR LETTERS

DAKOTA KAŜKAPI OKICIZE WOWAPI

Clifford Canku and Michael Simon

Introduction and Afterword by John Peacock

Minnesota Historical
Society Press

CLEAN
WATER
LAND &
LEGACY
AMENDMENT

Support for the translation of these letters was provided by the Institute for Regional Studies' Gunlogson Fund at North Dakota State University, with additional funding from the Shakopee Mdewakanton Dakota Oyate.

www.mhspress.org
The Minnesota Historical Society Press is a member of the Association of American University Presses.

10 9 8 7 6 5 4 3 2 1

∞ The paper used in this publication meets the minimum requirements of the American National Standard for Information Sciences—Permanence for Printed Library Materials, ANSI Z39.48-1984.

International Standard Book Number

ISBN: 978-0-87351-873-4 (paper)

Image credits: pages xii and 212 are from Post and Reservation File (#12 and #19, respectively), Davenport, Iowa, Record Group 92, National Archives. Courtesy Jim Jacobsen and Davenport Public Library. Letters on pages xviii and xx–xxi are from the Stephen R. Riggs and Family Papers, Minnesota Historical Society.

This book was designed and set in type by Wendy Holdman. The typeface is Minion Pro.
Lisa Himes wrote the index.

Library of Congress Cataloging-in-Publication Data

Canku, Clifford.
    The Dakota prisoner of war letters = Dakota Kaskapi Okicize Wowapi / Clifford Canku and Michael Simon ; introduction and afterword by John Peacock.
        pages   cm
    Includes bibliographical references and index.
    ISBN 978-0-87351-873-4 (pbk. : alk. paper)
        1. Dakota Indians—Wars, 1862–1865—Personal narratives. 2. Dakota Indians—Iowa—Davenport Region—Correspondence. 3. Indian prisoners—Iowa—Davenport Region—Correspondence. 4. Prisoners of war—Iowa—Davenport Region—Correspondence. 5. Dakota language—Translating into English. I. Title.
E83.86.C36   2013
973.7—dc23
                                                                                    2012051270

DEDICATION

Calling the spirits
Of the Dakota Prisoners of War,

Aŋpetu de nitawapi do
This is your day.

We are grandchildren in the present
To whom you give this responsibility:

These letters
you hand down to us
tell future generations
That the people may end their afflictions
and live.

A spirit
came in a vision
and told us to do this.

And when we doubted whether we could complete what he asked us to do
Wakaŋboide [To Make a Sacred Blaze] came in a dream to tell us:

Taŋyaŋ ecanupi do
You are doing good.
Wasaġiciyapi wo
Be strong.
Our relatives are watching over us.

We are humbled
as we honor our ancestors.

Woecon kiŋ de unyakupi do
We accept this responsibility you gave us.

We do this for you and for the students.

De unkiyepi do.
This is us.

Mato Watakpe   Charging Bear   Clifford Canku
Akicita Cistina   Little Warrior   Michael Simon
With the assistance of *Zitkadaŋ Sapa*   Black Bird   John Peacock

Contents

Spiritual Foundation
Dakota Prisoner of War Letters of 1862–1866

Dr. Clifford Canku

In 1998, a visitor came to me from the *Wanagi Makoce,* the spiritual world. At this time I was a faculty member of the Sisseton Wahpeton College (SWC). I was busy viewing student papers in order to assign grades to them when a spirit appeared by my desk for a moment, after which I looked up, and the spiritual visitor disappeared.

Ta-oyate-duta = His People Red

Afterward I received a call from Flandreau Santee Dakota elders, who asked me to assist them in translating letters in the Dakota language, which they had received from the Minnesota Historical Society (MHS). I agreed, and for two years we translated a total of twenty-four letters. Each time I came, the team felt the spirit of Ta-oyate-duta and Crows come around them. As translation team members felt the presence of Ta-oyate-duta's spirit, they recalled that his remains were buried at the First Presbyterian Church of Flandreau, South Dakota. The Dakota elders on this original translation team included William Beane, Syd Byrd, Ellen Weston, Elmer Weston, Margaret Weston, Mona Mayasota, and Agnes Ross. These letters remained with them in Flandreau.

After the funding ran out in Flandreau, I mentioned the importance of the Dakota POW letters to the administration at Sisseton Wahpeton College. With the help of then President Dr. Elden Lawrence and Dean Harvey DuMarce, we traveled sometime in 2005–6 to the archives of the Minnesota Historical Society, where we flagged about two hundred letters for photocopying. We hired Bill Iron Moccasin, a Lakota elder, and three other Dakota elders: Michael Simon, Hildreth Venegas, and Doris Robertson. Using the photocopies now filed in the SWC archives, this team translated over a hundred letters before the project ended.

Wakaŋboide = Sacred Blazing Fire

I retired from SWC in 2008, when I was recruited to teach at North Dakota State University (NDSU) that fall. The following spring, Michael Simon and I, with others, traveled once again to the MHS archives, this time to flag the Dakota POWs' letters so that the archives staff could send us electronically scanned copies. It was a dream of ours to finally get these letters translated and put into book form. The task was slow and started afresh, this time with grant funding from NDSU's Gunlogson Fund and the Shakopee Mdewakanton Dakota Oyate. We found about a hundred letters, but many of these letters were too faded to read and some were written by those outside the camp. In this book we have selected fifty of the most legible and interesting Dakota POW letters to translate into English. Many of them, written in clear handwriting, deal with Christianity, which is not surprising. Stephen R. Riggs was a Presbyterian missionary, and many of the prisoners who wrote to him had studied with him and the Pond brothers, Samuel and Gideon, starting in the 1840s. We found no letters written by Riggs to the prisoners.

In the winter of 2012, when the project seemed overwhelming, I had a dream. A spirit came to me in my dream. I was at the Sun Dance tree holding a bundle in my hands. An old Dakota man appeared with a small Dakota boy by his side. They came from the east gate/door, and they stopped four times to announce the old man's name. The man said, "*Wakanboide miye do.*" As he stood in front of me, he looked up at me. With a very handsome face, he said to me, "*Hau, wicohaŋ ecanupi kiŋ de waŝte do*" (Yes, The work you are doing is good, it is so). He said, smiling as he looked at me, "*Wacin ibosakapi ŝni po. Taku waŝte icanunpi do*" (Do not be discouraged for what you are doing is good, it is so). He turned around and walked back toward the east door.

It was apparent that what we have been doing with the Dakota POW letters is expected to be shared with others at this time. Dakota people who face this difficult past squarely and discover their own families' stories can move beyond anger and anguish. We hope that our work will encourage further research and study of other Dakota letters that lie untranslated in regional and national archives. Dakota students who learn their language and do the difficult work of translation will publish more books that take us all to a new age, where Dakota people tell their own history to the world.

Hau, mitakuyepi. We are chosen by our ancestors to do this translation project. It is truly an awesome task, and we have done our best to complete this task in a sacred manner. *Hau, mitakuye owasiŋ caŋte waŝteya nape ciyuzapi do.*

An oral version of this text was presented at the Dakota Legacy of Survival, Flandreau, SD, August 17, 2012, on the 150th anniversary of the first battle of the 1862 Dakota–U.S. War.

Translator's Preface

Michael Simon

Hau mitakuyepi caŋte etaŋhan owasiŋ iyuśkiŋyaŋ nape uniyuzapi (Yes, our relatives, from the heart we gladly shake your hand).

This book is dedicated to the Dakota *akicita wicakaśkapi* (prisoners of war). When the *Oyate* gathers together, there is an honoring song sung for Dakota warriors who have returned from war. The song goes like this:

> *Oyate ki kawitaya au ca, ecas mikśuyapo*
> When the people gather, you must remember me,
> *Dakota hokśina heya ka akicita iyaye*
> Saying this, Dakota boy went away to be a soldier.

There was great *oiyokiśica unkahinḣpayapi* (a great sadness fell upon our people) after the Dakota–U.S. War in 1862. The *akicita* prisoners, who suffered great injustice, were never honored. With honor, hope, and humbleness of heart we dedicate this song to some great akicita. Although death claimed them, they are still alive in spirit. They were not afraid to die because they lived as true warriors. They loved and wanted goodness for family and *Oyate*. It is only fitting that we remember them as they continue to live in these letters. Following the tradition of our Dakota *Oyate*, we translators show honor and respect and remember these warriors as we dedicate an honoring song composed by Ron, Shane, and Wambdi Cook, who are relatives of the translators.

Dakota Akicita Wicakaśkapi
Wicaunkiksuyapi Odowan—A Remembrance Song

> *Dakota akicita wicakaśkapi—niohan nauŋhoŋpi*
> Dakota warrior-prisoner—Your actions we have heard
> *Niye okiŋihan ka waŋiditaka*
> You are honorable—You are brave
> *Tuŋkaŋśidaŋ naŋikciziŋpi*
> The Great Spirit defended you

Prisoner Background

The Dakota *akicita wicakaśkapi* were imprisoned at Camp Kearney adjacent to Camp McClellan, Davenport, Iowa. The military commission, which sentenced the Dakota warriors to prison, were unrestrained when it came to sentencing. Approximately 265 men were sent to Camp Kearney, ranging in clusters of ages: 15–30, 31–50, 51–65+. In addition, there were sixteen women, plus two children. The women were listed as nurses (two), cooks (ten), and laundresses (four). Although the women were sent to the prison as workers, they were still listed as prisoners. One of the women was a daughter of Little Crow. The younger men were mostly students learning to read, write, and interpret both Dakota and English. These young men were considered promising scholars. One of the letter writers wrote about a number of these young men disappearing from camp one night, never to be heard or seen again. Although an inquiry was made to prison officials, there was no response.[1]

Some of the young and middle-aged men were being educated in religious studies, which included reading, interpretation of scripture, and preaching. The Rev. Dr. Thomas S. Williamson created a religious academy within the prison to educate some of the men to become preachers. One prisoner, named Caske/Robert Hopkins, was one of the most advanced students. He was taught to perform marriages and to administer the sacraments. The prison's religious academy became the forerunner for the Santee Normal Training School, established at Santee, Nebraska, to educate all Dakota persons interested in religious studies.[2] The value of this institution to the Dakota was that many learned to play the piano and organ and many became preachers and leaders in the church.

In time, many of the middle-aged men worked outside the prison under guard for the farmers and to do other manual labor jobs. However, in the first year and a half, the prisoners were confined to the prison, usually wearing shackles, and hardly ventured out; those who didn't work outside made trinkets, beadwork, woodcarvings, clothing, and mittens. Most of the articles were sold to local citizens. During the first two years, it appears that the men were not permitted to create warm clothing or blankets; as a result, many men froze to death during the winter. One of the letter writers writes about the prisoners being ordered to remove the stoves from the barracks. The prisoners thought they were going to be given new stoves and complied. Instead, they went without heat until the prisoners were allowed to reinstall the old stoves. Not all the guards were cruel, but some just couldn't resist inflicting punishment and pain on those unable to resist.

Indian Prisoners' Quarters, looking northeast, Camp Kearney, drawn by Henry Lambach, Davenport City Surveyor, probably late in 1865.

As a consequence, many prisoners died from sickness, while others froze to death. The prisoners write about the deaths in these letters, giving rough counts and naming those who have passed. Stephen R. Riggs, the Presbyterian minister to whom these letters were written, estimated that 120 Dakota people died in the camp; this may have included the deaths of others who were captured after the war and brought to the camp.[3]

Our Personal Experiences as Translators

This project was completed in the hope that the continuing mistreatment, the miscarriage of justice, and the oppressive and dominating mentality expressed and perpetrated toward Dakota people that caused the Dakota–U.S. War could change. However, in all too many cases, that mindset continues to live on in the current dominating mentality that influences U.S domestic and foreign policy today.

Dr. Canku tells elsewhere of the visions that have inspired and supported his work. When he shared his vision of Wakaŋboide with me, I became energized for two reasons:

1. At first, I thought I might be the cause of the translation project's floundering and the many obstacles that kept blocking our path, but now I realized it was not me, personally, but the spirit posed a challenge to each of us if we were going to see the project through to completion.

2. Wakaŋboide was my great-great-grandfather's son. I was taken back eight years to 2002, when, while I was engaged in a vision quest, the *Wakiŋyaŋ* (Thunderbeings) came and struck a tree near me and started it on fire. As it was thundering, I heard a voice say between the lull of thunder, "*Wakaŋboide de miye*" (Sacred Blazing Fire—this is me). This was my grandfather speaking. At the time, I did not know the reason, but now I realize why.

It was in 2002 that I became acquainted with the Dakota Prisoner of War letters and was recruited to work on the translation project. When I first read some of the letters I experienced a variety of emotions, which I express here in Dakota and translate to Modern Dakota English (MDE):

Dakota Akicita Wicakaśkapi Wowapi tokaheyaȟ bdawa uŋkaŋ iyomakiśica hehan caŋmaze hehan tawaciŋ ǫa caŋte maksawaha se ececa (When I first read the Dakota prisoner of war letters I grieved, then I became angry and finally brokenhearted).

There's a Dakota word, *caŋtiyapa aŋ* (injured feeling), for those that went through *wokakize* (suffering) and oppression and heartache. The way that I dealt with these emotions, so I could be rational rather than emotional, was by going into the *inipi* (sweat lodge).

Oinikaga wan mahed uŋkipi ǫa Tuŋkaŋśidaŋ okokiyakapi ǫa waceuŋkiyapi (We made a sweat lodge ceremony, went in, and told the Great Spirit, and prayed to him). In the *inipi*, one of spirits came to me and said, "*Caŋtesice śni wo tokśta ouniciyapi kta*" (Don't be sad; we will help you).

• • • •

The authors have considered development of this book as a religious search. The Dakota would call it "*taku wauŋkuwapi*," a search for Dakota justice for those who suffered greatly protecting their diminishing homeland, but it is also the beginning of a healing process. There must be justice before healing, an acknowledgment and acceptance, on both sides, of the tragedy of 1862. Dakota justice involves speaking or talking about the oppressive actions; the Dakota saying "*mitakuye owasiŋ*" (we are all related) must be practiced; here the communities must use different healing patterns. For the Dakota, these involve ceremonies such as the "Wiping of Tears." A return to traditional practices helps Dakota communities acknowledge their trauma.

The history of this war is told in other books, and people who want to read that story can find it elsewhere, including descriptions of the Doctrine of Discovery, Manifest Destiny, and all the "justifications" whites used to take the land. In this book, we show the prisoners' point of view and try to have the prisoners tell their own story. Some of them had probably wanted to go to war, and some of them had not. But all of them had experienced the four main reasons behind the Dakotas' decision to go to war: 1) the land was overwhelmed by the intrusion of white settlers, and both the U.S. federal government and Minnesota state government had reduced the Dakota land base by 24 million acres in deceitful treaties for fifty-seven years; 2) the annuities, agreed upon in the treaties and consisting of food, shelter, clothing, horses, cattle, poultry, and crop seed, were not paid on time, leading to starvation for the Dakota; 3) pressure to conform to Christian ways and values were leading to the loss of Dakota culture and religion; 4) reduction of hunting grounds plus depletion of fish in lakes, streams, and rivers led to the Dakotas' inability to physically support themselves and thus increasing dependence on the promised annuities.

The Dakota realized that the white settlers were not honest in their dealings with them and were determined to take the Dakota ancestral homeland because they were obsessed with greed and had a voracious appetite for the land. The American dream is illusory and economically discriminatory, but today it has become the basis for the judicial, legislative, and executive branches of government at both state and federal levels. In most legal cases involving Native Americans, which come before state or federal courts, the Native American often has no chance of winning.

As we consider the historical events of 150 years ago, very little has changed in regard to the attitudes and behavior of the average Euro-Minnesotan toward the Dakota people. There is no public showing of brotherly/sisterly love and affection. The Civil War battles of 1862 are part of the history taught to school kids, but the Dakota–U.S./Minnesota War's dark shadows on Minnesota history have often been deliberately ignored.

Tokata ektakiya taku kta he (What's in the Future?)

Dehaŋ decen uŋkaŋpi ǫa uŋnipi šta tóhiŋni wašteuŋdakapi kte šni kiŋ héoŋ tehikauŋdapi. Tuwe wauŋyakapi ǫa táku uŋkeyapi kta šta šúŋka iyecen waciŋuŋkiyuzapi kte ciŋhe sdonuŋkiyapi. (Although we are alive right now, they will never like us, and for us that's too difficult to live with. We realize that whoever sees us, and no matter what we say to try to defend ourselves, the white people will think of us as dogs.)

Waŝicuŋ owasiŋ uŋtapi cíŋpi tuka akeŝ úŋŝiuŋdapi ǫa dehaŋ ŝkaŋŝkaŋ uŋyakoŋpi. (At first the white people wanted to kill all of us, but since then, they relented and have compassion on us, and we're able to move around.)

—Wakanhdi Topa/David Faribault, May 18, 1863, Davenport, Iowa

In 1987 the State of Minnesota, urged by the Minnesota Historical Society and the Dakota Studies Committee, proclaimed a "Year of Reconciliation" for whites and Indians, attempting to heal the bitter heritage left by the war of 1862. In response to this gesture at "the idea" of reconciliation, some older Dakota leaders such Amos Owen, Ernest Wabasha, Eli Taylor (from Canada), Maude Bluestone Williams, and others were asked to react. Their responses can be summed up by Eli Taylor's words: "I hope it does some good. But I don't think it will. I don't think many people know about it. It was a long time ago and not many people care." In the words of Maude Bluestone Williams, "Way after my people came back here—my mother and father were married in 1910—they still walked the woods and went along the tops of the hills. They still tried to stay out of sight when they could, because it just wasn't good to be an Indian. But mostly, they [the whites] ignored us and we ignored them. I never had a white friend when I was growing up."[4] Amos Owen, Eli Taylor, and Maude Bluestone Williams have since passed to the spirit world.

In the words of Peter Clark of Roseville, Minnesota, "Our perceptions of Indians was changed forever, and attitudes of whites who had abused Indians for so many years left a lasting scar on our history." Norman Tegen of Hopkins, Minnesota, says, "Minnesota Nice is a phrase I don't like very well especially when I think about the Dakota Conflict. There is a painting in the Minneapolis Institute of Art titled Minnesota Nice against a backdrop of an 1862 map [with] silhouettes of the Mankato gallows, mounted soldiers and down cast Indians on foot in the direction of the Dakota Territory. On the right hand border is a long listing of treaties broken by the federal government."[5]

How long must a "lasting scar" last? Many names have been given to the war over the years: the Great Sioux Uprising, the Dakota Conflict, the U.S.–Dakota War, and now the Dakota–U.S. War. It is still Minnesota's most painful, most tragic story, and we all live with its consequences.

In 1987, the State of Minnesota proclaimed a year of reconciliation, but to date it has produced only token gestures toward accepting and restoring the aftereffects of the "tragic conflict" of 1862. Likewise, South Dakota proclaimed in February 1990 a "Year of Reconciliation" but has done little to bring out in the open the illegal taking of land and other abominations committed, all justified by Manifest Destiny and progress toward the "American Dream." In 1990, Ada Deer, a Menominee leader who later became head of the Bureau of Indian Affairs, responded to a *New York Times* article on South Dakota's attempts at reconciliation written by Jack Rosenthal: "If this is to be a sincere effort toward genuine reconciliation, the historic and compelling injustices involving broken treaties and broken promises must be addressed. Let us remember actions speak louder than words."[6]

• • • •

A Final Tribute

We have made great effort to be true to the letter writers, the Dakota *akicita wicakaśkapi,* so a fitting tribute to close with is a Dakota prayer song sung at Sun Dances and other ceremonies:

> *Wakaŋtaŋka oŋśimada*
> Great Spirit, have pity on me
> *Wani waciŋ ca decamon do*
> I want to live and I do this
> *Omakiya yo makakiże do*
> Help me, I am suffering

We have shared these Dakota *wowapi* (letters), for they personify the struggle of a people for their way of life. Our hope is that young Dakotas will learn their language, culture, history, and heritage so that they can stay within the *hocoka,* the center. It is sad when our young lose their cultural center because they then fall outside of the circle and become disconnected from the *Oyate.* This is known in Dakota as *onuniya uŋpi ce* (lost and wandering about). We need to get back to the *Caŋku Duta* (Red Road) and *piya akan maunipi kta* (we will walk on it in a new way).

This *wocekiye* (prayer) is inscribed on a plaque in Mankato's Reconciliation Park.

> Grandfather I come to you this day
> in a humble way to offer prayers
> for the thirty eight Dakota who perished
> in Mankato in the year 1862.
> To the West, I pray to the Horse Nation
> and to the North, I pray to the Elk people.
> To the East, I pray to the Buffalo Nation
> and to the South, the Spirit people.
> To the Heavens, I pray to the Great Spirit
> and to the Spotted Eagle.
> And Below, I pray to Mother Earth
> to help us in this time of reconciliation.
> Grandfather, I offer these prayers
> in my humble way.
> To all my relations.
>
> Amos Owen

Acknowledgments

This project has benefited from the work that Dr. Canku and Mr. Simon shared with other Dakota first speakers, and the translators gratefully acknowledge this debt. In 1998 William Beane and Mona Mayasota at the Flandreau Santee Sioux Reservation invited a number of elders to participate in a project to translate letters from the Riggs papers, funded by the Rosebud Sioux Tribe. The translators included William Beane, Syd Byrd, Clifford Canku, Ellen Weston, Elmer Weston, Margaret Weston, Mona Mayasota, and Agnes Ross. The elders on this project worked together, discussing the correct translation of each word, and learned much from each other about how to approach the challenging work. About twenty-four letters were fully translated in two years. The Flandreau project retains ownership and possession of those translations.

That project's funding ran out, and the translation work stopped. In the winter of 2005–6, Sisseton Wahpeton Tribal College, under the leadership of then President Dr. Elden Lawrence, began another translation project. Elders on the project included Bill Iron Moccasin (Lakota) and Sisseton Wahpeton Dakota elders Doris Robertson, Hildreth Venegas, Clifford Canku, and Michael Simon. In this project, translators worked on letters separately but consulted with and learned from each other. That project ended in 2008, and Sisseton Wahpeton Tribal College retains ownership and possession of those translations.

In 2009 a third translation project was started at North Dakota State University. With support from the Gunlogson Fund and the Shakopee Mdewakanton Sioux Community, Dr. Canku and Mr. Simon gathered a new set of copies of the letters and began a new translation project. Thus this work is separate from but deeply informed by the earlier projects.

Dr. Canku and Mr. Simon would also like to express *wopida taŋka,* many thanks, to Dakota transcriptionist Sandra (Sandee) Geshick from the Lower Sioux Dakota Community; to Šišokaduta Joe Bendickson from the Sisseton Wahpeton Dakota Nation and Caŋtemaza Neil McKay from the Spirit Lake Dakota Nation for proofreading and adding diacritical marks to the Dakota letters; to Glenn Wasicuna from the Sioux Valley Dakota Nation for reading the final manuscript; to English transcriptionists Jody Snow, Rebecca West, and Stash Hempeck; to translation team manager Dr. Bruce Maylath, professor of English, North Dakota State University; and to Pamela McClanahan and Ann Regan, director and editor in chief, respectively, of the Minnesota Historical Society Press.

Davenport Iowa
Apr 17. 1865.

S. R. Riggs

Mitakuye Ito wowa
cicage kta wacin Nakaha Wotanin
Naonhonpi Tonkansidan ktepi keyapi
tuka kecen tuwe taku tanyan onkokiye
kapi kta iye ece śni heon mitakuye
wowapi cicu eya taku wanjikji nawahon
wacin ga heon den wowapi kin cicage yedo
Tonkansidan he onsiondapi ga de hanyan
onyakonpi tuka hecen Nakaha ktepi
keyapi heon cante onsicapi tona onkiyu
kcanpi hecinhan hena cante onsicapi
hehan hecen isantanka kin hecen
token cante onkiyazapi kta nacece
idukcen hecinhan omayakidaka
wacin ga heon wowapi cicage yedo
hehan Tonkansidan Tonkansidan token
ktepi hecinhan he tanyan nawahon
kta wacinyedo hehan eya Anpetu
Wakan eca token owakihi hecen
wahokun wica wakiye. Henana epe kte
owasin Nape ciyuzapi

Mowis Itewakanhdiota
Hemiyi

Mowis Itewakaŋhdiota to S. R. Riggs, April 17, 1865 (Letter 37)

Introducing the Dakota Letters

John Peacock (Spirit Lake Dakota)

For participating in the Dakota–U.S. War of 1862, thirty-eight Dakota men were hanged at Mankato on December 26 of that year. The following April, approximately 265 more Dakota men, also condemned to death, but not executed, were marched in shackles into Camp McClellan, a military prison at Davenport, Iowa. There they wrote letters in the Dakota language. Fifty of these, written by more than three dozen of the condemned men, have now been translated into English by two of the letter writers' Christian Dakota descendants, Dr. Clifford Canku and Mr. Michael Simon, themselves members of the last generation in the United States of mother-tongue, fluent Dakota speakers.

Both translators were born on the Sisseton-Wahpeton Dakota Nation's reservation in South Dakota and grew up speaking Dakota as their first language. Now in their seventies, they are traditional Sun Dancers and retired Dakota Presbyterian ministers (Mr. Simon formerly headed the Dakota Presbytery). Both men have told me that their training at seminary in translating Biblical languages helped them translate the Dakota letters. They think of the letters not merely as historic documents but as *sacred texts*—as revelation of a Dakota apocalypse and as prophesy of the Dakota expulsion and exodus from their Minnesota homelands, the male letter writers to Davenport; their wives, children, and dependent elders first to a prison camp at Fort Snelling and then into the desert at Crow Creek.

These letters were written from a place of sadness and loss. As Mr. Simon says in his preface, the prisoners were held at Camp Kearney, a portion marked off from Camp McClellan in December 1863. The overcrowded barracks, built of green wood, offered little protection from the Iowa winter, and the prisoners were not provided adequate fuel. They were kept shackled for months. Sixteen Dakota women, brought along to cook and launder for the prisoners, also lived in the camp with their children. By 1864, men were taken out of the camp under guard to cut wood and work in nearby farm fields. That summer, a group of Dakota families—ninety men, women, and children who had been picked up at Pembina—were imprisoned with them. At least 120 people died of smallpox and other ailments at Camp Kearney. In the spring of 1866, President Andrew Johnson finally pardoned the men, who were then sent west to meet their families.[1]

The letter writers first learned to write in the Dakota language in prison at Davenport, earlier in another prison at Mankato, or earlier still in mission schools. In all these places, missionaries worked to convert Dakota people to Christianity, in part by teaching them to read and write their once entirely oral language, for which missionaries had created a writing system and into which they had translated the Bible and various Christian hymns and liturgies.

With the exception of a letter addressed to General Henry Hastings Sibley, most of the Davenport letters are addressed to *Tamakoce* (His Country), the name the Dakota had given to missionary Stephen Riggs, whom the writers also frequently address in the body of their letters as *mitakuye*, Dakota for "my relative."

In his own writings, Rev. Riggs often makes reference to the other prison at Mankato, where the prisoners had been incarcerated before being moved to Davenport, minus the thirty-eight

May Anpetu 3. th 1864.

Mitakoda Tamakoce
Nakaha ake Wowapi Cicage
Tuka dehan wacinciza tuka
anpetu kin, dehan nina
cante maśica waonyedo
mitawin tokinigaga tanin
śni keyapi kin heon nina
cante maśica tuka wanihan
mate kte keyapi nakaha he
naceskihon onkan dehan
koken awacin makeca tohan
mate kte cinhan kohannarin
wakantanka tikin ekta
wai kta e nikin miciye
śni ke epca tokeśta tuwe
mayaco kinhan tokeśta ićeya
he tokata woyaco kin chanin
kta epca ecin dehan wanikiya
eyapi kin he wacin waoyedo
hehan kicizapi kin he winohinca
hokśiyopa ko wicaktepi kin

Robert Hopkins Caske to Mitakoda Tamakoce (My friend Rev. S. R. Riggs),
May 3, 1864, page 1 (Letter 8)

heon ekta yeya i heon kehan
mate kta tuka naceca he
owotanna ecamon kta wacin
onkan he wiconte owade keca
ma kinpi kin he imaite tuka
heon makaikapi kin tohanyan
makizaikapi ini kin hehanyan
wicohan sica wanjidan ecamon
ini ke epca heon owotanna waon
kta wacin iho henana epe kta
micante on Nape Ciyuzapi
mitawin kici

mitakuze Robert Hopkins
Caske he mizeco

pehan ito woyute kin on
teriya onkanpi heen ito
tanyan waontapi yakuwa
wacin yeclo

Robert Hopkins Caske to Mitakoda Tamakoce (My friend Rev. S. R. Riggs),
May 3, 1864, page 2 (Letter 8)

executed at Mankato. The Davenport prisoners continued what they had begun at Mankato, which Riggs referred to as "one great school." In prison, Riggs writes, "these Sioux have made as much progress in education as in twenty six or twenty seven years" of missionary efforts before the war to teach Dakota how to read and write in their own language. At Mankato, the prisoners had also written some four hundred letters that Riggs's fellow missionary Thomas Williamson delivered to the male prisoners' relatives—mostly their wives and children—at the Fort Snelling prison camp.[2]

If any of these family letters still exist, they are carefully held in family hands; while none of the Davenport letters were written by any of the thirty-eight executed Dakota, their voices may some-day be heard through those family letters.

With the exception of the Sibley letter, which was found in the National Archives in Washington, DC, the letters translated here are from a total of approximately 150 such letters in the Riggs family papers at the Minnesota History Center. These fifty were selected mainly because they are among the most important of the faded handwritten manuscripts, others of which Dr. Canku and Mr. Simon may try to decipher and translate at some later date. The two men thought it appropriate to give readers the first fifty letters during the 150th anniversary of the Dakota–U.S. War of 1862 and its aftermath.

It is important to remember that the letters were written to Riggs, who had built a mission at Lac Qui Parle in 1837 and worked unceasingly to convert the Dakota to Christianity. In writing to Riggs, some prisoners protested their innocence on the grounds that either they had not fought in the war at all or that they had been forced to fight by more hostile Dakota. (Riggs and his colleague Williamson were able to persuade Abraham Lincoln to pardon over fifty of the prisoners in 1864, two years before Lincoln's successor Andrew Johnson freed the rest.) Other prisoners wrote asking for gospels to read and hymnals to sing in Dakota, and they promised Riggs they would attend communion and stop drinking. Some of the prison writers seemed to be very apt disciples of Rev. Riggs, or at least a literally captive audience to the trinity Riggs preached of Christ, literacy, and temperance.

After the fifty letters were selected, they were photocopied, painstakingly typed, and translated into literal word-for-word English, following the Dakota word order. The question then arose: should the final idiomatic English translation be in Standard English, Dakota English, or some combination of the two?

To answer this question first requires a few more words about the translators. They have spoken at innumerable conferences and lectured at tribal and mainstream colleges—Dr. Canku extensively, as instructor of Dakota language and culture at North Dakota State University. Both men speak Standard English in many of these contexts, but they also speak Dakota English on many informal tribal occasions—for example, at lunch at the tribal senior center and when ordering corn soup at the powwow fry bread stand. Their Dakota English is frequently laced with an informal version of the Dakota language, known as fast-speech, itself full of English loan words. As elders for whom the Dakota language is their mother tongue, they also speak formal Dakota on ceremonial occasions, singing Sweat Lodge songs, offering prayers there and at the Sun Dance.

Now, what exactly *is* Dakota English? Dakota English is a stable, well-documented, rule-governed, predictable dialect that has been spoken and written across the reservations of North and South Dakota for more than a century. Known colloquially as "Rez English," it is influenced in part by the way words are pronounced and sentences formed in the Dakota language itself. For example, in the Dakota English sentence *Long time ago when we talk Indian they wash our mouth out with soap,* past time is marked not by the Standard English verb tense suffix *–ed* (talk*ed* / wash*ed*) but by a past-tense adverbial phrase, *long time ago,* which in Dakota would be translated *ehanna,* placed at the beginning of a Dakota sentence.[3]

William Leap, author of *American Indian English,* suggests that a Dakota English sentence's variation from Standard English is primarily determined by the Dakota language's grammar and syntax. Linguist Beverly Olson Flanigan argues, however, that marking past time by adverbs rather than verb tenses is primarily a residue of many of the simplified pidgin Englishes that Anglophone explorers and traders once used to speak not only to Dakota but to other peoples around the globe in early contact relationships.

> That this contact language did not long continue to be used by all Indians in all areas is clear and not surprising: acculturation, intermarriage, and relatively peaceful contact in the eastern part of the United States led to the rapid demise of such a pidginized English, often within one or two generations. But in the [American] West, where wars, reservation confinement, and increased hostility toward the natives led to isolation and suppression, the forms used in the first contacts became in some areas relatively stable . . . as the English lexicon expanded and communicative needs increased.[4]

Leap's and Flanigan's perspectives are not mutually exclusive. But Leap's conclusion that Dakota English owes more to the Dakota language than to pidgin English is definitely sustained by how closely Dr. Canku and Mr. Simon's translations into Dakota English follow the original Dakota language of the Davenport prison letters, even with respect to three features of Dakota English that Flanigan says derive primarily from contact pidgin English.[5]

The first feature of Dakota English is multiple negation. (In the following example, as is true throughout this book, the first line presents the original Dakota; the second is a word-for-word English translation that preserves the Dakota word order; and the third is Dakota English.)

Tuka okini tuwedaŋ hecoŋ kta śni epca
But maybe nobody to do that will not I think
But I don't think nobody will do that.[6]

The second feature of Dakota English is possessive constructions by word order rather than case ending (as in standard English apostrophe *s*).

waŋna Waŋmdi Oŋpiduta tipi wikcemna om Ḣeipa ikiyedan ahdite kéyapi
Now Eagle Redtail family ten together Hillhead near settled they said.
Now they have said Redtail Eagle family of ten tipis camped near Hillhead.[7]

In Standard English, this might be translated, "Redtail Eagle's family of ten tipis is now camped near Hillhead, they said."

The third and most important feature of Dakota English pertains to what both Flanigan and Leap call topic/comment constructions. "The topic of a sentence . . . is stated first, with a comment [that] follow[s and] elaborates," writes Flanigan, who provides examples of simple Dakota sentences and their Dakota English equivalents: *He śuŋka kiŋ mitawa.* That dog, it is mine. *Wašte kiŋ icu wo!* The good one, take it![8] More complex sentences have been described by Franz Boas and Ella Deloria in their *Dakota Grammar*:

> The general syntactic structure is . . . the subject followed by all its qualifiers open[ing] the sentence which closes with the verb preceded by all its qualifiers . . . each . . . qualif[ying] the [next]: [e.g.,] 'carrying them ‖ nice place-a ‖ searching for ‖ he went'; i.e., he went searching for a nice place while carrying them.[9]

Such sentences are elaborated by what Flanigan and Leap both call backing and filling repetitions—the most common discourse feature to be found in the Davenport prison letters, both in the original Dakota and in the elders' Dakota English translations. Here is an example:

Wicaŝta	den	kaŝka	uŋkaŋpi	dena	waziyata	áye		ciŋ	oŋnuŋpapi
Men	here	imprisoned	we are	these	north	they go together		the	two of us

There are some men imprisoned here, if allowed, two of us can go with those going north

kiŋhaŋ	om	wóuŋhdakapi	kta	iyececa
if	with	talk to them	shall	like/such as

and speak to the authorities on our behalf.

In Standard English, this might be translated, "If two of us imprisoned here are allowed to go with those that are going north, we can speak to the authorities on our behalf."[10]

An English speaker reading such sentences in the original Dakota usually takes in the topic/ comment at the beginning of the sentence, then glances to the verbal construction at the end, and then reads the rest of the sentences from the end back to the beginning—right to left—continuing first with the verbal modifiers and then the modifiers of the original noun phrase topic. On one hand, Flanigan concludes that "such constructions are not, in themselves, evidence of pidgin origins, nor are they evidence of [D]akota transfer"; on the other hand, she says, "the [Dakota] syntax requires [such constructions]."[11] According to William Leap,

> Right-to-left syntactic constructions are common occurrences in [Dakota] English syntax, they are in [Dakota] language tradition, and persons who participate regularly in [Dakota] English conversations are accustomed to retrieving meaning from sentences and paragraphs constructed in these terms.[12]

Paragraphs are constructed in these terms not only when the topic of each sentences is repeated back and filled in by the predicate of the sentence, but also when all the sentences in the body of the paragraph repeat back and fill in the gist of the paragraph's topic sentence. Indeed some paragraphs in the body of the entire text repeat back and fill in the opening paragraph. At all of these levels, Dr. Canku and Mr. Simon's Dakota English translations remain faithful to the original Dakota language. This recursiveness is what Flanigan, in her analysis of other Dakota English texts, describes in a non-pejorative way as "a 'long windedness' which is typical of [D]akota story-telling."[13] Flanigan quotes the following story as an example:

My grandmother, close to bedtime, she would soak dried cherries and soak it and then pound it. She had a big round dried cowhide like a bowl. She used to pound cherries in that. Well, she put the cherries in that after they're soaked. Then she'd pound them. Then she'd make *wojapi* [pudding] and then we'd say. 'Oh, boy! Grandma's gonna *hunkanka* [tell stories] tonight!' She'd make fry bread, *wojapi* and we'd eat that. She'd put us all to bed and then she'd sit and *hunkanka*.[14]

A Standard English version of this paragraph might read, "When we saw Grandma soak cherries in her big dried cowhide bowl, and then pound them into pudding, we'd say, 'Oh, boy! Grandma's gonna tell stories tonight!' She'd make fry bread, and after we'd eaten the fry bread and pudding, she'd put us to bed and tell us stories." Comparing the two versions, the Standard English paragraph is two sentences, with Grandma mentioned twice by proper name and twice by the pronoun *she*. By contrast, the Dakota English paragraph contains nine sentences, with Grandmother mentioned by proper name or by pronouns a total of eleven times.

Listen now for backing/filling repetition not just within individual sentences but as an organizing feature of the whole text of the following Dakota English translation of one of the Davenport prison letters. This letter is addressed to *Tamakoce*, or "His Country," the Dakota name of missionary Stephen R. Riggs:

One of my relatives, His Country, I will write this letter to you—it is so. Because I will tell you how I am. Lately, I was very sick, but because God has pity on me, I am fine and he healed me—it is so. Recently, I am fine—it is so. So are you okay as well? I will pray for you—it is so.

Then, one of my relatives, recently, I want that one of your prayers will be written down, because it's been awhile. We have not been visited by any ministers—it is so.

Thus, one of my relatives, now, all negative thoughts, I will not have them—it is so. Thus, my relative, from here on, God will always pity me. I will say—it is so.

Thus, in the future, if I will join in communion, I want to take part. So from here, I will help you—it is so. Thus, if you tell me what not to do, I want to do what's right—it is so.

Then, I want to tell you one thing, recently Major Forbes wrote me a letter, saying soon you will be released. This he told me—it is so. So, my relative, I want you to see Major Forbes, and I want someone not related to me to tell me, because it is so. I have not participated in any bad things our Dakota have done, now I have suffered terribly for a long time, but maybe this is all in God's plan. God may want me to go through all this for his sake. Maybe if he pities me, I will go home. I want his help—it is so. That is all I will say. I shake your hand—it is so.

This is me, Antoine Provençalle[15]

I could see what Flanigan and Leap meant by backing/filling repetitions in the sentence *Thus, in the future, if I will join in communion, I want to take part. So from here, I will help you—it is so.* But I could not really perceive backing/filling repetitions as a discourse feature at the whole text level of this prison letter until I tried to turn Dr. Canku and Mr. Simon's Dakota English translation of the letter into the following Standard English:

My relative His Country,

I write to tell you I was very sick but am healed and doing fine now by the grace of our compassionate God, whom I pray will also keep you in good health.

For a long time no minister has visited us, so would you send a written prayer?

I am keeping from negative thoughts and want in the future to take communion. I will help you from here, so tell me what not to do; I want to do what's right.

The other thing I want to tell you is recently Major Forbes wrote saying I will be released soon, so I want you to see him and I want someone not related to me to tell me it is so. I have participated in none of the bad things our Dakota have done, though I have suffered a long time. It may be God's plan for me to go through all this for His sake, but perhaps His compassion will lead to my release. All I can say is I need His help.

I shake your hand, Antoine Provençalle

In turning the Dakota English into Standard English, I deleted twelve instances of "it is so" [in Dakota *do*], the rhetorical flourish with which a traditional Dakota man typically ends his declarative sentences. More significantly, I also cut the number of times that the term of address "my relative" appears in this letter from five down to one. In the Dakota English, as in the original Dakota, half of those five repetitions are then filled in in the rest of each sentence in which the term of address appears with what the letter writer is asking Riggs for: e.g., "one of my relatives, I want that one of your prayers will be written down"; "my relative, I want you to see Major Forbes." The remaining repetitions of "my relative" appear with what the letter writer is giving Riggs: e.g., "one of my relatives, I will write this letter to you . . ." In writing "one of my relatives, now, all negative thoughts, I will not have them—it is so. Thus, my relative, from here on, God will always pity me. I will say—it is so," Provençalle is giving Riggs what Riggs most wanted from the prisoners—evidence of a true conversion. The evidence is not just in Provençalle's message but in the epistolary medium for that message, literacy in general being the medium of missionization, and letters in particular being the evidence of literacy in prison. How pleased Riggs must have been to receive a letter that keeps repeating in so many ways and filling in its salutation to him, "One of my relatives, His Country." This repeated invocation of kinship is not just a term of address; kinship is the very topic of the letter, of every paragraph, of each sentence. The rest of every sentence, of the body of every paragraph, then addresses what is predicated on kinship—exchange between kin. In reducing those five repetitions of "my relative" down to one, I had unwittingly gutted the letter's structure as an elaborate kinship exchange, an exchange that Provençalle indicates he wants to keep going: "Thus, in the future, if I will join in communion, I want to take part."

Antoine Provençalle was one of my own ancestors. What Provençalle most wants from Riggs is help getting released from prison. Is Provençalle's Christian conversion the resignation of a defeated, apprehended, and convicted Dakota abandoning his culture? Or is Provençalle's Christian conversion and offer to take communion the signifying practice of a mixed-blood using the familiar bicultural resources of Christian conversion and Dakota traditional kinship exchange to negotiate his release?

In helping men like Provençalle commute their sentences, were Riggs and his colleague Thomas Williamson making conversion to Christianity a condition of release? If so, was this implicit bargain key to the far more numerous conversions Riggs and Williamson made among the prisoners than among free Dakota people before the war? In general, were the prisoners true converts, or dupes, or were they playing along in hopes of extricating themselves from jail? Were the prisoners, as has been suggested by recent historians without full access to the Davenport letters, engaging with Riggs and Williamson, their *wotakuyepi* or kinsmen of another kind, in ceremonially giving up their traditional gods in exchange for their skins?[16]

Were the prisoners converting to Christianity, not by way of assimilating to white culture but by way of adapting Christianity for their own purposes and according to their own practices, as Dakota people had done with so much else in the white man's world—his horses, his weapons, his tools, his trade goods?

Never would such questions have occurred to me had the Dakota English translation of Provençalle's letter finally been rendered into Standard English. In cutting repetitions of "my relative," I thought I was simply following an editorial instinct I had developed over years of editing my own writing—an instinct that I think of as *squeezing the water out* of my sentences, that is, reducing repetition by constructing longer sentences with relative clauses, so as not to have to keep repeating the subject of the sentence, even with pronouns. Instead of being "long winded," I have always wanted my writing to flow in sentences that drew the reader straight through left to right. It has never occurred to me to want readers to read my sentences in the way I have described reading a sentence in Dakota or in Dakota English. Anything of the kind would have suggested to me that my sentence had failed to be understood by the reader, never that this was a desirable way to read sentences, much less individual paragraphs, and certainly not whole texts.

I know I am not the only English-speaking reader with such assumptions. After one of our early conference presentations of the Dakota English translations, an academic in the audience gently suggested that the translations needed further work to make them more idiomatically "correct" in English. Dr. Canku and Mr. Simon made me aware of her concerns, and I attempted a sample edit. When I read it to them, they didn't say anything. They just winced. My notes from that meeting drew the distinction between the dialects for the first time: "Shall I discuss with Clifford and Mike their Dakota English versus my Standard English translation, and ask them why they thought I went too far?"

When we discussed the question, Dr. Canku and Mr. Simon revealed that many years ago, in their formal training in divinity school to be Presbyterian ministers, they both had had to struggle to get some of their non-Native professors to approve of the way they naturally wrote in Dakota English. Present at this discussion was Sandra Geshick, a Dakota woman who was helping transcribe the prison letters, and she chimed in that her own academic writing in English was currently receiving some of the same kinds of negative responses from non-Native professors in a graduate program she was in the process of deciding to leave. Ms. Geshick, Mr. Simon, and Dr. Canku all appeared visibly relieved when I responded by saying I was not going to edit any more of their translations so as to make them more "idiomatic" in Standard English, as opposed to what they had written, which we now started calling Dakota English.

Dakota English is, after all, closer to whatever English the letter writers might have heard or spoken in 1862 and to the way they had formed sentences in the Dakota language in which they originally wrote the letters.

Of course, the Dakota language in which they originally *wrote* the letters did not exactly correspond to how they *spoke* their language in 1862. At that time, the Dakota language had only existed in written form for thirty years, having been developed by Riggs and other missionaries in 1832 in order to translate the Bible into Dakota as a tool for conversion. The language of the Davenport prison letters is thus a hybrid of the Dakota the prisoners *spoke* and the Dakota they learned from the missionaries to *write,* observing some of the familiar conventions—salutation, ending, and so forth—of nineteenth-century letter writing.

Non-Native readers in general and non-Native academics, in particular, may hear Dakota English as flawed English, evidence of poor education or substandard ability.[17] This would be wrong. To paraphrase William Leap, those of us who strive to learn directly from Dakota people—"within culturally significant Dakota contexts"—need to follow Dakota rules for speaking, reading, and writing English, not impose expectations of correctness established in the non-Dakota world.[18] There are traditional Dakota speakers who are skeptical that a book in Standard English can ever be a culturally significant Dakota event. These translations in Dakota English are for them.

A Note on the Translations

The translators have used the oldest Dakota dictionary available, Stephen R. Riggs's *A Dakota-English Dictionary*, published in 1890, as their main resource. It is a fitting connection: Riggs taught the Dakota how to write, and they taught him Dakota. The orthography used to write Dakota words was changing in the 1860s, as the transcripts show, and conventions have continued to change since 1890.

Organization and Orthography

The Dakota version provided on the left page of each spread shows the translation process. The first line is a transcription of the original Dakota using modern spellings (employing a system developed by Dr. Canku, based on the Riggs dictionary), the second line is a word-for-word translation to English, and the third line presents a Modern Dakota English translation, as discussed in the introduction to this book. On the first line, non-standard accented syllables are marked, for the easier use of language learners, but the punctuation and capitalization of the original letters has been preserved. In addition, the version on the left sometimes includes corrections of errors made by the letter writers. In the first letter, for instance, Wiŋyaŋ writes "waoŋ niyakapi," which means, "you hate to live"; what she means is "waoŋ niwakapi" or "I hate to live." (*Wauŋ* and *waoŋ* are used interchangeably in the letters.) An arrow at the bottom of a page indicates that the letter continues without a break.

The Dakota text on the upper right-hand pages of this book reproduces, to the best of our ability, the exact Dakota text as originally written. The writers usually did not use capital letters to start sentences or periods to end them, and only a few writers used paragraphs, which are reproduced here with indented text. Many writers split words at the ends of lines without indicating word breaks. We have preserved the letters' original spellings (sometimes clearly erroneous), capitalization, punctuation, and orthography. Many of the writers use alternate characters for ċ (ç), ħ (ħ and r), ķ (q), ɋ (q), ṡ (ṡ and x), ŧ (ṭ and ţ), and ż (j). Some writers use both x and ṡ in the same letter. The letter writers often use *oŋ* where *uŋ* is now considered correct. A letter writer may sign his name as one word in one letter and as two words in another; we have followed the original spellings but used single words in the contents and headings. We have tried to standardize the translations of Dakota names, but there are many correct ways to translate them, and in a few cases we provide alternatives.

The layout of the letters in this book approximates the layout of the original letters. Each translation is signed with the translator's initials: Clifford Canku/Mato Watakpe is CC/MW, and Michael Simon/Akicita Cistina is MS/AC.

Dating and Locating the Letters

Forty-nine of the letters that are translated in this book are held in the Stephen R. Riggs and Family Papers at the Minnesota Historical Society, where they are available to researchers; Letter 2, the fiftieth, is in the National Archives in Washington, DC. As this book goes to press, the Riggs letters are being individually cataloged and prepared for posting online.

Several letters in the Riggs papers present particular challenges. Letters 15 and 16 are both written on the same sheet of paper, as are letters 30 and 31; Letter 21 is written across two different pages, with other letters written on their versos.

Dakota Alphabet

Accents on Dakota words usually fall on the second syllable. Variations are marked.

LETTER	SOUND	DAKOTA	ENGLISH
a	father	ate	father
b	boy	bdo	potato
c	chore	canku	road
ĉ	(exploded)	ciĉu	to give you
d	day	do	it is so
e	they	ŝákpe	six
g	give	ŝuŋgmanitu	wolf
ġ	(guttural)	hoġan	fish
h	hello	haŋpi	juice
ĥ	(guttural)	wówiĥa	funny
i	machine	ina	mother
k	kite	káta	hot
ķ	(exploded)	ķa	and
m	mouse	mni	water
n	new	nina	very
ŋ	(nasal) ink	táŋka	large
o	go	to	blue
p	party	aŋpetu	day
Þ	(exploded)	pow Þo	fog/mist
ɋ	(exploded)	ɋa	and
s	see	ska	white
ŝ	shower	ŝíca	bad
t	town	tonana	few
ŧ	(exploded)	ŧe	dead
u	choose	dúta	red
w	warn	wo´wapi	book
y	yellow	yam´ni	three
z	zebra	mázaska	money
ż	azure	pétiżanżan	lamp

The Dakota Prisoner of War Letters

Dakota Kaŝkapi Okicize Wowapi

1   April 25/63

2a pa yuȟa.   mitakuye   nakaha   wówapi   wanži   cícaǧe   ye
2b Curly Head   my relative   now   letter   one   make for you   it is so
2c My relative Curly Head, now I write a letter to you—it is so.

3a nakaha   nína   caŋte   maśice   ye   he nayahoŋ   kte   mdokehaŋ   táku   tehika
3b now   very   heart   sad/bad   it is so   you hear   will   last summer   thing   terrible
3c Now my heart is very broken—it is so.   Last summer, we all know one terrible event

4a wanži   sdononyapi   óŋkaŋ   óhiŋni   nina   caŋte   maśice   tuka   dehan   ake   iyotaŋ
4b one   we all know   and   always   very   heart   sad/bad   because   now   again   more
4c has occurred, and always we are very heartbroken, because now again,

5a nínahiŋ   caŋte   maśice   waniyetu   kiŋ   de   tehiya   oŋyakoŋpi   tuka   wacadan
5b very much   heart   sad/bad   winter   the   this   terrible   we all are   because   without
5c my heart is broken very much, because this winter we are without, we are all suffering.

6a waoŋ   niwakapi   ye   tóken   waŋna   tókiya   oŋkayapi   kte   ciŋhaŋ
6b I am   hate to live   it is so   and   now   where   take us   will   if
6c I hate to live—it is so.   And now where will they take us?

7a ehake   ȟiŋ   waoŋ   niwakapi   kte   nace   epca   tuka   mdokehaŋya   hdiya kupi
7b yet   very   I am   hate to live   will   maybe   thought   because   last summer   come home
7c Yet, I hate to live, because I thought last summer, if the

8a ḳehaŋ   wicahuŋka   wica atku   tóki   eȟpeya   iwicayaye   ciŋ   iyecen   nína   caŋte   maśice
8b when   men   fathers   here   taken   have gone   the   like   very   heart   sad/bad
8c men and fathers come home, where have they taken them?   My heart is very broken,

9a tuka   eciŋ   óhiŋni   caŋte   mayakiye   nakaś   hemacece   Tuka   waŋna
9b because   so   always   heart   consider me   and   I am like this   because   now
9c but always you are considerate of me, and I am like this because now

10a wókiyapi   kta   hehan   waŋciyakapi   kta   nace   epca   hehan   caŋte   waśteya
10b make peace   will   then   I see you   will   maybe   I thought   then   heart   good
10c they will make peace, I thought then, I will see you.   Then I am good hearted,

11a waoŋ   tuka   táku   wakaŋ   iye   óŋśioŋdapi   ḳa   waoŋkiciyakapi   tuka   dehan
11b I am   because   thing   sacred   him   pity us   and   we see each other   but   now
11c because the Holy Spirit has pitied us and is with us.   But now

12a tókiya   oŋkayapi   kta   sdonoŋkiyapi   śni   ḳa   héoŋ   waŋna   tóhiŋni
12b where   take us   will   we know   not   and   therefore   now   never
12c we don't know where they will take us, and therefore I thought maybe we will never

13a waŋciyakapi   kte   śni   nace   epca   óŋkaŋ   héoŋ   nínahiŋ   caŋte   maśice
13b see you all   will   not   maybe   I thought   and   therefore   very   heart   sad
13c see all of you, and therefore my heart is very sad.

>

1. Wįyaŋ, April 25, 1863

April 25/63

payuha. mitakuye nakaha wowapi wanji cicage ye nakaha nina cante maxice ye henayaron kte mdokehan taku terika wanji sdononyanpi onkan ohini nina cante maxice tuka dehan ake iyotan ninarin cante maxice waniyetu kin de teriya onyakonpi tuka wacadan waon niyakapi ye tokex wana tokiya onkayapi kte cinhan ehake rin waon niyakapi kte nace epca tuka mdokehanya hdiya kupi qehan wicahunku wica atku toki erpe ya iwicayahe cin iyecen nina cante maxice tuka ecin ohini cante mayakiye nakax hemacece Tuka wana wokiyapi kta hehan waciyakapi kta nace epca hehan cante waxteya waon tuka taku wakan iye onxiondapi qa waonkiciyakapi tuka dehan tokiya onkayapi kta sdononkiyapi xni qa heon wana tohini waciyakapi kte xni nace epca onkan heon ninarin cante maxice

>

· · · ·

1. A Woman, April 25, 1863

April 25/63

My relative Curly Head, now I write a letter to you—it is so. Now my heart is very broken—it is so. Last summer, we all know one terrible event has occurred, and always we are very heartbroken, because now again, my heart is broken very much, because this winter we are without, we are all suffering. I hate to live—it is so. And now where will they take us? Yet, I hate to live, because I thought last summer, if the men and fathers come home, where have they taken them? My heart is very broken, but always you are considerate of me, and I am like this because now they will make peace, I thought then, I will see you. Then I am good hearted, because the Holy Spirit has pitied us and is with us. But now we don't know where they will take us, and therefore I thought maybe we will never see all of you, and therefore my heart is very sad.

>

The version of each letter at top right is a letter-for-letter transcription of the original document. Spellings in the Dakota version on the left-hand page have been modernized. See p. xxix.

14a tuka eya maȟpi kiŋ héci táku wakaŋ óŋšioŋdapi kiŋhaŋ waoŋ kiciyakapi kte
14b but to say heaven the there thing holy pity us if I am be with will
14c But, I said, maybe there in heaven the Holy Spirit, if he pities us, I am thinking we will see

15a eciŋ waoŋ hécen tókiya éoŋhnakapi kta nayaȟoŋ héciŋhaŋ omayakidake kta waciŋ
15b I think I am thus where they place us will you hear if so tell me will I want
15c each other. Thus, if you hear where they plan to place us, I want you to tell me.

16a hehan wicakaškapi kiŋ tókiya éwicahnakapi héciŋhaŋ hena ḳoŋ odake kta waciŋ
16b then prisoners the where put them where ever these all you tell will I want
16c Then, I want you to tell me wherever they have put all these prisoners,

17a óhiŋni tuwe taŋyaŋ táku oŋkokiyakapi kiŋ hena oŋhnayapi cée héoŋ
17b always someone right thing tell us although these lie to us always therefore
17c although someone always tells us something good, they lie to us, therefore what's real,

18a tóken ȟiŋ nayaȟon kiŋ iye ceŋȟin omayakedaka waciŋ nakaha nicoŋkśi waŋži
18b what real hear the that truthful tell me I want recently your daughter one
18c I want you to tell me, you hear the truth. Recently, your daughter

19a ite okaġapi maḳu kiŋ wašte wadake ḳa piwada tohan yau ni waoŋ
19b face picture gave me the good I consider and thankful when you come alive I am
19c gave me a portrait, I think it's good, I am thankful. If I am alive that long,

20a kiŋ hehaŋyaŋ yuha waoŋ kte nakaha misuŋka waŋmdake šni eyayapi hécen
20b the that long have I am will recently my brother I saw not took him then
20c when you come, I will have it. Recently, I did not see my brother, then they took him,

21a nína waceye ḳa nína caŋte mašice óŋkaŋ nina pe mayazaŋ ḳa wamayazaŋ
21b very crying and very heart sad/bad and very head hurt and sick
21c and I was crying and very heartbroken, and my head hurt badly, and it seemed like I was sick.

22a kte sécece niš wówapi waŋži miye caġe kte waciŋ henana epe kte
22b will it seems you letter one me make will I want all say will
22c I want you to write me a letter, that's all I will say.

23a niciŋca om ape ciyuze ca i iciputake ye nitakuye wíŋyaŋ he miye
23b your son's with hand shake so kisses it is so your relative woman this me
23c I shake your son's hand with kisses—it is so. This is your relative Woman.

24a pa yuȟa AnaJune wówapi waŋži wécaġe tókiya oŋ kiŋ he sdonyaye
24b Curly Head AnaJune letter one make for where at the this you know
24c I wrote a letter to Curly Head AnaJune, you know where she is,

25a niye yeyakiye kta waciŋ dakota wówapi yawapi taŋyaŋ oŋspe šni kta
25b you send it will I want Dakota letter read good know not will
25c I want you to send it, she does not read Dakota well.

26a idukcaŋ kiŋhaŋ isaŋtaŋka ca oyakaġe ca yaku kta waciŋ
26b you think if long knife so writing so give him will I want
26c If you can write it in Long Knife [English], I want you to give it to her.

tuka eya marpi kin heci taku wakan onxiondapi kinhan waon kiciyakapi kte ecin waon hecen
tokiya eonhnakapi kta nayaron hecinhan omayakidake kta wacin hehan wicakaxkapi kin
tokiya ewicahnakapi hecinhan henakon odake kta wacin ohini tuwe tanyan taku onkokiyakapi
kix hena onhnayaupi cee heon token rin nayaron kin iye cenrin omayakedaka wacin nakaha
niconkxi wanji ite okagapi maqu ki waxte wadake qa piwada tohan yau niwaon kin hehanyan
yuha waon kte nakaha misunka wanmdake xni eyayapi hecen nina waceye qa nina cante maxice
onkan ninape mayazan qa wamazan kte seecece nix wowapi wanji miye cage kte wacin henana
epe kte nicinca om nape ciyuze ca iiciputake ye nitaku winya he miye

payuha AnaJune wowapi wanji we cage tokiya on kin he sdonyaye ni ye yeyakiye kta
wacin dakota wowapi yawapitanyan onspe xni kta idukcan kinhan isantanka ca oyakage ca yaqu
kta wacin

· · · ·

But, I said, maybe there in heaven the Holy Spirit, if he pities us, I am thinking we will see each
other. Thus, if you hear where they plan to place us, I want you to tell me. Then, I want you to
tell me wherever they have put all these prisoners, although someone always tells us something
good, they lie to us, therefore what's real, I want you to tell me, you hear the truth. Recently,
your daughter gave me a portrait, I think it's good, I am thankful. If I am alive that long, when
you come, I will have it. Recently, I did not see my brother, then they took him, and I was crying
and very heartbroken, and my head hurt badly, and it seemed like I was sick. I want you to
write me a letter, that's all I will say. I shake your son's hand with kisses—it is so. This is your
relative Woman.

I wrote a letter to Curly Head AnaJune, you know where she is, I want you to send it,
she does not read Dakota well. If you can write it in Long Knife [English], I want you to give it
to her.

CC/MW

1   Davenport Iowa
2   Camp McClellan – May 18th 1863

3   Gen. H. H. Sibley
4   Dear Sir   I will write you this letter in the Sioux Language again and
5   you will please to excuse us for writing you so often about this matter.

6a   Wópetoŋhaŋska – Táku waŋżi waŋna ókini   oiyapa   tuka   ake   nahaŋȟiŋ wówapi
6b   General Sibley   what one   now   perhaps proclaim but   again yet   letter
6c   General Henry H. Sibley—All the men are together on this, and we wanted to write this letter about

7a   uŋniĉupi wicaŝta owasiŋ yuwitaya hécen   uŋciŋpi Wicaŝta táku waŋżidaŋ eciyapi
7b   we give   men   all   together therefore   we want man   what one   called
7c   the news that has just come out.   There's a man named "That One"

8a   he   owotaŋna tuka wówapi uŋicaġapi úŋkaŋ wicaŝta waŋżidaŋ Caskedaŋ eciyapi he
8b   that   straight   but   letter   we make   and   man   one   First Son   called   that
8c   we are writing about—he's an honest and straight man, but there's one named "First Born Son,"

9a   S. R. Riggs wówapi ķu   hécen   he   tóken eya   eŝta   wicake ŝni.
9b   S. R. Riggs letter   gave therefore   that how   to say although truthful not
9c   who wrote a letter to S. R. Riggs, no matter what he says, he's not truthful.

10a   hehan wicaŝta kaŝka   uŋkaŋpi kiŋ witaya   tóken waciŋuŋyaŋpi he
10b   Then   men   imprisoned sitting here the   together how   depend upon   that
10c   These men sitting here in prison together depend upon you, and now

11a   waŋna nayaȟun. tuka wicaŝta ihdawapi   ķa   dakota tóna   om   taŋkan
11b   now   you heard   but   men   count one's self and   friends   which with   outside
11c   you have heard us.   But there's some men who consider themselves friends of those on the outside,

12a   yakonpi kiŋ hena wíkopapi   ókini táku waŋzigzi uŋ   ŝicaya caźeuŋyatapi
12b   they are the those they are afraid maybe what some   to be badly   mention by name
12c   but the Dakota are afraid of them, we are thinking, maybe they said something bad

13a   nace   uŋkeciŋpi   héoŋ   akihde   wówapi uŋniĉupi
13b   perhaps we are thinking therefore more than once letter   we give you
13c   about us, that's why we are continually writing to you.

14a   hena anawicayaġoptaŋpi kte   ŝni iyececa uŋdakapi.   he   de   táku
14b   those listen to them   shall/will not   like   our opinion   that this what
14c   In our opinion, you shouldn't listen to those persons.   There's one thing

15a   oŋdapi tuka ninaȟin   uŋciŋpi tuka he   táku waŝte ece   uŋciŋpi.
15b   we ask   but   exceedingly we want but   that what good   only   we want
15c   we really want and are asking for, and it's only good.

16a   Waziyata eyaye   ciŋ hena om   tacaŋ uŋwaŋżipidaŋ
16b   north   they have gone the   those with   body   we are one
16c   Those that have gone north, we remain one body with them.

>

2. Wakanhdi Topa/David Faribault, Jr., May 18, 1863

Davenport Iowa
Camp McClellan May 18th 63

Gen. H. H. Sibley

Dear Sir I will write you this letter in the Sioux Language again and you will please to excuse us for writing you so often about this matter.

Wopetonhanska—Taku wanji wanna onkini oiyapa tuka ake nahanhin wowapi oniçupi wicaxta owasin yuwitawa hecen uncinpi Wicaxta taku wanjidan eciyapi he owotanna tuka wowapi onicagapi unkan wicaxta wanjidan Caskedan eciyapi he S. R. Riggs wowapi qu hecen he token eya exta wicake xni. hehan wicaxta kaxka unkanpi kin witaya token wacinunyapi he wanna nayarun. tuka wicaxta ihdawa qa dakota tona om takan yakonpi kin hena wikopapi okini taku wanzigzi on xicaya cajaonyatapi nace onkecinpi heon akihde wowapi oniçupi hena anwicayaroptanpi kte xni iyececa ondakapi. he de taku ondapi tuka ninarin uncinpi tuka he taku waxte ece uncinpi. Waziyata eyaye cin hena om tacan onwanjipidan

>

• • • •

2. Four Lightning/David Faribault, Jr., May 18, 1863

Davenport Iowa
Camp McClellan—May 18th 1863

Gen. H. H. Sibley

Dear Sir I will write you this letter in the Sioux Language again and you will please to excuse us for writing you so often about this matter.

General Henry H. Sibley—All the men are together on this, and we wanted to write this letter about the news that has just come out. There's a man named "That One" we are writing about—he's an honest and straight man, but there's one named "First Born Son," who wrote a letter to S. R. Riggs, no matter what he says, he's not truthful. These men sitting here in prison together depend upon you, and now you have heard us. But there's some men who consider themselves friends of those on the outside, but the Dakota are afraid of them, we are thinking, maybe they said something bad about us, that's why we are continually writing to you. In our opinion, you shouldn't listen to those persons. There's one thing we really want and are asking for, and it's only good. Those that have gone north, we remain one body with them.

>

17a   ǫa   takuwicuŋyaŋpi   tuka   iye   káǧapi   ǫa   dehaŋ   iyotaŋhaŋiyeuŋkiyapi
17b   and   our relatives   but   he/she   have made   and   now   we are experiencing difficulty
17c   Our relatives have caused the war, but now we are experiencing great difficulty because of it.

18a   ǫa   mdokehaŋ   taŋhaŋ   hokšiyopa   winuĥiŋca   takuwicuŋyaŋpi   wahdag
18b   and   last summer   since   children   women/wives   our relatives   to see one's own
18c   Since last summer, we have not seen our children, wives, and relatives,

19a   uŋkicakiżapi   ǫa   teĥike   uŋdapi   tuka   iye   he   takuwicuŋyaŋpi
19b   we have suffered   and   hard to bear   consider   but   he/she   that   our relatives
19c   and we feel it's too difficult of a burden to bear.   Some of our relatives [Mdewakanton]

20a   apa   káǧapi   ǫa   wicohaŋ   šíca   waŋ   dehaŋ   yuštag   uŋkakiżapi.
20b   some   they made   and   deed   bad   a   now   vanquished   we are suffering
20c   have done bad deeds, now we're defeated and suffering because of it.

21a   takomni   he   ikce wicašta   wicohaŋ   kiŋ   he   yušicapi   ǫa   owasiŋ   uŋtapi   iyececa
21b   always   that   common man   deed   the   that   they spoiled   and   all   we die   like
21c   They have already ruined the work of the common man, for that we will probably all die.

22a   tuka   dehaŋ   niuŋkaŋpi   unkiyepi   šni   tuka   dena   héca   wiuŋcaštapi   nakaeš.
22b   but   now   we are alive   we ourselves   not   but   these   such   we are men   truly/indeed
22c   Indeed, we are all alive at this time because we're not like them, but we are men.

23a   wašicuŋ   owasiŋ   uŋtapi   cíŋpi   tuka   akeš   úŋšiuŋdapi   ǫa   dehaŋ
23b   white men   all   we die   they want   but   again   they pity us   and   now
23c   At first the white people wanted to kill all of us, but since then, they relented and have compassion

24a   škaŋškaŋ   uŋyakoŋpi.   hécen   héoŋ   uŋkiš   táku   wašte   waŋżi
24b   to stir/move about   we are   so   therefore   we   what   good   one
24c   on us, and we're able to move around.   For that reason, if there's one thing good

25a   ecawicuŋkicuŋpi   uŋkokihipi   kiŋhaŋ   he   ecen   ecuŋkuŋpi   uŋciŋpi.
25b   we can do for them   we are able   if   that   so   we will do   we want
25c   we can do for them, we want to do this.

26a   ǫa   wašicuŋ   iyepi   uŋ   etaŋhaŋ   owasiŋ   uŋtapi   kta   iyececa   héoŋ
26b   and   white men   they   to be   from   all   we die   shall   like/such as   therefore
26c   The white men think we should have all been killed because of what happened, but we were not, so

27a   etaŋhaŋ   ece   ecuŋkuŋpi   iyececa.   uŋdakapi   ǫa   héoŋ   óta   uŋkeyapi.
27b   from   usually   we will do   like/such as   our opinion   and   therefore   many   we say this
27c   in our opinion, we should go ahead and do it.   And many of us are saying we should.

28a   wicašta   den   kaška   uŋkaŋpi   dena   waziyata   áye
28b   men   here   imprisoned   we are   these   north   they go together
28c   There are some men imprisoned here, if allowed, two of us can go with those

29a   ciŋ   oŋnuŋpapi   kiŋhaŋ   om   wóuŋhdakapi   kta   iyececa
29b   the   two of us   if   with   talk to them   shall   like/such as
29c   going north and speak to the authorities on our behalf.

>

qa takuwicunyapi tuka iye kagapi qa dehan iyotahaniyeonkiyapi qa mdokehantahan hokxiopa
winurinca takuwicunyanpi wahdag onkicakijapi qa terike ondapi tuka iye he takuwicunyanpi
apa kagapi qa wicoran xica wan dehan yuxtag onkakijapi—takomni he ikcewicaxta wicoran
kin he yuxicapi—qa owasin onṭapi iyececa tuka dehan niunkanpi unkiyepi xni tuka dena heca
wiuncaxtapi nakaex—waxicun owasin ontapi cinpi tuka akex onxiundapi qa dehan xkanxkan
onyakonpi—hecen heon unkix taku waxte wanji ecawiconkicunpi onkokihipi kinhan he ecen
econqonpi uncinpi—qa waxicun iyepi on etanhan owasin unṭapi kta iyececa heon etanhan ece
econqupi iyececa—undakapi qa heon ota onkeyapi—wicaxta den kaxka unkanpi dena waziyata
aye cin onupapi kinhan om wounhdakapi kta iyececa

>

• • • •

Our relatives have caused the war, but now we are experiencing great difficulty because of
it. Since last summer, we have not seen our children, wives, and relatives, and we feel it's too
difficult of a burden to bear. Some of our relatives [Mdewakanton] have done bad deeds, now
we're defeated and suffering because of it. They have already ruined the work of the common
man, for that we will probably all die. Indeed, we are all alive at this time because we're not
like them, but we are men. At first the white people wanted to kill all of us, but since then, they
relented and have compassion on us, and we're able to move around. For that reason, if there's
one thing good we can do for them, we want to do this. The white men think we should have
all been killed because of what happened, but we were not, so in our opinion, we should go
ahead and do it. And many of us are saying we should. There are some men imprisoned here, if
allowed, two of us can go with those going north and speak to the authorities on our behalf.

>

30a   qa   iye   taŋkan   yakoŋpi   qa   tóna   om   dápi   kte   ciŋ   hena
30b   and   he/she/it   outside   they are   and   how many   with   they go   shall   the   those
30c   Those on the outside that are going north and those going with them

31a   tóhiŋni   om   wóhdakapi   kte   śni   nacece   eciŋ   hena
31b   when   with   they talk   shall   not   probably   suppose   those
31c   probably will not speak up for us, we are saying this because those on the outside

32a   wicahnayaŋpi   kta   keciŋpi   kte   ciŋ   héoŋ   heuŋkiyapi   kaiś
32b   they deceive them   shall   they think   will   the   therefore   we said that   or
32c   will think the white people will just fool them again; or

33a   hécen   wókiyapi   śni   kiŋhan   isaŋtaŋka   tóken   tápi   kiŋhan
33b   so/therefore   making peace   not   if/when   Long Knives   how   what way die   if/when
33c   if there's no peaceful relations, then, in what manner the soldiers die,

34a   unkiś   dena   owasiŋ   iyecen   uŋtapi   uŋciŋpi.   takuwicuŋyaŋpi   śta
34b   ourselves   these   all   like   we die   we want   our relatives   although
34c   we ourselves want to die in the same way.   Although the white men

35a   tokawicuŋyaŋpi   kte   waśicuŋ   om   etaŋhan   owasiŋ   uŋtapi   kiŋhan
35b   our enemies   shall   white men   with   from   all   we die   if/when
35c   are not our relatives but our enemies, if we were to die with them,

36a   taŋkaya   caże   uŋkotaŋiŋpi   kta   qa   hécen   waŋżi   uŋnipi   kiŋhan
36b   greatly   name   become known   shall   and   therefore   one   we live   if/when
36c   our name will become greatly known.   Therefore, if one of us can stay alive,

37a   wicaśta   iyecen   unyakoŋpi   kte.   hehan   décen   uŋkaŋpi   qa   uŋnipi
37b   man   like/such as   we are   shall   now   so/this   we are   and   we live
37c   we can, eventually, live free like other people.   Although we are alive right now,

38a   śta   tóhiŋni   waśteuŋdakapi   kte   śni   kiŋ   héoŋ   tehikauŋdapi.
38b   although   when   they won't like us   shall   not   the   therefore   we think it difficult
38c   they will never like us, and for us that's too difficult to live with.

39a   tuwe   wauŋyakapi   qa   táku   uŋkeyapi   kta   śta   śúŋka   iyecen   waciŋuŋkiyuzapi
39b   Who   see us   and   what   we say   shall   although   dog   like   they think of us
39c   We realize that whoever sees us, and no matter what we say to try to defend ourselves,

40a   kte   ciŋhe   sdonuŋkiyapi.   takuwicuŋyaŋpi   waŋna   Miniśośe   ohnayaŋ
40b   shall   if/when   we realize/know   our relatives   now   Missouri River   upon
40c   the white people will think of us as dogs.   We want our relatives now imprisoned

41a   wicahnakapi   hena   iye   nípi   uŋciŋpi   qa   mdokehaŋna   wiconte
41b   imprisoned   those   they   live   we want   and   summer   death
41c   at the Missouri River [Crow Creek] to remain alive.   Last summer we

42a   ehpeuŋkiyayapi   qa   wicaśta   ta   iyecen   tacaŋ   tawaiĉiye   śni   uŋkaŋpi.
42b   we left behind   and   man   die   like   body   to be free   not   we are
42c   left death behind and with no freedom to do what we wanted, we were like dead men.

qa iye takan yakonpi qa tona om dapi kte cin hena tohinni om wohdakapi kte xni nacece
ecin hena wicahnayanpi kta kecinpi kte cin heon heunkiyapi qaix hecen wokiyapi xni kinhan
isantanka token ṭapi kinhan unkix dena owasin iyecen ontapi uncinpi—takuwicunyanpi xta
tokawicunyanpi kte waxicun om etanhan owasin unṭapi kinhan tankaya caje onkotanipi kta qa
hecen wanji unipi kinhan wicaxta iyecen onyakonpi kte—hehan decen unkanpi qa unipi xta
tohini waxteondakapi kte xni kin heon terikaondapi—tuwe waunyakapi qa taku onkeyapi kta
xta xunka iyecen wacinunkiyuzapi kte cinhe sdononkiyapi—takuwicunyanpi wanna Minixoxa
ohnayan wicahnakapi hena iye nipi uncinpi qa mdokehanna wiconṭe erpeunkiyapi qa wicaxta
ṭa iyecen tacan tawaiçiye xni unkapi—

>

. . . .

Those on the outside that are going north and those going with them probably will not speak
up for us, we are saying this because those on the outside will think the white people will just
fool them again; or if there's no peaceful relations, then, in what manner the soldiers die, we
ourselves want to die in the same way. Although the white men are not our relatives but our
enemies, if we were to die with them, our name will become greatly known. Therefore, if one
of us can stay alive, we can, eventually, live free like other people. Although we are alive right
now, they will never like us, and for us that's too difficult to live with. We realize that whoever
sees us, and no matter what we say to try to defend ourselves, the white people will think of us
as dogs. We want our relatives now imprisoned at the Missouri River [Crow Creek] to remain
alive. Last summer we left death behind and with no freedom to do what we wanted, we were
like dead men.

>

43a ókiŋni   he   hécen   ecuŋpi   kiŋhaŋ   nauŋżicapi   kta
43b maybe   that so/therefore they did it if/when we escape   shall
43c The white men were maybe afraid we would try to escape,

44a wašicuŋ   ikopapi   šta   tóhiŋni   hokšiyopa   eȟpeya   nawicuŋżicapi   kte
44b white man   afraid   although never   children   leave/left we escape   shall
44c but we would never do that, because we would not leave the children

45a šni   hécen   he   ikoyapapi   kte   šni   Wašicuŋ   kízapi   uŋciŋpi
45b not   so/therefore that you not afraid shall not   White man fought   we want
45c behind, so you don't have to be fearful of that.   If we wanted to fight

46a kiŋhaŋ   mdokehaŋ   en   uŋkupi   kte   šni   tuka   wašicuŋ   ehna   uŋkicaġapi
46b if/when   last summer in   we come   shall not   but   white man   among   we grew up
46c the white people, we would have never come in last summer, also

47a ḳa   tacaŋ   waŋżidaŋ   om   uŋkihdawapi   iyecen   uŋyakoŋpi   kiŋ   héoŋ
47b and   body   one   with   we count ourselves like   we are   the   therefore
47c we consider ourselves as one body with them, because we grew up with them, so

48a kici   uŋkicizapi   uŋciŋpi   šni   ḳa   en   itoheya   anawicuŋpapi   tuka
48b with   we fight   we want   not   and   at   towards   we run to for protection but
48c we would never fight them.   We are much like them, therefore, we would never fight

49a teȟiya   iyeuŋkicizapi   tuka   táku   wašte   waŋżi
49b with difficulty   they fought us   but   what   good   one
49c them, instead we run to them for protection.   They're the ones who fought us, causing

50a ecoŋkupi   uŋkokihipi   he   ecoŋkupi   uŋciŋpi   kiŋ   heceedan.   niš   nišnana
50b we can do   we are able to that we did   we want   the   only that   you   you alone
50c great difficulty for us; if there's one good thing we can do, we want to do that.   You alone,

51a Wakpa   minišota   ohna   initaŋcaŋ   ḳa   dakota   wicoȟaŋ   taŋyaŋ
51b river   grayish water into/on chief/ruler and   Dakota   work/custom   well
51c General H. H. Sibley, are the Commander in the Minnesota River area and know the

52a sdonwicayaye   héoŋ   nína   waciŋuŋniyaŋpi.   ḳa   héoŋ   waŋna
52b know/have knowledge of therefore   very   we depend upon   and   so   now
52c Dakota custom well, that's why we depend upon you.   We are serious about

53a núŋpa   wówapi   uŋničupi   ḳa   nínaȟin   hécen   uŋciŋpi.   Dakota   taŋkan
53b two   letter   they give and   seriously so   we want   friends   outside
53c wanting peace, that's why we've written twice.   We said to one another,

54a yakoŋpi   he   ecadaŋ   om   wauŋkiciyakapi   kta   keoŋkiciyapi   ḳa   nakuŋ
54b they are   that soon   with   we see each other shall we said to each other   and   also
54c we will soon see each other and be with those on the outside.   The white men

55a wašicuŋ   heyapi   tuka   tóken   uŋkeniciyapi   heceedan   awaciŋ   uŋkaŋpi.
55b white man said that but   how   we say to you   that alone   to think of   we are
55c said to us, no matter what, think only about what we've said to you.

>

okini he hecen ecanupi kinhan naunjicapi kta waxicun ikopapi xta tohini hokxiopa erpeya
nawicunjicapi kte xni hecen he ikoyapapi kte xni Waxicun kizapi uncinpi kinhan mdokehan
en unkupi kte xni tuka—waxicun ehna unkicagapi qa tacan wanjidan om onkihdawapi
iyecen unyakonpi kin heon kici onkicizapi uncinpi xni qa en itoheya anawicunpapi tuka
teriya iyeonkicizapi tuka taku waxte wanji ecunqonpi onkokihipi he ecunqonpi uncinpi kin
heceedan—nix nixnana Wakpa minisota ohna initancan qa dakota wicoran tayan sdonwicayaye
heon nina wacinuniyanpi—qa heon wanna nupa wowapi nicupi qa ninarin hecen uncinpi—
Dakota takan yakonpi he ecadan om waunkiciyakapi kta keonkiciyapi qa nakun waxicun heyapi
tuka token onkeniciyapi heceedan owacin unkanpi—

>

• • • •

The white men were maybe afraid we would try to escape, but we would never do that, because
we would not leave the children behind, so you don't have to be fearful of that. If we wanted to
fight the white people, we would have never come in last summer, also we consider ourselves
as one body with them, because we grew up with them, so we would never fight them. We are
much like them, therefore, we would never fight them, instead we run to them for protection.
They're the ones who fought us, causing great difficulty for us; if there's one good thing we can
do, we want to do that. You alone, General H. H. Sibley, are the Commander in the Minnesota
River area and know the Dakota custom well, that's why we depend upon you. We are serious
about wanting peace, that's why we've written twice. We said to one another, we will soon see
each other and be with those on the outside. The white men said to us, no matter what, think
only about what we've said to you.

>

56a	heceedan	ohna	táku	waŝte	ecuŋkupi	kta	iyecece	uŋdapi	ḳa	tuwe
56b	that alone	in	what	good	we have done	shall	like/such as	we think	and	who
56c	We think that's the only way we can do something good.							And all		

57a	ikcekcen	wicaŝta	tóna	tokahanpi	hena	owasiŋ	he	caże	uŋkokiciwapi	kte.
57b	common	man	how many	who are elderly	those	all	that	name	we write/wrote	shall
57c	the elderly common men here will sign their names.									

58a	Wambdi Táŋka		Maȟpiyawakaŋhdi	Wabashaw's Son
58b	Big Eagle		Lightning Cloud	Red Cap's Son

59a	Heȟaka máza		Aŋpetu waŝte	Red Owl's Son
59b	Iron Elk		Good Day	Red Owl's Son

60a	Makanaȟtake	Son of Maȟpiya Wicaŝta	Tukaŋ ahnamani	Caske ptécedaŋ
60b	Kick the Earth	Son of Cloud Man	Walks with Stone	Short First Son

61a	Hokŝidaŋ dúta	Taiyanku	Napiŝtaŋyaŋ
61b	Scarlet Boy	Comes Home Openly	Lays Violent Hands On

62a	Tate ibomdu	Maȟpiya waŝicuŋ	Iyotaina	Son of Waziamani
62b	Blowing Wind	White Cloud Man	Great One	Son of Walks on Pine

63a	Kaȟo
63b	Throw

64a	Tate winaȟon		Oyemaza	Wakuta	Basden
64b	Hears the Wind		Iron Track	Shooter	Splits with Knife

65a	Wicaŋȟpi dúta	Crow band
65b	Red Star	

66a	Yellow Medicine Man	Maȟpiya Oicaȟmani
66b		Walks Among the Clouds

67a	Hepaŋ Dúta
67b	Scarlet Second Son

68a	Tapeta Táŋka
68b	His Big Fire

69a	Tahoȟpi wakaŋ
69b	His Sacred Nest

70   The different bands—everyone will do just as these [men] will say—

heceedan ohna taku waxte ecunqonpi kta iyecece ondapi qa tuwe ikcekcen wicaxta tona tokahanpi hena owasin he caje onkokiciwapi kte—

Wamdi tanka		Marpiyawakanhdi	Wabashaw Son
Heraka maza		Anpetu waxte	Red Owl Son
Makanartake	son of Marpiya Wicaxta	Tukan ahnamani	Caske ptecedaŋ
Hokxidaŋ dúta	Taiyanku	Nanpi staye	
Tate ibomdu	Marpiya waxicun	Iyotaina	Son of Waziamani
	Karo		
Tate winaron		Oyemaza	Wakuta	Basden
Wicarpi duta	crow band		
Yellow Medicine Man	Marpiya oicarmani		
	Hepan Duta		
	Tapeta Tanka		
	Tahorpi wakan		

The different bands—every one will do just as these will say—

>

• • • •

We think that's the only way we can do something good. And all the elderly common men here will sign their names.

Big Eagle		Lightning Cloud, Red Cap's Son	
Iron Elk		Good Day, Red Owl's Son	
Kick the Earth, Son of Cloud Man		Walks with Stone	Short First Son
Scarlet Boy	Comes Home Openly	Lays Violent Hands On	
Blowing Wind	White Cloud Man	Great One, Son of Walks on Pine	
	Throw		
Hears the Wind		Iron Track	Shooter	Splits with Knife
Red Star	Crow band		
Yellow Medicine Man	Walks Among the Clouds		
	Scarlet Second Son		
	His Big Fire		
	His Sacred Nest		

The different bands—everyone will do just as these [men] will say—

>

71a   Dear Sir   Wicaŝta   tóken   eniciyapi   kiŋ   he   nína   hecen   waciŋ   qa   heoŋ
71b   man   how   they call you   shall/will   that   very   therefore   I want   and   therefore
71c   As a man what is your name, therefore I want to know, that's

72a   nína   epe   do.   takomni   nakahaŋ   kehaŋ   waŝicu   iyecen   wauŋ   waciŋ
72b   very   I say   it is so.   nevertheless   now/lately   then   white man   like   I, to be   want
72c   why I ask so strongly.   However, lately, I want to be like the white man.

73a   qa   tuktedaŋ   miyohaŋ   ŝice   ŝni   úŋkaŋ   dehan   wicohaŋ   ŝica   waŋ   icaga
73b   And   nowhere   my action   bad   not   and   now   work/habit   bad   a   grew/grow
73c   My deeds or affairs were never bad, but now a bad controversy arose

74a   úŋkaŋ   mix   iyoma waża   ŝni   tuka   dehan   opeya   makakiże   qa   woiŝteca
74b   and   I   concerned about   not   but   now   together   with suffering   and   shame
74c   and I am concerned about it and suffering alongside of them.   Now there's great shame

75a   táŋka   sdonwaye   qa   teĥike wadake   teĥiya   wani   ŝta   waŝicuŋ
75b   great   know   and   hard to bear   with difficulty/badly   I live   although   white man
75c   for me, and I find it hard to endure.   Although I live with difficulty, I would

76a   iyecen   wauŋ   kte   imaŝtece   héoŋ   tóken   Dakota   úŋpi   qa
76b   like   to be   shall/will   I am shamed   therefore   however   friends   they be   and
76c   be ashamed to be like the white man.   Therefore, how the Dakota live and

77a   tóken   tapi   kihaŋ   he   iyecen   mate   kta   eciŋ   wauŋ   do.
77b   however   die   to treat   that   like them   I die   shall/will   thinking   about this   it is so.
77c   how they die, I want to die like them, that's what I'm thinking.

78a   tohaŋ   ecanuŋpi   kte   ciŋ   wówapi   waŋżi   unyaķupi   qa   oŋkoyakidakapi
78b   When   you do this   shall/will   the   letter   one   give us   and   tell us about it
78c   When you do this, if you send us a letter and tell us,

79a   uŋkaŋŝ   pida   uŋyayapi   kta   tuka   nínaĥiŋ   waciŋuŋniyaŋpi   qa
79b   if   thankful   you will make us   shall/will   but   especially   we depend upon you   and
79c   you will make us happy and thankful.   We are very dependent upon you here and

80a   ekta   etuŋwaŋ   uŋkaŋpi   kta.
80b   at/to   look towards   we wait here   shall/will
80c   will look forward to seeing you.

81a   Yours   Wakaŋhdi Tópa or David Faribault Jr.
81b   Four Lightning

Dear Sir Wicaxta token eniciyapi kin henina hecen wacin qa heon nina epe do. takomni nakahan qehan waxicu iyecen waun wacin qa tuktedan miyoran xice xni unkan dehan wicoran xica wan icaga onkan mix iyoma waja xni tuka dehan opeya makakije qa woixteca tanka sdonwaye ka terike wadake teriya wani xta waxicun iyecen waun kte imaxtece heon token Dakota unpi qa token ṭapi kihan he iyecen maṭe kta ecin waun do—tohan ecanupi kte cin wowapi wanji unyaqupi qa onkoyacidakapi unkanx pida unyayapi kta tuka—ninarin wacinuniyanpi qa ekta etunwan unkanpi kta.

Yours—Wakanhdi Topa or David Faribault Jr.

• • • •

Dear Sir As a man what is your name, therefore I want to know, that's why I ask so strongly. However, lately, I want to be like the white man. My deeds or affairs were never bad, but now a bad controversy arose and I am concerned about it and suffering alongside of them. Now there's great shame for me, and I find it hard to endure. Although I live with difficulty, I would be ashamed to be like the white man. Therefore, how the Dakota live and how they die, I want to die like them, that's what I'm thinking. When you do this, if you send us a letter and tell us, you will make us happy and thankful. We are very dependent upon you here and will look forward to seeing you.

Yours Four Lightning or David Faribault Jr.

MS/AC

1   Davenport Iowa

2   June 26th 1863

3   Rev. S. R. Riggs

4a   Takuuŋyaŋpi kiŋ óta kana wówapi uŋnicaġapi do
4b   Our relatives the many those letter we write it is so
4c   Many of our relatives have written this letter—it is so.

5a   Dehaŋ tóken uŋyankoŋpi kiŋ he nayaĥoŋ kta uŋciŋpi do
5b   Then how we are the that to listen to shall we want it is so
5c   Then we want you to listen, as we tell you, how we are living here in prison—it is so.

6a   Huŋkayapi ąa huŋkayapi śni kóya mniuŋkiciyapi ąa wówapi kiŋ de
6b   the elders and elders not together we met/meet and letter the this
6c   The elders and non-elders met together and wrote this

7a   uŋnicaġapi do Táku waŋżi ecoŋkupi ąa waŋna uŋhduśicapi ąa Dehan
7b   we write it is so What one we did and now we made it bad and now
7c   letter—it is so. We did one thing, and it was wrong what we did, and now

8a   uŋkażużupi Den wicaśta ąa winuĥca kóya uŋyakoŋpi kiŋ owasiŋ
8b   we are paying for (this) here men/man and women together we are here the all
8c   we are paying for this. The men and the women that are living here together

9a   wóhduze ecoŋkoŋpi kte śni tuka owasiŋ wóhdakapi do
9b   holy communion we have done shall not but all they talked it is so
9c   met and talked, they said they will not take their communion—it is so.

10a   Tóken Táku wakaŋ waciŋyaŋ úŋpi he owasiŋ ohdakapi
10b   How Great Spirit depend to be they that all they told
10c   They told how they all depend upon the Great Spirit.

11a   Huŋkayapi wicaśta wicayuhapi owasiŋ hécen ecoŋpi Aŋpetu wakaŋ óhiŋniyan
11b   The elders men they have all therefore/so they did Day sacred always
11c   Therefore, the elders that watch over them did the same. We ask

12a   he wóhdag wicoŋkeyapi do Hécen wicaśta owasiŋ akepiya
12b   that talk we make them it is so therefore men/man all again make new
12c   them to talk every Sunday—it is so. So all the men have again recommitted.

13a   Táku wakaŋ waciŋyapi hecen nina caŋte unwastepi eciciyapi
13b   Great Spirit trusting in/faith so/therefore very we are glad/joyful we say to you
13c   So we are telling you we are very glad we trust the Great Spirit.

>

3. Itewakaŋhdióta umaŋ hena, June 26, 1863

Davenport Iowa
June 26th 1863

Rev. S. R. Riggs

Takuonniyapi kin ota kana Wowapi onnicagapi do Dehan token unyankonpi kin he nayaḣon kta oncinpi do. Honkayapi qa Honkayapi śni koya Mnionkiciyapi qa Wowapi kin de onnicagapi do Taku wanji Econqonpi qa Wanna onhdusicanpi qa Hehan onkagapi Den Wicaśta qa Winuḣca koya onyakonpi kin owasin Wohduze Econqonpi kte śni tuka owasin Wohdakapi do Token Taku wakan Wacinya onpi he owasin ohdakapi Honkayapi wicaśta wicayuḣapi owasin Hecen econpi Anpetu wakan ohinya he Wohdag Wiconkeyapi do Hecen wicaśta owasin akepiya Taku wakan wacinyapi Hecen Nina Cante onwastepi ciciyepi

>

• • • •

3. Many Lightning Face and others, June 26, 1863

Davenport Iowa
June 26th 1863

Rev. S. R. Riggs

Many of our relatives have written this letter—it is so. Then we want you to listen, as we tell you, how we are living here in prison—it is so. The elders and non-elders met together and wrote this letter—it is so. We did one thing, and it was wrong what we did, and now we are paying for this. The men and the women that are living here together met and talked, they said they will not take their communion—it is so. They told how they all depend upon the Great Spirit. Therefore, the elders that watch over them did the same. We ask them to talk every Sunday—it is so. So all the men have again recommitted. So we are telling you we are very glad we trust the Great Spirit.

>

14a   waniyetu   wikcemna yamni   hehaŋyaŋ   Dakota   ekta   taku wakaŋ   oie   kiŋ   ayaipi
14b   Winter   thirty   so long   Dakota   at/to   something sacred   a word   the   they took to
14c   You took the Great Spirit's Word to the Dakota people for over thirty years,

15a   tuka   Dakota   ota   ciŋpi   šni   tuka   uŋkiyepi   dehan   kaška oŋyakoŋpi   kiŋ
15b   but   Dakota   many   they want   not   but   we/us   now   we that are in prison   the
15c   but many Dakota persons did not want His Word.   But those of us in prison

16a   onetanhan   waŋna   taku wakaŋ   oie   kiŋ   ocowasiŋ   uŋhapi
16b   therefore/for that cause   now   Great Spirit   a word   the   whole thing   to have/own entirely
16c   now want the Great Spirit's Word, therefore we now have His Word entirely.

17a   Hécen   waŋna   dehaŋ   wicašta   kiŋ   dena   ikce wicašta   ekta
17b   So/therefore   now   thus far   men   the   these   common man   at/to
17c   So if these men here in prison go to where the common people are on the outside,

18a   ípi kiŋhaŋ   Táku wakaŋ   oie   kiŋ   taŋkan   áyapi   kta   okihipi
18b   To have gone to   Great Spirit   his word   the   out of doors   they take   shall   they are able
18c   and they take the Great Spirit's Word, they can do it, because they will be

19a   kta   iyecece   do
19b   shall/will   like/such as   it is so
19c   very capable of doing that—it is so.

20a   Hehan   wéhaŋ   wótaŋiŋ   waŋži   wašte   naoŋhoŋpi   tuka   tókiya
20b   then   last spring   news   one   good   we heard   but   where
20c   Then we heard good news last spring, but we don't know what became of it—

21a   iyayataŋiŋ   šni   Hécen   ito   he   dehaŋ   naoŋhoŋpi   kta   uŋciŋpi
21b   to have gone/to appear   not   therefore   come/well   that   now   we heard   shall   we want
21c   it just disappeared.   Therefore we would like to hear about it now—

22a   tuka   do   Wópeton háŋska   kici   pahiŋ   en   nayapiŋpi   ḳa   tóken   yaciŋpi
22b   but   it is so   General Sibley   with   the head   at   wear around   and   how   they want
22c   it is so.   You usually do what you want, as it is, you can wear General Sibley

23a   ca   ecen   ecanupi   ece   Hécen   dehaŋ   waciŋuŋniyapi   táku   waŋži
23b   when   so/as it was   they do   usually   So/therefore   now   we depend upon you   what   one
23c   around your head.   We depend upon you, so if there's anything

24a   nayahoŋpi   héciŋhaŋ   he   naoŋhoŋpi   kta   uŋciŋpi   ḳa   wówapi   kiŋ   de   uŋnicaǧapi   do
24b   they heard   if   that   to hear   shall   we want   and   letter   this   we write   it is so
24c   you hear concerning us, we want to hear the same thing, that's why we write you this letter—it is so.

25a   Hehan   Tuŋkaŋšidaŋ   ake   nakaha   takeya   nace   heoŋkiyapi   uŋ   táku
25b   then   grandfather   again   lately   he said   perhaps   we said   to be   what
25c   We want to know what the President has in mind, and if he said anything

26a   caŋte   yúza   waŋna   sdonyaya   héciŋhaŋ   he   naoŋhoŋpi   kta   uŋciŋpi   do
26b   heart   to take hold of   now   you know   if   that   we want to hear   shall   we want   it is so
26c   concerning us, that's what we want to hear about—it is so.

>

Wanetu wikcemna 30 Hehaya Dakota ekta Taku wakan Oie kin Ayaipi tuka Dakota ota cinpi śni tuka oŋkiyepi dehan Kaśka onyakonpi kin onetanhan Wanna Taku wakan oie kin Ocowasiŋ onhapi Hecen Wanna Dehan Wicaśta kin Dena Ikce wicaśta ekta Ipi kinhan Taku wakan oie kin Tankan ayapi kta okihipi kta Iyecece do

Hehan Wehan Wotanin wanji waśte naonĥonpi tuka tokiya Iyaya tanin śni Hecen Ito He Dehan naonĥonpi kta oncinpi tuka do Wopeton hanska kici Pakin en nayapinpi qa token yacinpi ca ecen ecanupi ece Hecen Dehan Wacinonniyapi taku wanji nayaĥonpi Hecinhan he naonĥonpi kta oncinpi qa Wowapi kinde onnicagapi do

Hehan Tonkanśidan ake nakaha takeya nace Heonkiyapi on taku Cante yuza wanna Sdonyaya Hecinhan he naonĥonpi kta oncinpi do

>

• • • •

You took the Great Spirit's Word to the Dakota people for over thirty years, but many Dakota persons did not want His Word. But those of us in prison now want the Great Spirit's Word, therefore we now have His Word entirely. So if these men here in prison go to where the common people are on the outside, and they take the Great Spirit's Word, they can do it, because they will be very capable of doing that—it is so.

Then we heard good news last spring, but we don't know what became of it—it just disappeared. Therefore we would like to hear about it now—it is so. You usually do what you want, as it is, you can wear General Sibley around your head. We depend upon you, so if there's anything you hear concerning us, we want to hear the same thing, that's why we write you this letter—it is so.

We want to know what the President has in mind, and if he said anything concerning us, that's what we want to hear about—it is so.

>

27a   Waŋna   henana   uŋkeyapi   kta   Den kaśka   uŋyakoŋpi caŋte oŋyakiyapi
27b   Now   that is all   we will say   will   here imprisoned   we are   love/have affection for
27c   Now that is all we will say.   We ask that you have a heart for those of us here in prison.

28a   Den   kaśka uŋyakoŋpi owasiŋ caŋte uŋ   nape   uŋiyuzapi   do
28b   here   we imprisoned   all   heart to be hand we take hold of it is so
28c   Those of us here in prison all shake your hand with good feelings—it is so.

29a   Itewakaŋhdi óta   Kawaŋke
29b   Many Lightning Face   Knocks Down

30a   Waśte inape   Wicaŋȟpi duta
30b   Comes Out Good   Red Star

31a   Ėhnamani   Maka Ohomni Ku
31b   Walks Among   Comes Back Around the Earth

32a   Aŋpetu waśte   Máza waśicuŋ
32b   Good Day   Iron Whiteman

33a   Maza Kiŋyaŋ hiyaye   Tawamni waśte
33b   Iron Flyer Flying By   His Good Water

34a   Waśicuŋ máza   Kicos mani
34b   Iron Whiteman   Calls as He Walks

35a   Wicaȟca máza   Tatoheya
35b   Old Iron Man   Against The Wind

36a   Wasu Wakaŋhdi
36b   Sacred Lightning Hail

37a   Hena   nape   oŋniyuzapi   do
37b   Those hand   we shake your   it is so
37c   Those [of us above] shake your hand—it is so.

Wanna Henana onkeyapi kta Den kaśka onyakonpi Cante onyakiyapi
Den kaśka unyakonpi Owasin Cante on nape oniyuzapi do

Itewakaŋhdiota
Waśte inape
Ehnamani
Aŋpetu waśte
Mazakiŋyaŋ hiyaye
Waśicuŋ maza
Wicaḣca maza
Wasu wakaŋhdi

Kawaŋke
Wicaŋḣpi duta
Maka Ohomni Ku
Maza waśicoŋ
Tawamni waśte
Kicos mani
Tatoheya

Hena nape onniyuzapi do

• • • •

Now that is all we will say. We ask that you have a heart for those of us here in prison.
Those of us here in prison all shake your hand with good feelings—it is so.

Many Lightning Face
Comes Out Good
Walks Among
Good Day
Iron Flyer Flying By
Iron Whiteman
Old Iron Man
Sacred Lightning Hail

Knocks Down
Red Star
Comes Back Around the Earth
Iron Whiteman
His Good Water
Calls as He Walks
Against The Wind

Those [of us above] shake your hand—it is so.

MS/AC

1a Tamakoce mitakoda ake wówapi cícaġe yedo ito táku waŋżi eciciye kte
1b His Country my friend again letter give you it is so well thing one say to you will
1c My friend His Country, again I give you a letter, one thing I will say to you—

2a ye do Dakota kaśka yukaŋpi kiŋ he táku aiyapi kiŋ he token eyapi
2b it is so Dakota jailed setting here the this thing they talk the this how they say
2c it is so. The Dakota imprisoned here, they talk about something. What they say

3a kiŋ he ociciyake kte ye do he ꝙa kéyapi ye do waziyata isaŋtaŋka áye
3b the this tell you and will it is so this and they say it is so north long knife say
3c is this, I want to tell you—it is so. They say, in the north, amongst the U.S. soldiers, they say

4a ciŋ om uŋyaŋpi ꝙa ihaśiŋ wicaśta wicohaŋ śíca káġapi kiŋ waŋżi isaŋtaŋka
4b the among we go and greasy lips man works bad they make the one Long Knife
4c we were among the traders who did bad acts, and one soldier

5a kiŋ niyake yúzapi kte ye do éyapi ꝙa héoŋ wéhaŋ heyapi tuka héceŋ
5b the alive taken will it is so they say and for that last fall they say but thus
5c was captured alive—it is so. They say this occurred last fall, but we could

6a okihipi śni ye do tuka ake nakuŋ eyapi ye do úŋkaŋ nakaha oŋspa
6b they cannot it is so but again also they say it is so now again part
6c not have done it—it is so. Also, but they say—it is so. Now again I have heard part

7a nawaȟuŋ ye do táku héceŋ iyomakipi śni yedo iyecetu kta tuka héceŋ okaȟ
7b I heard it is so. thing thus happy not it is so right will thing these action
7c of it—it is so. Thus, there is something I don't like, it is not right, these actions.

8a iteȟeya uŋkayapi kta kéyapi nawaȟuŋ ye do iho hena héceŋ eyapi e owasiŋ
8b terrible we are will they said I heard it is so well these thus they say these all
8c They say we are going to be treated bad, I heard—it is so. Well, this is what they said, all this

9a ociciyake ye do héceŋ taŋyaŋ iyukcaŋpi ꝙa śicaya iyukcaŋpi héciŋhaŋ
9b I tell you it is so these good thinking and bad thinking if it is so
9c I tell you—it is so. Whether their thinking will be good or their thinking will be bad, if it is so.

10a hena nayaȟoŋ kta e ociciyake ye do henana epe kte ye do
10b these you hear will I tell you it is so all I say will it is so
10c These are for you to hear—it is so. This is all I will say—it is so.

11a héceŋ inśiŋ tóken idukcaŋ kiŋhaŋ wówapi mayaꝁu waciŋ ye do
11b thus since how you think if letter give me I want it is so
11c Thus, let me know what you think, if you write me a letter, I want to know what you think—it is so.

12a Iyożaŋżaŋ he miye
12b Glowing Light it is me

13a Tamakoce mitakuye waŋżi nape ciyuze ye do Mowis Itewakaŋhdióta hemiye
13b His Country my relatives one hand shake it is so
13c His Country, one of my relatives, I shake your hand—it is so. Moses Many Lightning Face, it is me

4. Iyożaŋżan, [wiyawapi sni, 1863]

Tamakoce mitakoda ake Wowapi cicage yedo ito taku wanji eciciye kte ye do Dakota kaxka
yukanpi kin he taku aiyapi kin he token eyapi kin he ociciyake kte ye do he ka ken eyapi ye
do waziyata isantanka aye cin om unyanpi qa ihaxin wicaxta wiconran xica kagapi kin wanji
isantanka kin niyake yuzapi kte ye do eyapi qa heon wehan heyapi tuka hecen okihipi xni ye
do tuka ake nakun eyapi ye do unkan nakaha unxpa nawarun ye do tuka hecen iyomakipi xni
yedo iyecetu kta tuka hecen okar itoheya unkayapi kta keyapi nawarun ye do iho hena hecen
eyapi e owasin ociciyake ye do hecen tanyan iyukcanpi qa xicaya iukcanpi hecin han hena yarun
kta e ociciyake ye do henana epi kte ye do hecen inxin token idukcan kinhan wowapi mayaqu
wacin ye do

iyojanjan he miye

tamakoce mitakuye wanji nape ciyuze ye do
Mowis Itewakanhdiota hemiye

• • • •

4. Glowing Light, [undated, 1863]

My friend His Country, again I give you a letter, one thing I will say to you—it is so. The Dakota
imprisoned here, they talk about something. What they say is this, I want to tell you—it is so.
They say, in the north, amongst the U.S. soldiers, they say we were among the traders who did
bad acts, and one soldier was captured alive—it is so. They say this occurred last fall, because of
that we could not have done it—it is so. Also, because they say—it is so. Now again I have heard
part of it—it is so. Thus, there is something I don't like, it is not right, these actions. They say we
are going to be treated bad, I heard—it is so. Well, this is what they said, all this I tell you—it is
so. Whether their thinking will be good or their thinking will be bad, if it is so. These are for you
to hear—it is so. This is all I will say—it is so. Thus, let me know what you think, if you write me
a letter, I want to know what you think—it is so.

Glowing Light, it is me

His Country, one of my relatives, I shake your hand—it is so.
Moses Many Lightning Face, it is me

CC/MW

1a   Tamakoce   ito   táku   waŋżi   ociciyake   kta
1b   His Country   well   what   one   tell you   shall/will
1c   His Country, there is one thing I will tell you.

2a   eya   wicaṡta   wókcaŋ   waŋ   iwohdagwakiya   ciŋ   ito   ociciyake   kta
2b   also   man   a prophet   a/an   I made him talk   the   well   I tell you   shall/will
2c   Also, I will tell you about a man, who is a prophet, whom I asked to talk.

3a   tokaheya   heye   do   coŋkaṡke   kiŋ   en   yai   kéyapi
3b   first   he said   it is so   prison   the   in   you went   they said
3c   The first thing, he said, was that you were at the prison.

4a   eya   tuka   ówaŋpi   ṡni   do   epe   do   óŋkaŋ   akeṡ   heye   wicayaka
4b   also   but   to go with   not   it is so   I said   it is so   and   again   he said   are you truthful
4c   I said, but I was not present—it is so.   Once again, he said, are you sure you're

5a   he   eye   do   ho   epe   do   hehan   wayezu wakpa   en
5b   look here   he said   it is so   yes   I said   it is so   then   Rush River   at
5c   telling the truth?   Yes, I said—it is so.   Then he said, they said you were at

6a   kicizapi   kiŋ   óyape   keyapi   eye   do   hiya   ówape   ṡni   do
6b   they fought   the   to join   they said   he said   it is so   no   to go with   not   it is so
6c   the battle at Rush River [near Henderson]—it is so.   No, I said, I did not

7a   epe   do   úŋkaŋ   akeṡ   heye   akaŋsaŋpa   Taŋpa wakpa   en
7b   I said   it is so   and   again   he said   across   Birch Coulee Creek   at
7c   participate—it is so.   And then, he said, you were at Birch Coulee Creek and

8a   makaoķa   kiŋ   en   kicizapi   kiŋ   en   óyape   kéyapi   eye   do
8b   Dig the Earth   the   at   they fought   the   at   to join with   they said   he said   it is so
8c   again when they fought at Dig the Earth, this is what they said—it is so.

9a   ho   ówape   do   epe   úŋkaŋ   tóna   yakuta   he   eye   do
9b   yes   to go with   it is so   I said   and   how many   you shoot   that   he said   it is so
9c   Yes, I said, I was with them—it is so.   And how many did you shoot? he asked.

10a   he   caŋĥdi   manice   nakaṡ   epa   tka   ecen   ito   inina   naŋke
10b   yes   gun powder   I have none   truly   I said   but   so   well   be silent   you be
10c   Truthfully, I didn't have any gunpowder, I said.   He said, well, you should be quiet

11a   kta   eye   do   tuwe   he   caĥdi   nícaŋ   eṡta   mazopiye
11b   shall/will   he said   it is so   who   that   gunpowder   have none   though   store house
11c   about it—it is so.   He said, even though someone is without gunpowder,

12a   etaŋhaŋ   caĥdi   icupi   kiŋ   oŋġe   ķupi   kta   iyececa   eye   do
12b   from   gunpowder   they took   the   some   gave   shall   like   he said   it is so
12c   they took gunpowder from the trading post and would give them some—it is so.

>

5. Ninaiyopte, [1863 or 1864]

Tamakoce ito taku wanji ociciyake kta eya wicaxta wokcan wan wohdagwakiya cin ito ociciyake kta tokaheya heye do conkaxke kin en yai keyapi eya tuka owanpi xni do epe do onkan akex heye wicayakahe eye do ho epe do hehan wayeju wankpa en kicizapi kin oyape keyapi eye do hiya owape xni do epe do onkan akex heye akansanpa Tanpa wankpa en makaoqe kin en kicizapi kin en oyape keyapi eye do ho owape do epe onkan tona yakute he eye do ho canrdi manice nakax epa tka ecen ito inina nake kte eye do tuwe he canrdi nican exta mazopiye etanhan canrdi icupi kin ongequpi kta iyecece eye do

>

• • • •

5. Truly Passes On, [1863 or 1864]

His Country, there is one thing I will tell you. Also, I will tell you about a man, who is a prophet, whom I asked to talk. The first thing, he said, was that you were at the prison. I said, but I was not present—it is so. Once again, he said, are you sure you're telling the truth? Yes, I said—it is so. Then he said, they said you were at the battle at Rush River [near Henderson]—it is so. No, I said, I did not participate—it is so. And then, he said, you were at Birch Coulee Creek and again when they fought at Dig the Earth, this is what they said—it is so. Yes, I said, I was with them— it is so. And how many did you shoot? he asked. Truthfully, I didn't have any gunpowder, I said. He said, well, you should be quiet about it—it is so. He said, even though someone is without gunpowder, they took gunpowder from the trading post and would give them some—it is so.

>

13a   hécen   oŋmatókiyataŋhaŋ   nayaźiŋ   he   eye   do

13b   therefore   one or other/from what place   you stand   that   he said   it is so

13c   So from what side were you standing, he asked—it is so.

14a   ho   tíŋtan   kiŋ   eciyataŋhaŋ   nawaźiŋ   do   epe   haŋ   caŋpanhmihma

14b   yes   on prairie   the   from side   I stand   it is so   I said   yes   wagon

14c   Yes, I said I was standing from the prairie side—it is so.   Yes, he said,

15a   caŋtka   waŋke ya   wicaśta   waŋźi   tukte   yakute   he   eye   do

15b   left   to be/lie   man   one   which   you shoot   that/do   he said   it is so

15c   did you shoot a man from the left side of the wagon—it is so.

16a   ho   núŋpa   wakute   tuka   he   téhaŋtu   nakaś   iwakam   mdúza   ǫa   wakute

16b   yes   two   I shoot   but   that   far off   truly   above   held   and   I shoot

16c   Yes, it was a long distance, so I held the gun above him and shot twice—

17a   do   epe   do   tuka   he   caŋĥdi   manice   képe   ciŋ he

17b   it is so   I said   it is so   but   that   gunpowder   none have   that I said   if/when

17c   it is so, I said.   But I said that I didn't have any gunpowder left, and I was

18a   wicawake   do   tuka   he   kicizapi   śni   kiŋ   ĥaĥatoŋwaŋ

18b   to speak truth   it is so   but   that/those   they fight   not   the   village at the falls

18c   telling the truth—it is so.   But they were not fighting, because they left for where the

19a   ti   típi   kiŋ   ekta   iyaya uŋkiyayapi   hakam   kicizapi   do

19b   to live   house   the   at   they let us go   afterwards   they fought   it is so

19c   Ojibwe live.   They allowed us to leave, so we went, they fought afterward—it is so.

20a   hécen oŋhdipi   úŋkaŋ   waŋna   Mdewakaŋtoŋwaŋ   peźihutaziziƙapi   kiŋ   en   naźiŋca

20b   so   we came back   and   now   Mdewakantonwan   yellow medicine   the   at   escaped

20c   When we came back, the Mdewakantonwan escaped to Yellow Medicine and

21a   étipi   hehan   en oŋhdipi   do   úŋkaŋ   waŋna   ake   kicizapi

21b   camped   then   at   we came back   it is so   and   now   again   fight they

21c   camped there, then we came home—it is so.   They said, now

22a   aye   kta   kéyapi   úŋkaŋ   tuwe   ópe   śni   kiŋhan   ktépi   kta

22b   they go together   will   they said   and   anybody   to join with   not   if   they kill   shall

22c   they will go and fight again, and if anybody didn't join with them, they would kill them,

23a   kéyapi   do   hécen   oŋ etaŋhaŋ   ówape   ca   dehan   iyotaŋhaŋiyewakiye   do

23b   they said   it is so   so   therefore   I joined   and   now   I'm having a hard time   it is so

23c   they said—it is so.   Therefore, I took part in the battle, and now I'm suffering greatly for it—it is so.

24a   iho   mihuŋkawaŋźi   hena   hécetu   yedo   ninaiyopte   miyedo

24b   be it so   my brother   those   truth   it is so

24c   So, my brother, that is the truth—it is so.   Truly Passes On, this is me—it is so

hecen onmatokiyatanhan nayajin he eye do ho tintan kin eciyatanhan nawajin do epe han
canpanhmima xantka wanke ya wicaxta wanji tukte yakute he eye do ho nunpa wakute tuka
he tehantu nakax iwakam mduze qa wankute do epe do tuka he canrdi manice kepe cinhe
wicawake do tuka he kicizapi xni kin raratunwan ti tipi kin ekta iyaya onkiyayapi hankam
kicizapi do hecen onhdipi onkan wanna mdewakantonwan pejuhutanziziqyapi kin en
najinca etipi hehan en onhdipi do onkan wanna ake kiciza aye kta keyapi onkan tuwe ope
xni kinhan ktepi kta keyapi do hecen onetanhan owape ça dehan iyotanhan iyewakiye do iho
mihunkanwajin hena hecetu yedo ninaiyopte miyedo

· · · ·

So from what side were you standing, he asked—it is so. Yes, I said I was standing from the
prairie side—it is so. Yes, he said, did you shoot a man from the left side of the wagon—it is
so. Yes, it was a long distance, so I held the gun above him and shot twice—it is so, I said. But
I said that I didn't have any gunpowder left, and I was telling the truth—it is so. But they were
not fighting, because they left for where the Ojibwe live. They allowed us to leave, so we went,
they fought afterward—it is so. When we came back, the Mdewakantonwan escaped to Yellow
Medicine and camped there, then we came home—it is so. They said, now they will go and fight
again, and if anybody didn't join with them, they would kill them, they said—it is so. Therefore,
I took part in the battle, and now I'm suffering greatly for it—it is so. Truly Passes On, this is
me—it is so

MS/AC

1   Davenport Iowa indian Camp March 20th 1864

2a Tamakoce   mitakuye   Nakaha Wówapi Cícaǧe   do   tuka   he   mitakuye
2b His Country my relative now   letter   I make for you it is so because this my relative
2c His Country, my relative, now I make this letter for you—it is so.   Because, my relative,

3a he   tóken Waoŋ kiŋ he   ociciyake kte do   eya   nína   Wawicayazaŋka
3b this how   I am   the this I tell you will it is so to say very   sickness
3c this is how I am.   I tell you, there are a lot of sicknesses here—it is so.

4a tuka   hécen táku Wakaŋ óŋšimada ǫa hécen tákudaŋ mayazaŋ šni Waoŋ do
4b because then   thing sacred pity me   and thus   nothing   hurts me   not I am   it is so
4c The Holy Spirit has pity on me and nothing hurts me, I am fine—it is so.

5a hécen niš mitakuye   iyecen zaniyaŋ naŋke kta de   Wówapi en mi Wakaŋtaŋka
5b Thus   you my relative like   healthy   sit   will this letter   at   God
5c Thus, my relative, are you being well?   I pray to God

6a iceWakiye do   hehaŋ mitakuye táku Waŋži eca miye ca kta Waciŋ ǫa
6b pray to   it is so then   my relative thing one   do   me   for will I want and
6c for you—it is so.   Then, my relative, I want you to do something for me,

7a Wówapi de   cícaye   do   Ate   Fort Abercrombie   héciyataŋhaŋ
7b letter   this take for you it is so father Fort Abercrombie   where from
7c I ask you to take this letter to the officer in charge at Fort Abercrombie.   He gave me

8a mázaska 3 yámni maǩu   tuka hécen makoce kiŋ den yúzapi šni hécen
8b money   3 three   gave me but   thus   country the here caught not thus
8c three dollars because they did not hold the treaty money.

9a mitakuye   héciya he   mázaska kiŋ he   Wašte kéyapi
9b my relative there   this money   the this good   they say
9c My relative, they say that this money is good,

10a hécen he ciču kta niš mitakuye hécen déciya mázaska
10b thus   give you will you my relative this   here   money
10c thus, I will give you this money.

11a Waŋži mayaǩu kta Waciŋ ǫa   niye Wówapi ciču   do
11b one   give me will I want and you   letter   I give you it is so
11c You can give me one dollar, thus, I write this letter to you, it is so.

12a eciŋ   niye Wauŋšiyada nakaš héoŋ   cicida   do
12b thus   you   pity   and   reason I ask you this it is so
12c Thus you pity me, so therefore I ask this.

13a hécen mitakuye dehán teȟika nakaš hécen kohaŋna mayaǩu kiŋhaŋ
13b thus   my relative now   terrible thus   this   soon   give me   if
13c If you can, give the money to me because it is terrible here.

>

6. Augustin Fresneir, March 20, 1865

Davenport Iowa indian Camp
March 20th 1864

Tamakoce mitakuye Nakaha Wowapi Cicage do tuka he mitakuye he token Waon kin he
ociciyake kte do eya nina Wawicayazanka tuka hecen taku Wakan onximada qa hecen tokidan
maya zan xni Waon do hecen nix mitakuye iyecen zaniyan nake kta de Wowapi en mi
Wakantanka ice Wakiye do hehan mitakuye taku Wanji eca miye can kta Wacin qa Wowapi
de cicaye do Ate Fort Abercrombie heciyatanhan mazaska 3 yamn i maqu tuka hecen makoce
kin den yuzapi xni hecen mitakuye he ciya he mazaska kin he Waxte keyapi hecen he ciçu kta
nix mitakuye hecen deciya mazaska Wanji mayaqa kta Wacin qa niye Wowapi ciçu do ecin
niye Waonxiyada nakax heon cicida do hecen mitakuye dehan terika nakax hecen kohanna
mayaqa kinhan

>

• • • •

6. Augustin Fresneir, March 20, 1864

Davenport Iowa Indian Camp
March 20th 1864

His Country my relative, now I make this letter for you—it is so. Because, my relative, this is
how I am. I tell you, there are a lot of sicknesses here—it is so. The Holy Spirit has pity on me
and nothing hurts me, I am fine—it is so. Thus, my relative, are you being well? I pray to God
for you—it is so. Then, my relative, I want you to do something for me, I ask you to take this
letter to the officer in charge at Fort Abercrombie. He gave me three dollars because they did
not hold the treaty money. My relative, they say that this money is good, thus, I will give you
this money. You can give me one dollar, thus, I write this letter to you, it is so. Thus you pity me,
so therefore I ask this. If you can, give the money to me because it is terrible here.

>

14a   pidamayaye   kte   do   takomni   mitakuye   tákudaŋ   oyag pica
14b   I thank you   will   it is so   even so   my relative   nothing   say least
14c   I will thank you—it is so.   My relative, it is dangerous

15a   šni   nakeš iapi   henana   eciciye   kte   do   Nape   ciyuze   do
15b   not   saying   that all   say to you   will   it is so   Hand   shake   it is so
15c   to tell you anything, that is all I say to you, well, this is so.   I shake your hand—it is so.

16a   Wóniya   Wakaŋ   nícioŋ   nuŋwe   nitakuye
16b   Holy   Spirit   be with you   so be it   your relative
16c   May the Holy Spirit be with you, may it be it so.   I am your relative.

17a   Wówapi   mayaku   kiŋhaŋ   décen   macaże   éyahnake   kte   do
17b   letter   give me   if   thus   my name   put it   will   it is so.
17c   If you give me a letter, you can put my name on it—it is so.

18a   Augustin Fresneir

19a   He miye   do
19b   It is me—it is so

pidamayaye kte do takomni mitakuye takudan oyag pica xni nakax iapi henana eciciye kte do
Nape ciyuze do Woniya Wakan nicion nunwe nitakuye Wowapi mayaqu kinhan decen macaje
eyahnake kte do

Augustin Fresneir

    he miye do

    • • • •

I will thank you—it is so. My relative, it is dangerous to tell you anything, that is all I say to you,
well, this is so. I shake your hand—it is so. May the Holy Spirit be with you, may it be it so. I am
your relative. If you give me a letter, you can put my name on it—it is so.

Augustin Fresneir

    It is me—it is so

                                              CC/MW

1a　　Dakota　Wíyapi　Magaskada　Wimimi en　　1864
1b　　Dakota　moons　white geese　round moon　1864
1c　　April full moon 1864

2a　　Tamakoce　mitakuye　hécen　eha　Ake　wówapi　cicaġe　　ecin　táku
2b　　His Country　my relative　then　also　again　letter　I made for you　suppose　something
2c　　His Country, my relative, I write this letter to you.　　　　　They say the Holy

3a　　wakan　eyapi　kin　hecedan　iyotan　　héon　dehan　koŝka　　unyakunpi　wicaŝta
3b　　sacred　they say　the　he alone　most great　therefore　now　prisoner　we are　　men
3c　　Spirit alone is most great, I suppose for that reason, now we men are in prison.

4a　　wanżikŝi　Tehika　eyapi　tuka　　miŝ　kaken　epca　waun　Wakantanka　hée
4b　　several　terrible　they say　because　myself　like this　I think　I am　Great Spirit　that is
4c　　Several said it is terrible.　　For myself, I think God is

5a　　iyotan　　qa　waŝte　qa　eya　ótakiya　awacin　waun　heon　　wicunte　inonpa
5b　　most great　and　good　and　to say　frequently　I think　I am　therefore　death　second
5c　　most Great and Good.　　　　Frequently I think about the second death [Judgment Day],

6a　　hée　táku　　maka　akan　tehika　iyecece　ŝni　hée　tehika　héon　　onkiŝnana
6b　　that　something　earth　upon　terrible　fitting　not　that is　terrible　therefore　we alone
6c　　that is something upon earth it's not terrible, it's terrible for us alone.

7a　　óunniciyapi　qa　Canku　wiconi　kin　he　　ohna　ománipi　kte　ake únpi　ókini　　tokata
7b　　help you　　and　road　life　the　that is　in　　they walk　will　they live　perhaps　future
7c　　We help you on the road of life and they will walk, they will live.　　　Maybe if

8a　　wanżi　ni　kinhan　ókini　ksápi　kte　epca　tuka　wanna　óta　ápi　wówapi　unspepi
8b　　one　live　if　　perhaps　wise　will　I think　but　now　a lot　died　letter　they learn
8c　　one lives in the future, he will be wise, I think.　　But now a lot of young men who learned

9a　　kin　koŝka　　ece　tápi　he　cin　mitakuye　iyomakiŝice　ye do　ake　omdake kte
9b　　the　young men　always　die　that is　the　my relative　I am saddened　it is so　again　tell of me
9c　　to write are always dying.　　I am saddened, my relative—it is so.　　Again, tell me,

10a　　ye do　déciya　onhipi　ehantan　Wikcemna Tópa sánpa záptan　45　hena　tápi　nakun　ota
10b　　it is so　over here　we came　since　ten four plus five　　　45　these　died　also　lot
10c　　since we have come here, forty-five and more have died, and a lot

11a　　tapi　kta　iyecen　wankapi　wanna　tónana　unkayapi　　zitkada　waŝte　de hi　　qa
11b　　died　will　like　laying here　now　few　　we are getting　bird　good　here came　and
11c　　will die.　　Those of us laying here are getting few.　　Good Bird came and

12a　　odowan　onspewicakiye　qa　wanna　mazanapcupe　kaŝpapida　qa　wanna　mnayanpi　qa
12b　　songs　taught them　and　now　metal finger ring　dime　　also　now　collect　and
12c　　taught them songs, and now they are also collecting rings and dimes

13a　　wanna　owasin　yuha　kinhde　Wówapi　wakan　yakaġa　keyapi　ni　unkunpi
13b　　now　all　take　home　letter　sacred　you made　they say　alive　we are
13c　　to take home.　　They say you are making a sacred book.　We are alive.

>

7. Ruban Tahoȟpi Wakaŋ, April [22], 1864

Dakota wiyapi magaokada wimima en 1864

Tamakoce mitakuye hecen eha Ake wowapi cicage ecin taku wakan eyapi kin hecedan iyotan heon dehan koska unyakunpi wicasta wanjiksin Tarikaeyapi tuka mis kaken epca waun Wakantanka hee iyotan qa waste qa eya otakiyan awacin waun heon wicunṭe inonpa hee taku maka akan terika iyecece sni hee terika heon onkixnina ooniciyapi qa canku wiconi kin he ohna omanipi kte ekeenpi okini tokata wanji ni kinhan okini ksapi kte epca tuka wanna ota ṭapi wowapi unspepi kinkoska ece ṭapi he cin mitakuye iyomakisice ye do ake omdake kte ye do deciya onhipi ehantan Wikcemna Topa sanpa zaptan 45 hena ṭapi nakan ota ṭapi kta iyecen wankapi wanna tonana unkayapi zitkada waste de hi qa odowan ospewicakiye qa wanna mazanapcupe kaspapida ko wanna mnayanpi qa wanna owasin yuha kihde Wowapi wakan yakaga keyapi ni onkanpi

>

• • • •

7. Ruban His Sacred Nest, April [22], 1864

April full moon 1864

His Country, my relative, I write this letter to you. They say the Holy Spirit alone is most great, I suppose for that reason, now we men are in prison. Several said it is terrible. For myself, I think God is most Great and Good. Frequently I think about the second death [Judgment Day], that is something upon earth, it's not terrible, it's terrible for us alone. We help you on the road of life and they will walk, they will live. Maybe if one lives in the future, he will be wise, I think. But now a lot of young men who learned to write are always dying. I am saddened, my relative—it is so. Again, tell me, since we have come here, forty-five and more have died, and a lot will die. Those of us laying here are getting few. Good Bird came and taught them songs, and now they are also collecting rings and dimes to take home. They say you are making a sacred book. We are alive.

>

14a iyehaŋ waŋuŋyakapi ḳeŝ oŋkiciŋpi ǫa hehan ake aŋpetu wakaŋ ehaŋ uŋkipi
14b in time we will see you we think and then again day sacred that time
14c I think we will see you on Sunday.   When

15a kiŋhaŋ wóhduze ecuŋkuŋpi kte ǫa he yuŝtaŋpi kiŋhaŋ hehan Peżihuta wicaŝta
15b when communion they do will and thus finish when then doctor
15c we get there, we will take communion, and when they finish, Dr. Williamson

16a Tókiya ye kta kéya Aŋpetu wakaŋ isaŋpa hehan ye kta kéya nakaha
16b where go will he said day sacred past then go will he said now
16c said where he will go.   Then he said he will go after Sunday.   Now

17a mniŝoŝe eciyataŋhaŋ wówapi óta ahipi tuka Takomni táku
17b Missouri River from letter lots they brought but nevertheless something
17c they have brought lots of letters from the Missouri River [Crow Creek], but nevertheless

18a waŝte nahuŋpica ŝni wadake winohca óŋŝikapi ǫa nihiŋciyapi ǫa
18b good good to hear not I think women pitiful and they are frightened/scared and
18c I think we will hear bad news, we are imprisoned, the women are pitiful and frightened, and

19a óta táku yútapi ŝni nażiŋcapi ǫa ecenkcaŋ táku wakaŋ kiksuyapi ŝni
19b a lot something not eat flee and as it is something sacred remember not
19c some have not eaten, they flee, and several have not remembered the Holy Spirit.

20a wicayapi henana kiya omdecahapi he tehike wada óŋŝikapi epce
20b they are getting these separate scattered this is terrible I think they are pitiful I think
20c They are getting scattered and separated, they are pitiful, and I think this is terrible, I think

21a ciŋ héoŋ Táku waŝte kiŋ hée waŝte ǫa táku ŝíce wakakiŝye ciŋ sáŋpa
21b the therefore thing good the it is good and thing bad suffering the further
21c something is good, that is good, and something bad further causes suffering,

22a waŝtedaka-aya ece hecen wicota waciŋ táku waŝte ece ekta
22b like habitual always thus consensus I want something good at
22c it's always habitual, so I want the crowd, if they can only

23a owasiŋ inażiŋ oŋkaŝ waŝte kta tuka mitakuye niŝ wówapi mayaḳu
23b all stand if only good will but my relative your letter you give me
23c all stand for only good, but it will be good, my relative.   You wrote me a letter,

24a óŋkaŋ he nína waŝte wadake ye do Ecin tokiyataŋhaŋ tuweda wówapi
24b and this very good I think it is so because from where no one letter
24c I think it is very good—it is so.   Because nobody writes

25a maḳupi ŝni ece mazanapcupe nom ciĉu henana epe kta
25b give me not always ring two I give you all say will
25c me a letter, I will give you two rings, that is all I will say.

26a   mitakuye nape ciyuze ye do   Ruban Tahohpi Wakaŋ
26b   my relative hand I shake it is so
26c   My relative, I shake your hand—it is so.   Ruban His Sacred Nest

iyehan wanunyakapi queś onkicinpi qa hehan ake anpetu wakan ehan unkipi kinhan wohduze ecunkunpi kte qa he yuśtanpi kinhan hehan Pejihuta wicaśta Tokiye ye kta keya Anpetu wakan isanpa hehan ye kta keya nakaha miniśośe eciyatanhan wowapi ota ahipi tuka Takomni taku waśte nagunpica śni wadake winonrca onśikapi qa nihinciyapi qa ota taku yutapi śni najincapi qa ecenkcan taku wakan kiksuyapi śni wicayapi henana kiya omdecahapi he terike wada onśikapi epce cin heon Taku waśte kin hee waśte qa taku śica wakakiśye cin sanpa waśtedakaaya ece hecen wicota wacin taku waśte ece ekta owasin inajin onkaś waśte kta tuka mitakuye niś wowapi mayaqu onkan he nina waśte wadake ye do ecin tokiyatanhan tuweda wowapi maqupi śni ece mazanapcupe nom ciçu henana epe kta

> nitakuye nape ciyuze ye do
> Ruban Tahohpi wakan

. . . .

I think we will see you on Sunday. When we get there, we will take communion, and when they finish, Dr. Williamson said where he will go. Then he said he will go after Sunday. Now they have brought lots of letters from the Missouri River [Crow Creek], but nevertheless I think we will hear bad news, we are imprisoned, the women are pitiful and frightened, and some have not eaten, they flee, and several have not remembered the Holy Spirit. They are getting scattered and separated, they are pitiful, and I think this is terrible, I think something is good, that is good, and something bad further causes suffering, it's always habitual, so I want the crowd, if they can only all stand for only good, but it will be good, my relative. You wrote me a letter, I think it is very good—it is so. Because nobody writes me a letter, I will give you two rings, that is all I will say.

> My relative, I shake your hand—it is so.
> Ruban His Sacred Nest

CC/MW

1a	May Aŋpetu 3th 1864	
1b	May 3rd 1864	

2a	Mitakoda	Tamakoce
2b	My friend	His Country
2c	My friend	Rev. S. R. Riggs

3a   Nakaha   ake   wówapi   cíkaġe
3b   Today   again   letter   to make/compose
3c   Today, I am writing you a letter.

4a   Tuka   dehán   waciŋciyaŋ   tuka   aŋpetu   kiŋ   dehán   nína   caŋte   maŝica   wauŋ   ye do
4b   But   now   depend upon   but   day   the   now   very   heart   sad/bad   to be   it is so
4c   I am very sad today, and also very dependent upon you for my existence—it is so.

5a   mitawiŋ   tokiyaiyaya   taŋiŋ   ŝni   kéyapi   kiŋ   héoŋ   nína   caŋte   maŝica.
5b   my wife   where/nowhere   to appear   not   they said   the   therefore   very   heart   sad/bad
5c   They said my wife has disappeared, therefore I am very heartbroken.

6a   tuka   wanihaŋ   mate   kta   kéyapi   nakahaŝ   he   nawakiĥoŋ   óŋkan   hehaŋ   kaken
6b   but   last winter   I die   will   they said   lately   that   I heard   and   thus   like this
6c   Last winter, they said I was going to die.   Lately, I just heard that, and then I began

7a   awaciŋ   makica   tohaŋ   mate   kte   ciŋhaŋ   kohaŋna hiŋ   wakaŋtaŋka
7b   to think   to become/suddenly   when   I die   shall   if/when   quickly/very soon   Great Spirit
7c   to suddenly think, when will I die?   When I die, I hope it is quickly and I shall go

8a   ti   kiŋ   ekta   wai   kta e   nihiŋmiĉiya   ŝni   ke epca   Tokeŝta   tuwe
8b   His home   the   at   to have gone to   will   to be frightened   not   I think   Presently   who
8c   to be with the Great Spirit in His home.   I think I will not be afraid.   At that time,

9a   mayaco   kiŋhaŋ   tókeŝta   iŝ   eya   he   tokata   wayaco   kiŋ   ehan i
9b   judge me   if/when   presently   he/she   also   that   future   judge   the   there/to have been at
9c   whoever judges me, in the future, will receive judgment just like me,

10a   kta   epca   eciŋ   dehan   wanikiya   eyapi   kiŋ   he   waciŋwayedo   Hehan
10b   will   I think   today   now   Savior   they say   the   that   I depend upon it is so   Then
10c   I think.   Today, I now depend upon the one they call Savior—it is so.   I was, then,

11a   kicizapi   kiŋ   he   winuĥiŋca   hokŝiyopa   ko   wicaktepi   kiŋ   heoŋ   ekta   wai
11b   battle   the   that   women   children   too/also   killing   the   therefore   at/to   I went to
11c   at the battle because they were killing women and children, that's why I went there.

12a   héoŋ   mate   kta   tuka   naceca   he   owotaŋna   ecamoŋ   kta   waciŋ
12b   therefore   I die   shall/will   but   perhaps/may   that   straight   to do   will   I want
12c   Therefore, I may die, but there is one thing I want to set straight.

13a   óŋkaŋ   he   wicoŋte   owade   kecaŋmakiŋpi   kiŋ   he   imate
13b   and   that   death   I look for/seek for   suitable they   the   that   kill me
13c   I am looking forward to death and my execution at the appropriate time.

\>

8. Robert Hopkins/Caske, May 3, 1864

May Anpetu 3th 1864

Mitakoda Tamakoce

Nakaha ake Wowapi cikage
Tuka dehan wacinciyan tuka anpetu kin dehan nina cante maśica waun ye do mitawin
tokiyaiyaya tanin śni keyapi kin heon nina cante maśica tuka wanihan maṭe kta keyapi
nakaha he nawakiħon onkan hehan kaken awacin makica tohan maṭe kte cinhan kohanna rin
wakantanka ti kin ekta wai kta e nihinmiciya śni ke epca tokeśta tuwe mayaco kinhan tokeśta iś
eya he tokata wayaco kin ihunni kta epca ecin dehan wanikiya eyapi kin he wacinwaye do hehan
kicizapi kin he winorinca hokśiyopa ko wicaktepi kin heon ekta wai heon maṭe kta tuka naceca
he owotanna ecamon kta wacin onkan he wiconte owade kecanmakinpi kin he imaśte

>

• • • •

8. Robert Hopkins/First Born Son, May 3, 1864

May 3rd 1864

My friend Rev. S. R. Riggs

Today, I am writing you a letter.
I am very sad today, and also very dependent upon you for my existence—it is so. They said my
wife has disappeared, therefore I am very heartbroken. Last winter, they said I was going to die.
Lately, I just heard that, and then I began to suddenly think, when will I die? When I die, I hope
it is quickly and I shall go to be with the Great Spirit in His home. I think I will not be afraid. At
that time, whoever judges me, in the future, will receive judgment just like me, I think. Today, I
now depend upon the one they call Savior—it is so. I was, then, at the battle because they were
killing women and children, that's why I went there. Therefore, I may die, but there is one thing
I want to set straight. I am looking forward to death and my execution at the appropriate time.

>

14a tuka   héoŋ   makaŝkapi   kiŋ   tohaŋyaŋ   makiyuŝkapi   ŝni   kiŋ   hehaŋyaŋ
14b but   therefore put me in prison the   how long   [they] pardon/free me not   the   so far/so long
14c As a result they will confine me to prison.   As long as they don't set me free,

15a wicohaŋ ŝica waŋżidaŋ ecamoŋ   ŝni   ki   epca   héoŋ   owotaŋna   waoŋ
15b work   bad   one   to do/work not   to/for I think   therefore straight   to be
15c I know I haven't committed one bad action, and I think I shall and want to be honest

16a kta   waciŋ   iho   henana   epe   kta
16b shall/will I want desire come/see there only so much I say will
16c and good.   All right, that is all I will say.

17a micaŋte oŋ   Nape ciyuzapi mitawiŋ kici
17b my heart with hand I shake   my wife with
17c My wife and I shake your hand with good feeling.

18a   nitakuye Robert Hopkins Caske he miye do
18b   Your relative, Robert Hopkins the First Born Son, it is me—it is so

19a   hehaŋ ito   wóyute kiŋ oŋ   tehiya   oŋkuŋpi   hecen   ito
19b   Then   well/so food   the   with with difficulty to be/exist therefore well/so
19c   We are living in great difficulty with little or no food, therefore

20a taŋyaŋ waoŋtapi yakuwa   waciŋ   ye do
20b well   we eat   you hunt/pursue   I want it is so
20c I want you to pursue getting us plenty of food to eat—it is so.

tuka heon makaśkapi kin tohanyan makiyuśkapi śni kin hehanyan wicoran śica wanjidan ecamon śni ki epca heon owotanna waon kta wacin iho henana epe kta micante on Nape ciyuzapi mitawin kici.

nitakuye Robert Hopkins Caske he miye do
hehan ito woyute kin on teriya onkunpi hecon ito tanyan waontapi yakuwa wacin ye do

• • • •

As a result they will confine me to prison. As long as they don't set me free, I know I haven't committed one bad action, and I think I shall and want to be honest and good. All right, that is all I will say. My wife and I shake your hand with good feeling.

Your relative, Robert Hopkins the First Born Son, it is me—it is so
We are living in great difficulty with little or no food, therefore I want you to pursue getting us plenty of food to eat—it is so.

MS/AC

1a   Wiwożupi wi 4   canin   en
1b   Moon when They Plant 4   end of woods   at
1c   May 4, at end of Woods

2a   Tamakoce   mihuŋkawaŋżi   ake   Wówapi   cícaǥe   do   yahi   kta   kéyapi
2b   His Country   my brother   again   letter   I make you it is so   you come   shall   they said
2c   His Country, my brother, I am writing you a letter again—it is so.   They said you were coming,

3a   úŋkaŋ   hécen   waŝtewadake   do   ǫa   pežihutawicaŝta   kici   oŋyakoŋpi
3b   and   therefore   I love that   it is so   and   doctor   with   we are here
3c   and so I really loved to hear that—it is so.   We are here with Dr. Thomas Williamson,

4a   tuka   tuŋkaŋŝidaŋ   he   ekta   iyaye   do   tuka   táku   okihi   kta
4b   but   grandfather/president that   at   went   it is so but   what   to be able   will
4c   but he left to go and see the President—it is so.   What he will be able to accomplish,

5a   sdonwaye ŝni   tuka   ókinni   iyehe   Táku wakaŋ óŋŝioŋdapi   kiŋhaŋ   wótaŋiŋ   waŝte
5b   to know   not   but   maybe   he/she   Great Spirit   to have mercy on if   news   good
5c   I don't know.   If the Great Spirit has compassion on him, maybe we will hear

6a   naoŋȟoŋpi   kta   ǫa   hehan   tohaŋ   yau   kta   kiŋhaŋ   taŋke   tipi   he
6b   we hear   will   and   then   when   you come shall   if   my older sister   house   there
6c   some good news.   And when you come, if you would stop at my older sister's home,

7a   yai   kiŋhaŋ   hánpa   waŋżi   mayakahi   kta   waciŋ   do
7b   to have gone to if   shoes/moccasins one   you bring me shall/will I want it is so
7c   I want you to bring me a pair of shoes—it is so.

8a   ǫa   mitaŋkŝi   he   wahokoŋwicayakiye   kta   waciŋ   ǫa   mitoŝka
8b   and   my younger sister that   to counsel them   shall   I want and my nephew
8c   And I would like you to counsel my younger sister's family.   If you are able to,

9a   Wówinape   he   tóken   oyakihi   he   Tuŋkaŋŝidaŋ   en   cażedate   waciŋ
9b   A Refuge   that   how   you are able to that   Grandfather   at   mention   I want
9c   I want you to mention my nephew A Refuge [Wowinape, a son of Little Crow] to the President—

10a   tuka   do   henana   epe   kta   óhiŋni   Ateyapi ǫa   ciŋhiŋtkuyápi
10b   but   it is so   only so much I say shall/will   always   Father   and   their Son
10c   it is so.   That is all I will say—may the Father, Son, and Holy Spirit and his

11a   ǫa   Wóniya wakaŋ   towaŝake   nícipi   uŋ   nuwe
11b   and   Holy Spirit   his strength with you to be let it be so
11c   power always be with you—may it be so.

12a   mitawaciŋ   uŋ   Nape   cihduzapi   do   nihuŋka waŋżi
12b   with my mind   to be hand   shake   it is so   your brother
12c   With my mind and being I shake your hand—it is so.   Your brother,

13a   Peter Tapetataŋka   he miye   do
13b   Peter His Big Fire, that is me—it is so.

9. Peter Tapetataŋka, May 4, [1864]

Wiwojupi wi 4 can in en

Tamakoce mihunkawanji ake Wowapi cicage do yahi kta keyapi onkan hecen waśtewadake
do ḣa pejihutawicaśta kici onyankonpi tuka tunkanśidan he ekta iyaye do tuka taku okihi kta
sdonwaye śni tuka onkini iyehe Taku wakan onśiondapi kinhan wotanin waśte naonḣonpi
kta qa hehan tohan yau kta kinhan tanke tipi he yai kinhan hanpa wanji mayakahi kta wacin
do qa mitanksi he wahonkonwicayakiye kta wacin ḣa mitośka Wowinape he token oyakihi
he Tunkanśidan en cajeda wacin tuka do henana epe kta ohinni Ateyapi ka cinhintkuyapi qa
Woniyan wakan towaśake nicipi un nuwe mitawacin on Nape cihduzapi do nihunka wanji

Peter Tapetatanka hemiye do

· · · ·

9. Peter His Big Fire, May 4, [1864]

May 4, at end of woods

His Country, my brother, I am writing you a letter again—it is so. They said you were coming,
and so I really loved to hear that—it is so. We are here with Dr. Thomas Williamson, but he left
to go and see the President—it is so. What he will be able to accomplish, I don't know. If the
Great Spirit has compassion on him, maybe we will hear some good news. And when you come,
if you would stop at my older sister's home, I want you to bring me a pair of shoes—it is so. And
I would like you to counsel my younger sister's family. If you are able to, I want you to mention
my nephew A Refuge [Wowinape, a son of Little Crow] to the President—it is so. That is all I
will say—may the Father, Son, and Holy Spirit and his power always be with you—may it be so.
With my mind and being I shake your hand—it is so. Your brother

Peter His Big Fire that is me—it is so.

MS/AC

1   Davenport May 17th 1864

2a   Mr S. R. Riggs   Tamakoce
2b   Mr. Stephen R. Riggs   His Country

3a   Nakaha wówapi cícaǧe kte   ǫa iapi   waŋžigži
3b   Now   letter   I make shall/will and language/talk some
3c   I will write you a letter and I will say a few words to you.

4a   epe   kta   eya uŋkiyepi   he ikce wicaŝta   wiwicatkotkoka ǫa
4b   I say shall/will also we ourselves that common man act foolishly   and
4c   Also, we the common men have been acting foolishly, as a result

5a   teȟiya   uŋyakoŋpi   tuka niyepi he tóken ecuŋuŋyaŝipi owasiŋ
5b   with difficulty we are   but   you   that How   you told us   all
5c   we are now living in great difficulty.   You and Dr. Williamson told us what we must do,

6a   ecen econkuŋpi   tuka uŋkiye pežihutazizi   he   tóken
6b   we did as you told us   but   we   Yellow Medicine there how
6c   so we did as you instructed us.   You told us what to do at Yellow Medicine and

7a   econ uŋyaŝipi   he   aiĉiciya   econkoŋpi tuka Dehaŋ waŋna
7b   they told us to do that make effort we did it but   now   now
7c   we have made great effort to do as you said, but because of that

8a   iwauŋŝakapi ŝni   dehaŋ itokaȟ de kta   he   tóna
8b   we are strong not   now   south   you are going that how many
8c   we have become weak.   We're told you are going south, and the group that were

9a   tokaheya wauŋspekiyapi he   ito   cažedate   kta   uŋciŋpi
9b   first   they taught   that well/come mention name shall/will we want
9c   first taught, we would like you to mention their names.

10a   Ǫa   ȟaȟamdote   en Misuŋka   kaŝkayaŋke ciŋ he   eya
10b   And the mouth of the Minnesota at my younger brother in prison   the that too
10c   My younger brother is in prison at the mouth of the Minnesota River, and I want you to

11a   taŋyaŋ wauŋspekiya   tuka tacaŋ ocowasiŋ   ŝíca ǫa   uŋ
11b   well   teach/taught they but   body   all/the whole thing bad   and to be
11c   teach him well.   His whole body is sick and in a weakened condition, and I

12a   téhaŋ   iwaŝake   kte ŝni epca he cažedate   kta waciŋ
12b   for how long not strong shall not I think that mention name will I want
12c   don't expect him to last too long, I'm thinking.   I want you to mention his name.

13a   James hepaŋ Wakaŋ
13b   James the Sacred Second Son

10. James Hepaŋ Wakaŋ, May 17, 1864

Davenport May 17th 1864

Mr S. R. Riggs Tamakoce

Nakaha wowapi cicage kte qa iapi wanjigji epe kta eya onkiyepi he ikce wicaxta wiwicatkotkoka qa Teriya onyakonpi tuka Niyepi he token ecununyaxipi owasin ecen econqunpi tuka onkiye pejuhutazizi he token econunyaxipi he aiciciya econqonpi tuka Dehan wanna iwaunxakapi xni dehan itokar dekta he tona tokaheya waunspekiyapi he ito cajedate kta oncinpi qa raramdote en misunka kaxkayanke cin he eya tanyan waunspekiya tuka tancan ocowasin xica qa on tehan iwaxake kte xni epca he cajedate kta wacin

James hepan Wakan

• • • •

10. James the Sacred Second Son, May 17, 1864

Davenport May 17th 1864

Mr. Stephen R. Riggs His Country

I will write you a letter and I will say a few words to you. Also, we the common men have been acting foolishly, as a result we are now living in great difficulty. You and Dr. Williamson told us what we must do, so we did as you instructed us. You told us what to do at Yellow Medicine and we have made great effort to do as you said, but because of that we have become weak. We're told you are going south, and the group that were first taught, we would like you to mention their names. My younger brother is in prison at the mouth of the Minnesota River, and I want you to teach him well. His whole body is sick and in a weakened condition, and I don't expect him to last too long, I'm thinking. I want you to mention his name.

James the Sacred Second Son

MS/AC

1   Davenport June 12, 1864

2a   Tamakoce
2b   His Country
2c   Stephen R. Riggs

3a   Nakaha   Ito   wówahdake kte Wicaŝta waŋ Hiŋhaŋduta Eciyapi he   etaŋhaŋ
3b   Now/today   well   I speak   will man   a   Owl Red   named   him   from
3c   Well today I will speak, as a man.   I am a descendent of the man named Red Owl—

4a   Imacaġe   do.   wicaŝta kiŋ he   tóken ohaŋ   ḳa   tóken tawaciŋ   kiŋ
4b   I grew up it is so man   the this how   character/ways and   how   thinks/mind the
4c   it is so.   From this man's actions/character, and how he thinks,

5a   hena   owasiŋ   miniŝota   oyate   kiŋ sdoŋyapi   do   ate   óhiŋni
5b   these/those all   cloudy water people   the you know this it is so father always
5c   all these are Minnesota people.   You know this—it is so.   Fathers [leading men]

6a   tuŋkaŋŝidaŋyapi kiŋ tóken ecoŋŝi kiŋ owasiŋ anaġoptaŋ ḳa   wicohaŋ wanżigżi waŝte
6b   their grandfather the how   orders the all   listen/obey and   work   several   good
6c   always do what the President orders them to do, all listen and obey and work.   Several have

7a   káġe   do.   óhiŋniyaŋ ate   akicita oŋ ḳa   tohaŋ táku   tehika   icaġe
7b   make   it is so   always   father soldier be and   when   things hard/difficult grew
7c   made good—it is so.   Father has been a soldier, and when difficult situations happened,

8a   ciŋhaŋ en Isaŋtaŋka tóken yakoŋpi   ḳa   tukte tápi   kiŋhaŋ ate   iŝ   Iyecen te
8b   if   at long knives how   they are and   where die   if   father he   like   die
8c   U.S. soldiers die, then Fathers die likewise,

9a   ate   kéya   úŋkaŋ   ate   ta ehaŋ táku tehika Icaġe ḳa   waŋna heciŋ
9b   father he said and if Father when he dies terrible grew and   now   I thought
9c   father said, and here when the Fathers died, terrible things occur, and now I thought

10a   dakota kiŋ owasiŋ tápi miŝ   ate   tóken tawaciŋ kiŋ Iyecen
10b   Dakota the all   die   me/myself father how   thinks   the right/that way
10c   all the Dakota died, myself.   I think like Father thinks, likewise,

11a   mitawa ciŋ ḳa   taku   tehika   Icaġe tka miŝ   hécen epe   do
11b   I think   and   something difficult grew   but myself   what I said it is so
11c   I think this way as well, and when difficult situations occur, what I have said—it is so.

12a   Isaŋtaŋka   taku tawapi oŋ dena   oŋkicaġapi   ce   Iho po   ekta
12b   Long Knives what is theirs because of these they make for us always consider at
12c   What the U.S. Cavalry experiences, they make us do, we have always considered going home,

13a   oŋhdapi   ḳa   tóken Isaŋtaŋka kiŋ e tápi kiŋhaŋ om   oŋtapi
13b   we have come and   where Long Knife the die   if   amongst   die
13c   and where if the U.S. Cavalry may die, we die amongst them.

>

11. Aŋpetuwaŝte, June 12, 1864

Davenport June 12th 1864

Tamakoce

Nakaha Ito wawahdake kte Wicaṡta wan Hinhanduta Eciyapi he etanhan Imacage do wicaxta kin he token oran qa token tawacin kin hena owasin miniṡota oyate kin sdonyapi do ate ohni i tunkanxidan yapi kin token econxi kin owasin anagoptan qa wicoran wanjigji waxte kage do ohniyan ate akicita on qa tohan taku terika Icage cinhan en Isantanka token yakonpi qa tukte ṭapi kinhan ate ix Iyecen ṭe ate keya unkan ate ṭa ehan takuterika Icage qa wanna hecin dakota kin owasin ṭapi miṡ ate token tawacin kin Iyecen mitawa cin qa takuterika Icaga tka mix hecen epe do Isantanka takutawapi on dena onkicagapi ce Iho po ekta onhdapi qa token Isantanka kin e ṭapi kinha om onṭapi

>

• • • •

11. Good Day, June 12, 1864

Davenport June 12, 1864

Stephen R. Riggs

Well today I will speak, as a man. I am a descendent of the man named Red Owl—it is so. From this man's actions/character, and how he thinks, all these are Minnesota people. You know this—it is so. Fathers [leading men] always do what the President orders them to do, all listen and obey and work. Several have made good—it is so. Father has been a soldier, and when difficult situations happened, U.S. soldiers die, then Fathers die likewise, father said, and here when the Fathers died, terrible things occur, and now I thought all the Dakota died, myself. I think like Father thinks, likewise, I think this way as well, and when difficult situations occur, what I have said—it is so. What the U.S. Cavalry experiences, they make us do, we have always considered going home, and where if the U.S. Cavalry may die, we die amongst them.

>

14a kta ce epe qa héoŋ Isaŋtaŋka ekta wahdi do
14b will also even though and that's why Long Knife at come back/arrive it is so
14c Even so, we also may die. And that is why I came back to the U.S. Cavalry—it is so.

15a únkaŋ hécen mitahokŝidaŋ kiŋ waŋna ta takudaŋ Iwawiŋdaŋ
15b and here then my son the now die nothing hinders
15c I arrived here—it is so. And so a lot of my sons have died. Nothing hinders

16a wicayapiŋ ŝni tápi kiŋ héoŋ nína caŋte maŝice dena hokŝidaŋ kiŋ
16b upon them not die the because very heart broken/bad these boys the
16c them no way as they die, because their hearts are broken, these boys.

17a Isaŋtaŋka om tacaŋ waŋżidaŋ Idawapi qa tóken dehan zu yakoŋpi
17b long knives with body one consider and how these we the warriors
17c You consider the Americans as one body, and so our warriors

18a oŋkiŝ Iyecen yakoŋpi ciŋpi tka okihipi sni wicaŝte ŝíca wicawapi Nakaŝ
18b us fight they are they want but they can not men bad count and
18c fight and live as one. They want, but they cannot, because we are amongst bad men and

19a tohaŋyaŋ ded niyukaŋpi kiŋ hehaŋyaŋ wótaŋiŋ waŝte Nahoŋpi kiŋ he awaciŋ
19b from here we live the this far news good hear the I think
19c we live far away from the news. We are thinking about hearing good news.

20a yakoŋpi kta ce wikcemŋa yámni om makaŝkapi tka waŋna akezaptaŋ tápi do
20b they are will ten three us are jailed but now fifteen die it is so
20c Those who live here are about thirty. I am among the prisoners, but now about fifteen died—it is so.

21a Wapaŝa tahokŝidaŋ kiŋ dena etaŋhan e hake nioŋkaŋpi do
21b Red Cap's boys these we are from we are left alive it is so
21c We are from Wabasha's boys, we are left alive—it is so.

22a hécen oŋkiŝ ake Wakaŋtaŋka oie kiŋ taŋyaŋ Naoŋĥuŋpi hécen waŝte
22b thus we again God word the good we heard thus good
22c Again we hear God's Word. We consider good what we have

23a oŋdakapi do onkiŝ tóken oŋkokihipi kiŋhaŋ hécen Iyae ciŋ niŋcin onka
23b we consider it is so we how we are able if then to say the want to live
23c heard—it is so. If we are able to say, we will

24a oŋkaŋpi kte do he ociciyake do
24b we are will it is so this tell you it is so
24c live here—it is so. This I tell you—it is so.

25 Good Day

26a Aŋpetuwaŝte he miye
26b Good Day it is me

kta ce epe qa heon Isantanka ekta wahdi do unkan hecen mitahokxidan kin wanna ṭa takudan Iwawindan wicayapin xni ṭapi kin heon nina cante maxice dena hokxidan kin Isantanka om tancan wanjidan Idawapi qa token dehan zu yakonpi inkix Iyecen yakonpi cinpi tka okihipi xni wicaxte xica wicawapi Nakax tohanyan den niyukanpi kin he hanyan wotanin waxte Naronpi kin he awacin yakonpi kta ce wikcemna yamni om makaxka pi tka wanna akezaptan ṭapi do Wapaxa tahokxidan kin dena etanhan e hake nionkanpi do hecen onkix ake Wakantanka oie kin tanyan Naonranpi hecen waxte ondakapi do onkix token onkakihipi kinhan hecen Iyae cin niŋcin onka onkanpi kte do he ociciyake do.

Good Daye
Anpetuwaxte he miye

• • • •

Even so, we also may die. And that is why I came back to the U.S. Cavalry—it is so. I arrived here—it is so. And so a lot of my sons have died. Nothing hinders them no way as they die, because their hearts are broken, these boys. You consider the Americans as one body, and so our warriors fight and live as one. They want, but they cannot, because we are amongst bad men and we live far away from the news. We are thinking about hearing good news. Those who live here are about thirty. I am among the prisoners, but now about fifteen died—it is so. We are from Wabasha's boys, we are left alive—it is so. Again we hear God's Word. We consider good what we have heard—it is so. If we are able to say, we will live here—it is so. This I tell you—it is so.

Good Day
Good Day it is me

CC/MW

1   Davenport Iowa

2   June 1864

3a   Tamakoce   Mihuŋkawaŋżi

3b   His Country   My One Brother

3c   Rev. Stephen R. Riggs   My brother,

4a   Nakaha   wówapi   cícaġe   do   Táku   waŋżi   waciŋniye

4b   Now/today letter   I make   it is so   That   one   depend upon you

4c   Today, I am writing you a letter—it is so.   That One who depends upon you,

5a   wakiŝice   do   ito   ociciyake kte   do

5b   to drive out or kick out   it is so   come/well tell you   shall/will it is so

5c   I had to chase him out—it is so.   Well, I will tell you—it is so.

6a   waŋciyake   Cehaŋ   táku   waŋżi ociciyake kiŋ he   wake   do

6b   to have seen if/when what one   tell you   the that mean that it is so

6c   When I see you, there is one thing which I will tell you, that's what I mean—it is so.

7a   waŋna nína tewahiŋda   tuka owakihi   ŝni do

7b   now   very   to value very much but   to be able to not it is so

7c   Now, there are things I cherish very much, but there's nothing I can do about it—it is so.

8a   miniwakaŋ kiŋ he   wicaŝta apa   yatkaŋpi   tuka he   owakihi   ŝni

8b   liquor   the that man   to go with they drink but   that to be able to not

8c   The men here [in prison] drink liquor, but there's nothing I can do to stop it.

9a   wicota owasiŋ Wakaŋtaŋka awaciŋpi tuka waŋżikżi miniwakaŋ yatkaŋpi   kiŋ   he

9b   many   all   Great Spirit they think but   some   liquor   they drink the that

9c   Many, almost all of them, think about the Great Spirit, but then some continue to drink liquor,

10a   iyomakipi ŝni do   he   ómayakiye kta   waciŋ do   he   tóken

10b   I like   not it is so that help me   shall I want it is so   that   how

10c   and I don't like that—it is so.   I want you to help me with this—it is so.   Whichever way

11a   idukcaŋ   kiŋhaŋ akicita taŋcaŋ   kiŋ wówapi yaķu   kte   waciŋ do

11b   you think if/when soldier head one the letter   you give shall I want it is so

11c   you think about it, I want you to write a letter to the commander of the soldiers—it is so.

12a   wicaŝta tóna   miniwakaŋ yatkaŋpi   kiŋhaŋ taŋkata yapi ŝni waciŋ

12b   Man   how many liquor   they drink if/when outside go   not I want

12c   These men, if they want to drink liquor, will not be permitted to go outside the prison, that's what

13a   do   owakihi   kiŋ hena kohaŋna wówapi mayaķu   waciŋ do

13b   it is so   If I am able the those very soon letter   you give me I want it is so

13c   I want—it is so.   If I can do this, I want you to write me a letter as soon as you can—it is so.

>

12. Heȟaka Maza, June, 1864

Davenport Iowa
June 1864

Tamakoce   Mihunkawanzi

Nakaha wowapi cicage do Taku wanji waciniye wakixice do ito ociciyake kte do wanciyake
Cehan taku wanji ociciyake kin he wakedo wanna nina tewarinda tuka owakihi xni do
mniwakan kin he wicaxta apa yatkapi tuka he owakihi xni wicota owasin Wakantanka awacinpi
tuka wanjikji mniwakan yatkapi kin he iyomakipi xni do he omayakiye kta wacin do he token
idukcan kinhan akicita tancan kin wowapi yaqu kta wacin do wicaxta tona mniwakan yatkanpi
kinhan tankata yapi xni wacin do owakihi kinhan kohanna wowapi mayaqu wacin do

>

· · · ·

12. Iron Elk, June, 1864

Davenport Iowa
June 1864

Rev. Stephen R. Riggs   My brother,

Today, I am writing you a letter—it is so. That One who depends upon you, I had to chase him
out—it is so. Well, I will tell you—it is so. When I see you, there is one thing which I will tell
you, that's what I mean—it is so. Now, there are things I cherish very much, but there's nothing
I can do about it—it is so. The men here [in prison] drink liquor, but there's nothing I can do to
stop it. Many, almost all of them, think about the Great Spirit, but then some continue to drink
liquor, and I don't like that—it is so. I want you to help me with this—it is so. Whichever way
you think about it, I want you to write a letter to the commander of the soldiers—it is so. These
men, if they want to drink liquor, will not be permitted to go outside the prison, that's what I
want—it is so. If I can do this, I want you to write me a letter as soon as you can—it is so.

>

14a   Wakaŋtaŋka óhaŋ   kiŋ he   owicayakidake hécen   miŝ nina epa   tuka
14b   Great Spirit   action/work   the   that   you told them   so/therefore   I   very   I said   but
14c   You have told them about the work of the Great Spirit, so now, I also told all of them, and

15a   nakaha   owasiŋ ociciyake kte   do   wambditaŋka aŋpetu hokŝidaŋ   waziakannaziŋ
15b   now/today   all   I tell you   shall   it is so   Big Eagle   Day Boy   Stands on Pine
15c   now I am telling you—it is so.   Big Eagle, Day Boy, Stands on Pine,

16a   utuhu ótapi tuka mniska   manica   apa   henana
16b   Oak   many   but   white water   I have none   some/a part of   only so much
16c   The Oak, there are many, but I have no white writing paper, so that's all

17a   ociciyake kte   do   he   owotaŋna idukcaŋ   kiŋhaŋ   wówapi mayaḳu waciŋ   do
17b   tell you   shall   it is so   that   straight   you think   if/when   letter   give me   I want   it is so
17c   I will tell you—it is so.   If you think this out, carefully, I want you to write me a letter—it is so.

18a   ḑa   akicita taŋcaŋ   kiŋ oyakihi   kiŋhaŋ   wówapi yaḳu   waciŋ   do
18b   and   soldier   head one   the   you are able to   if   letter   you give   I want   it is so
18c   And if you are able to, I want you to write a letter to the commander of the soldiers, it is so.

19a   Waŝicoŋ haŋska Iyazahinŝbedan Peẑuhutawicaŝta niye   nakuŋ   hena   oŋnipi   yaciŋpi
19b   tall white man   hairy all over   doctor   you   also   those   we live   you want
19c   That tall white man, one that's Hairy All Over, the doctor [Williamson], and you, you want us to live

20a   teĥiya   yaoŋpi   do   hécetu   kiŋhaŋ   ómayakiyapi waciŋ   do
20b   great difficulty   you are   it is so   so/right   if/when   you help me   I want   it is so
20c   so that you go through great difficulty—it is so.   If that's true, I want you to help me—it is so.

21a   Caskedan   Wicaĥcamaza taŋiŋyaŋku   hena   ómakiyapi   tuka   do
21b   First Born Son   Old Iron Man   Comes Back Plainly   those   they help me   but   it is so
21c   First Born Son, Old Iron Man, Comes Back Openly, those are the men who help me—it is so.

22a   Heĥaka máza   he miye   do
22b   Iron Elk, that's me—it is so

23a   Henana   ociciyake kte   do
23b   Only so much   I tell you   shall/will   it is so
23c   That is all I will tell you—it is so.

24a   Nape   ciyuze   do
24b   hand   I shake   it is so
24c   I shake your hand—it is so.

25a   nakuŋ   hepaŋna   nape   mduze   do
25b   Also   Second Son   hand   shake his hand   it is so
25c   I also shake Second Son's hand—it is so.

26a   Heĥaka máza   he miye   do
26b   Iron Elk, that's me—it is so

Wakantanka oran kin he owicayakidake hecen mix nina epa tuka nakaha owasin ociciyake kta
do wanmditanka anpetu hokxidan waziakannaji untuhu otapi tuka mniska manica apa henana
ociciyake kte do he owotanna idukcan kinhan wowapi maqu wacin do qa akicita tancan kin
oyakihi kinhan wowapi yaqu wacin do Waxiconhonska Iyarahinxbedan pejita wicaxta niye
nakon hena onnipi yacinpi teriya yaonpi do hecetu kinhan omayakiyapi wacin do Caskedan
Wicarcamaja taninyanku hena omakiyapi tuka do

    Heraka maza hemiyedo

Henana ociciyake kte do
Nape ciyuze do
nakun hepanna nape mduze do

Hehaka maza hemiyedo

• • • •

You have told them about the work of the Great Spirit, so now, I also told all of them, and now
I am telling you—it is so. Big Eagle, Day Boy, Stands on Pine, The Oak, there are many, but I
have no white writing paper, so that's all I will tell you—it is so. If you think this out, carefully, I
want you to write me a letter—it is so. And if you are able to, I want you to write a letter to the
commander of the soldiers, it is so. That tall white man, one that's Hairy All Over, the doctor
[Williamson], and you, you want us to live so that you go through great difficulty—it is so. If
that's true, I want you to help me—it is so. First Born Son, Old Iron Man, Comes Back Openly,
those are the men who help me—it is so.

    Iron Elk, that's me—it is so

That is all I will tell you—it is so.
I shake your hand—it is so.
I also shake Second Son's hand—it is so.

Iron Elk, that's me—it is so

MS/AC

| 1a | | Wíyawapi | Aug 20th 1864 |
| 1b | | Month | Aug 20th 1864 |

2   Mr. S. R. Riggs

3a	mitakoda	ito	wówapi	cístiŋna	cícaġe	kta	waciŋ	niciŋkśi	wéco	tuka
3b	My friend	well	letter	little/short	make	you will	I want	your son	invite	because
3c	Well, my friend, I will write a short letter.					I want to invite your son, because				

4a	dakota	iapi	kiŋ	taŋyaŋ	okihi	śni	kéya	om	akiyaka	ǫa	hehaŋ
4b	Dakota	speaking	the	good	can	not	he said	among	struggle	and	then
4c	he cannot speak Dakota well, he said.					He is among those who struggle,					

5a	hécen	eya	ate	ecadaŋ	u	kte	mnisota	etaŋhaŋ	u	kta	hécen
5b	thus	he said	father	soon	come	will	Minnesota	from	come	will	thus
5c	he said soon Father will come from Minnesota, then he will go to										

6a	Davenport	ekta	i	kta	naceca	enakiya	hécen	iyuśkiŋyaŋ	maŋke	ye do
6b	Davenport	at	go	will	maybe	gave up	thus	happy	I am sit	it is so
6c	Davenport prison.		He may change his mind, I am happy here—it is so.							

7a	wóhduze	ecamoŋ	kta	waciŋ	héon	tokiyataŋhaŋ	kaśta	waŋżi	yahipi
7b	communion	I will do	will	I want	because	from where	even so	one	you come
7c	I want to and will take communion whenever you come,								

8a	nína	waciŋ	hena	waŋna	ecamoŋ	kta	naceca	tuka	ito	ake	waŋżi	en
8b	very	I want	these	now	I do	will	maybe	because	well	again	one	here
8c	I want this very soon.			Maybe I will do this.			Well again, I really want one					

9a	yahipi	kta	he	nína	waciŋ	hehaŋ	ǫa	nakoŋ	odowaŋ	wówapi	sápa	2
9b	you all come	will	this	very	I want	then	and	also	song	book	black	two
9c	of you to come visit, then lastly, I also want you to bring two black song books,											

10a	ayahi	kta	hehaŋ	odowaŋ	wówapi	kaśpapi	waŋżidaŋ	héca	6	ahi wo	hehaŋ
10b	you bring	will	then	song	book	change	one	that is	six	you bring	then
10c	then song book you bring change for six, and then										

11a	wicaśta	waŋ	wakiŋyaŋmaza	eciyapi	kiŋ	he	odowaŋ	wówapi	ciŋ	ǫa	nakaŋ
11b	man	a	Thunder Iron	they call him	the	this	song	book	want	and	also
11c	a man, they call him Thunder Iron, he wants a song book and										

12a	wówapi	wakaŋ	téca	káġapi	kiŋ	he	waŋżi	ciŋ	hécen	kaŋġi	káġapi	maķu
12b	book	holy	new	they make	the	this	one	want	then	crow	they make	gave me
12c	a new Bible, he wants one, so then Makes Crow gave me one of them.											

>

13. Robert Hopkins, August 20, 1864

Wiyawapi Aug 20th 1864

Mr. S. R. Riggs

mitakoda ito wowapi cistinna cicage kta wacin nicinkśi weco tuka dakota iapi kin tanyan
okihi śni keya om akiyaka qa hehan hecen eya ate ecadan mnisota etanhan u kta hecen
Davenport ekta i kta naceca emakiya hecen iyuśkinyan make ye do wohduze ecamon kta wacin
heon tokiyatanhan kaśta wanji yahipi nina wacin hena wanna ecamon kta naceca tuka ito
ake wanji en yahipi kta he nina wacin hehan nakon odowan wowapi sapa 2 ayahi kta hehan
odowan wowapi kaspapi wanjidan heca 6 ahiwo hehan wicaśta wan wakinyanmaza eciyapi
kin he odowan wowapi cin qa nakan wowapi wakan teca kagapi kin he wanji cin hecen kangi
kagapi maqu

>

• • • •

13. Robert Hopkins, August 20, 1864

Month Aug 20th 1864

Mr. S. R. Riggs

Well, my friend, I will write a short letter. I want to invite your son, because he cannot speak
Dakota well, he said. He is among those who struggle, he said, soon Father will come from
Minnesota, then he will go to Davenport prison. He may change his mind, I am happy here—it
is so. I want to and will take communion whenever you come, I want this very soon. Maybe
I will do this. Well again, I really want one of you to come visit, then lastly, I also want you to
bring two black song books, then song book you bring change for six, and then a man, they call
him Thunder Iron, he wants a song book and a new Bible, he wants one, so then Makes Crow
gave me one of them.

>

13a	hécen	iapi		ata epe	śni	tónana	epa	ǫa	hecen	wówapi	cícaǧe	tuka
13b	therefore	they speak		I said	not	few	hits	and	so	letter	I write	because

13c   So this is what they said, I said a few words, and so I write this letter because

14a	he	wamdake	śni	naceca	epca	eya	odowaŋ wówapi	kiŋ
14b	I see		not	maybe	I thought	to say	song book	the

14c   I didn't see the song books.

15a	tona	oyakihi	ahi	wo	iho	mitakoda	henana epe	kta
15b	some	you can	bring	it is so	well	my friend	that's all I say	will

15c   Bring as many as you can, my friend.   Well, that is all I have to say.

16a	nitawiŋ Nicinca	ko	Nape ciyuzapi	Wówapi	zi	a b c d e héca	nakuŋ
16b	wife/son	both	shake their hands	letter	brown	Dakota alphabet	that is also

16c   Your wife and son, I shake their hands.   Also bring one of the brown Dakota alphabet books,

17a	waŋźi ayahi	waciŋ
17b	one you bring	I want

17c   I want that.

18a		Robert Hopkins	miye	do
18b		Robert Hopkins	I am	it is so

18c   I am Robert Hopkins—it is so.

19a	hehaŋ	winoĥiŋca	teĥiya	wicakuwapi	iśtiŋme	śni	wicakuwapi
19b	then	woman	terrible/bad	they treat	sleep	no	they treat them

19c   Then they treat the women terrible here.   They don't allow them to sleep, that is why

20a	hécen	awicayapi	waciŋ	taŋke	matata	he	típi	kiŋ	he	wake	ye do
20b	then	they take them	I want	my sister	Martha	that	they live	the	that	I mean	it is so

20c   I want them out of here, my sister Martha.   How they live is what I mean—it is so.

hecen iapi ata epe śni tonana epa qa hecen wowapi cicage tuka he wandake śni naceca epca eya odowan wowapi kin tona oyakihi ahi wo iho mitakoda henana epe kta nitawin Nicinca ko Napeciyuzapi Wowapi zi a b c d e heca nakon wanji ayahi wacin

      Robert Hopkins miye do

hehan winonĥinca teĥiya wicakuwapi iśtinbe śni wicakuwapi hecen awicayapi wacin taŋke matata he tipi kin he wake ye do

• • • •

So this is what they said, I said a few words, and so I write this letter because I didn't see the song books. Bring as many as you can, my friend. Well, that is all I have to say. Your wife and son, I shake their hands. Also bring one of the brown Dakota alphabet books, I want that.

      I am Robert Hopkins—it is so.

Then they treat the women terrible here. They don't allow them to sleep, that is why I want them out of here, my sister Martha. How they live is what I mean—it is so.

CC/MW

1   Davenport Iowa August 22 1864

2a   camp Indianes   Tamakoce   mihuŋka Waŋżi miŝ nakaha   Wówapi cícaġe kte do
2b   Indian Camp   His Country relative one   me   recently letter   make   will it is so
2c   Dakota POW Camp   One of my relatives, His Country, I will write this letter to you—it is so—

3a   tuka   he   tóken   Waoŋ   kiŋ   he   ociciyake   kte   do   Aŝkatudaŋ nína   Wamaya
3b   because this how   I am   the   this tell you   will it is so   lately   very   getting
3c   because I will tell you how I am.   Lately, I was

4a   eyaŋka tuka   hécen Wakaŋtaŋka óŋŝimada ḳa   taŋyaŋ Asni maye do
4b   to say   because then   God   pity me   and fine   heal   me   it is so
4c   very sick, but because God has pity on me, I am fine and he healed me—it is so.

5a   hécen nakaha taŋyaŋ Waoŋ do   hécen niŝ   iyecen taŋyaŋ yaoŋ   kta
5b   thus   now   fine   I am   it is so thus   you   are   fine   you are will
5c   Recently, I am fine—it is so.   So are you okay as well?   I will

6a   Wakaŋtaŋka icewakiye do   hehaŋ mihuŋka Waŋżi nakaha   Wócekiye nitawa
6b   God   pray   it is so then   my relative one   recently prayer   your
6c   pray for you—it is so.   Then, one of my relatives, recently, I want that one of your prayers

7a   kiŋ en   ówape   kta Waciŋ tuka   hecen Waŋna téhaŋ Waŝicuŋ Wakaŋ Waŋżidaŋ
7b   the   at   written will I want because thus   now   long   Minister holy   none
7c   will be written down, because it's been awhile.   We have not

8a   Waoŋ yakapi ŝni do   hécen mihuŋka Waŋżi Waŋna táku owasiŋ eciŝniyaŋ
8b   I am   they sit not it is so thus   relative one   now   thing all   wrong
8c   been visited by any ministers—it is so.   Thus, one of my relatives, now, all negative

9a   mitawaciŋ kiŋ hena Waŋna ecamoŋ kte ŝni do   hécen mihuŋka detaŋhaŋ
9b   thoughts   the these now   I do   will not it is so thus   my relative from
9c   thoughts, I will not have them—it is so.   Thus, my relative, from

10a   óhiŋni Wakaŋtaŋka úŋŝimada kta ice   wakiye kte do   hécen tokata
10b   always God   pity me   will always say to   will it is so thus   future
10c   here on, God will always pity me.   I will say—it is so.   Thus, in the future,

11a   Wóhduze   ecuŋpi kiŋhaŋ ówape kta Waciŋ do   héoŋ   etaŋhaŋ   óciciyake
11b   communion they do if   join   will I want it is so therefore from here help you
11c   if I will join in communion, I want to take part.   So from here, I will help you—

12a   do   hécen niŝ tóken ecuŋmayaŝi   kiŋhaŋ ecen ecamŋo kta Waciŋ do
12b   it is so thus   you   how   tell me to them if   right I do   will I want it is so
12c   it is so. Thus, if you tell me what to do, I want to do what's right—it is so.

>

14. Antoine Provençalle, August 22, 1864

Davenport Iowa August 22 1864

Camp Indianes   Tamakoce mihunka Wanji mix nakaha Wowapi cicage kte do tuka he token Waon kin he ociciyake kte do Axkatudan nina Wamaya eyanka tuka hecen Wakantanka onximada qa tanyan Asni maye do hecen nakaha tanyan Waon do hecen nix iyecen tanyan yaon kta Wakantanka icewakiye do hehan mihunka Wanji nakaha Wocekiye nitawa kin en owape kta Wacin tuka hecen Wanna tehan Waxicun Wakun Wanji dan Waon yakapi xni do hecen mihunka Wanji Wanna taku owasin ecixniyan mitawacin kin hena Wanna ecamo kte xni do hecen mihunka detanhan ohini Wakantanka onximada kta ice wakiye kte do hecen tokata Wohduze ecunpi kinhan owape kta Wacin do heon etanhan ociciyake do hecen nix token ecunmayaxi kinhan ecen ecamo kta Wacin do

>

• • • •

14. Antoine Provençalle, August 22, 1864

Davenport Iowa August 22 1864

Dakota POW Camp   One of my relatives, His Country, I will write this letter to you—it is so—because I will tell you how I am. Lately, I was very sick, but because God has pity on me, I am fine and he healed me—it is so. Recently, I am fine—it is so. So are you okay as well? I will pray for you—it is so. Then, one of my relatives, recently, I want that one of your prayers will be written down, because it's been awhile. We have not been visited by any ministers—it is so. Thus, one of my relatives, now, all negative thoughts, I will not have them—it is so. Thus, my relative, from here on, God will always pity me. I will say—it is so. Thus, in the future, if I will join in communion, I want to take part. So from here, I will help you—it is so. Thus, if you tell me what to do, I want to do what's right—it is so.

>

13a	hehaŋ	táku	Waŋżi	ociciyake	kte	do	nakaha	major Forbes	Wówapi	maķu
13b	then	thing	one	tell you	will	it is so	now	Major Forbes	letter	gave me

13c Then, I want to tell you one thing, recently Major Forbes wrote me a letter,

14a	óŋkaŋ	Waŋna	ecadaŋ	niciyuŝkapi	kta	ce emakiye	do	heceŝ	mihuŋka Waŋżi
14b	and here	now	soon	release you	will	say to me	it is so	thus	my relative one

14c saying soon you will be released.   This he told me—it is so.   So, my relative,

15a	niŝ	Major Forbes	Waŋdake	kta	ạa	Waciŋ	ạa	niŝ	mihuŋka Waŋżi	niŝ
15b	you	Major Forbes	see	will	and	I want	and	me	my relative one	you

15c I want you to see Major Forbes, and I want someone related to me

16a	omayakiye	kta	Waciŋ	tuka	do	miyeŝ	Dakota	táku	ŝíca	ecuŋpi
16b	say to me	will	I want	because	it is so	myself	Dakota	something	bad	doings

16c to tell me, because it is so.   I have not participated in any bad things

17a	kiŋ	tukudaŋ	ecamuŋ	ŝni	tka	hécen	Waŋna	téhaŋ	makakiże
17b	the	nothing	I do	not	but	thus	now	long time	terrible/suffering

17c our Dakota have done, now I have suffered terribly for a long time,

18a	tuka	takomni	Wakaŋtaŋka	iye	hécen	ciŋ	ạa	hécen	makaŋi	eece	tuka
18b	but	maybe	God	Him	thus	want	and	thus	brings me	always	because

18c but maybe this is all in God's plan and God may want me to go through all this for His sake.

19a	ókini	óŋŝimada	kiŋhaŋ	makiyuŝke	kta	ice	Waki	ye do	ómakiye	kta
19b	maybe	pity me	if	release me	will	can	go home	it is so	help me	will

19c Maybe if He pities me, I will go home—it is so.   I want His

20a	Waciŋ	do	henana	epe	kte	do	nape	ciyuze	do
20b	I want	it is so	all	say	will	it is so	hand	shake	it is so

20c help—it is so.   That is all I will say.   I shake your hand—it is so.

21   Antoine Provençalle

22a he miye
22b it is me

hehan taku Wanji ociciyake kte do nakaha major Forbs Wowapi maqu onkan Wanna ecadan
niciyuxkapi kta ce emakiye do hecen mihunka Wanji nix Major Forbs Wandake kta qa Wacin
qa nix mihunka Wanji nix omayakiye kta Wacin tuka do miyex Dakota takuxica ecunpi kin
tukudan ecama xni tka hecen Wanna tehan makakije tuka takomni Wakantanka iye hecen cin
qa hecen makani eece tuka okini onximada kinhan makiyuxke kta ice Waki ye do omakiye kta
Wacin do henana epe kte do nape ciyuze do

Antoine Provençalle
he miye

• • • •

Then, I want to tell you one thing, recently Major Forbes wrote me a letter, saying soon you will
be released. This he told me—it is so. So, my relative, I want you to see Major Forbes, and I want
someone related to me to tell me, because it is so. I have not participated in any bad things our
Dakota have done, now I have suffered terribly for a long time, but maybe this is all in God's
plan and God may want me to go through all this for His sake. Maybe if He pities me, I will go
home—it is so. I want His help—it is so. That is all I will say. I shake your hand—it is so.

Antoine Provençalle
it is me

CC/MW

1a   Wíyawapi Aug 24th 1864

1b   Month   Aug 24th 1864

2a   Waśte inape   miye   do

2b   Appears Good, it is me—it is so

3a   Wówapi kiŋ mitawa   hécen   ito   tóken huŋkayapi   úŋpi   kiŋ

3b   letter   the   my/mine therefore well   how   elders/ancestors they are the

3c   Well, this letter comes from me, so I will tell you how the elders are doing and how

4a   ówicawakiye   ciŋ hena Wówapi kiŋ den   wakaġe   ca   Mduhe

4b   help them   the those letter   the here I make/made and   I have/own

4c   I am helping them, that's why I am writing this letter and it's from me.   I am

5a   kta huŋkayapi   kiŋ hemaca śni tuka Wakaŋtaŋka oie   kiŋ icaġe

5b   shall elders/ancestors the I am   not but   Great Spirit his word the   grow

5c   not an elder, but I want the Great Spirit's Word to grow so they can work

6a   kta   waciŋ   hécen   Wakaŋtaŋka oie   kiŋ en ĥtanipi   kiŋ ówicawakiye

6b   shall I want therefore Great Spirit his word the at   they work the I help them

6c   for God, that's why I am helping them.

7a   Ca   nimiĉiciya   hécen   ito   miye wiwicawaŋġapi   kiŋ hena   ecamoŋ ġa

7b   and save my life therefore well me/I question them about the those I did/do and

7c   I am saved, therefore, I am asking them a question about their life, and those

8a   tóna   owotaŋna uŋpi   kiŋ hena om   wauŋ   kta   ġa   hena

8b   how many straight   they are the those with I am/to be shall and those

8c   living an honest and straight life, I will be with them.   And if they

9a   Wakaŋtaŋka tacaŋku omanipi   kiŋhaŋ ówape kta   waciŋ. hécen

9b   Great Spirit his path they walk if   I join shall I want therefore

9c   are walking God's path, I want to join them.   Therefore

10a   tóna   iapi iwicawakiye ciŋ hena   wówapi kiŋ den   caźepi   kiŋ

10b   how many word said to them the those letter   the here their names the

10c   those that I gave God's Word to, I have written their names down

11a   wakaġe   kta. hécen   tóken ĥtawani kiŋ hena wicaśta   sdonyapi

11b   I make/made shall therefore how I work   the those men/man they know

11c   in this letter.   I would like these men to see and know how I work

12a   kiŋ héoŋ   etaŋhaŋ caźepi   kiŋ mduhe kta   waciŋ.   Itaŋcaŋ   mitawa

12b   the therefore from   their names the I have shall I want   chief   my

12c   for the Lord, so that's why I have written their names down that I have.   My Protector

13a   Robert Hopkins   he e   Ninaiyopte

13b   Robert Hopkins, it is he   Truly Moves On

14a   Waśteinape   Duwe Dabce

14b   Appears Good   They Ask For

>

15. Waŝteinape ꞓa Robert Hopkins, August 24, 1864

Wiyapi Aug 24th 1864

Waŝteinape miyedo

Wowapi kin mitawa hecen ito token honkayapi onpi kin owicawakiye cin hena Wowapi kin den wakage ca Mduhe kta honkayapi onpi kin hemaca ŝni tuka Wakantanka oie kin icage kta wacin hecen Wakantanka oie kin en Rtanipi kin owicawakiye ca nimiꞓiciya hecen ito miye wiwicawangapi kin hena ecamon qa tona owotanna onpi kin. hena om waun kta qa hena Wakantanka tacanku omanipi kinhan owape kta wacin. hecen tona iapi iwicawakiye cin hena wowapi kin den cajepi kin wakage kta hecen token ḣtawani kin hena wicaŝta sdonyapi kin heon etanhan cajepi kin mduhe kta wacin Itancan mitawa

Robert Hopkins   he e   Ninaiyopte
Waŝteinape   Duwe Dabce

>

• • • •

15. Appears Good and Robert Hopkins, August 24, 1864

Month Aug 24th 1864

Appears Good, it is me—it is so

Well, this letter comes from me, so I will tell you how the elders are doing and how I am helping them, that's why I am writing this letter and it's from me. I am not an elder, but I want the Great Spirit's Word to grow so they can work for God, that's why I am helping them. I am saved, therefore, I am asking them a question about their life, and those living an honest and straight life, I will be with them. And if they are walking God's path, I want to join them. Therefore those that I gave God's Word to, I have written their names down in this letter. I would like these men to see and know how I work for the Lord, so that's why I have written their names down that I have. My Protector

Robert Hopkins, it is he   Truly Passes On
Appears Good   They Ask For

>

| 15a | | Waŝteŝte | Hmoŋyaku |
| 15b | | Good-Good | Hums as He Comes Home |

| 16a | | Iyożaŋżaŋ | Wakaŋhdiota |
| 16b | | Glowing Light | Many Lightning |

| 17a | | Cótaŋkamaza | Toŋkaŋġidaŋ |
| 17b | | Iron Flute | Brown Stone |

| 18a | | Tinazipewakaŋ | Wicitemaza |
| 18b | | His Sacred Bow | His Iron Face |

| 19a | | Ótadaŋ | Pataina |
| 19b | | Many | Takes Care of His Mother |

| 20a | | Tawahiŋkpeota | Otinayapamani |
| 20b | | His Many Arrows | Walks Bumping into House |

| 21a | | Toŋwaŋokawiŋġedaŋ | Hepanduta |
| 21b | | Looks Around Clearly | Scarlet Second Son |

| 22a | | Hupahu | Iwakaminażiŋ |
| 22b | | Knee | Stands Above |

| 23a | | Waŝicoŋiŝnana | Tatehiyayedaŋ |
| 23b | | White Man Alone | Wind That Goes By |

| 24a | | Taŋcaŋceyawakaŋ | Henry Toŋwaŋbobdumani |
| 24b | | Sacred Being Cries | Henry Walks and Sees the Blowing Wind |

25a	hena	wicapi	
25b	Those	men	
25c	Those are the men.		

| 26a | | Hápastiŋna | Wamduŝkatokecawiŋ |
| 26b | | Third Daughter | Different Bug Woman |

| 27a | | Maĥpiyamazawiŋ | Wikomaŝke |
| 27b | | Iron Cloud Woman | [I am] Young Woman |

| 28a | | Wawicaĥyewiŋ | Icaġohiyayewiŋ |
| 28b | | Creating Woman | Goes By Mark Woman |

| 29a | | Napewakaŋhdiwiŋ | |
| 29b | | Lightning Hand Woman | |

30a	iho		denakeca	Wakaŋtaŋka	Ti	kiŋ	ekta	awicamde		kta	Waciŋ.
30b	Come/see there		so many	Great Spirit	his	house	at	take them there		shall	I want
30c	I want these ones to know God, personally, so I want to lead them to God's house to live.										

>

Waśteśte
Iyojanjan
Cotankamaza
Tinazipewakan
Otadan
Tawahinkpeota
Tonwanokawingedan
Hupahu
Waśiconiśnana
Tancanceyawakan

Hmonyaku
Wakanhdiota
Tonkangidan
Wicitemaza
Pataina
Otinayapamani
Hepanduta
Iwakaminajin
Tatehiyayedan
Henry Tonwanbobdumani

Hena wicapi

Hapastinna
Mahpiyamazawin
Wawicahyewin
Napewakanhdiwin

Wamduśkatokecawin
Wikomaśke
Icagohiyayewin

iho denakeca Wakantanka Tikin ekta awicamde kta Wacin.

>

• • • •

Good-Good
Glowing Light
Iron Flute
His Sacred Bow
Many
His Many Arrows
Looks Around Clearly
Knee
White Man Alone
Sacred Being Cries

Hums as He Comes Home
Many Lightning
Brown Stone
His Iron Face
Takes Care of His Mother
Walks Bumping into House
Scarlet Second Son
Stands Above
Wind That Goes By
Henry Walks and Sees the Blowing Wind

Those are the men.

Third Daughter
Iron Cloud Woman
Creating Woman
Lightning Hand Woman

Different Bug Woman
[I am] Young Woman
Goes By Mark Woman

I want these ones to know God, personally, so I want to lead them to God's house to live.

>

31a	tuka	wanikiya	eyapi	kiŋ	ómakiye	ciŋhaŋ	owakihi	kta
31b	But	Savior	they said	the	help me	if/when	I am able to	shall

31c I think I can accomplish this if the One they call the Savior helps me, I know

32a	naceca	epca.
32b	Perhaps/probably	I think/thought

32c I will, probably, be able to do this.

33a	Hopkins	Waŝteinape
33b	Hopkins	Appears Good

34a	he miye	do
34b	that is me, it is so

35a	Hehan	nakaha	dena	wówapi	yawawicawakiya
35b	Then	now	these	letter	I made them read

35c Just now, I was able to get these men to read these letters:

36a	Maĥpiyatokcadaŋ
36b	Different Cloud

37a	Caska
37b	First Born Son

38a	Tahaŋpiŝica
38b	Bad Moccasin

39a	Tiyopa	4
39b	Four Door

tuka wanikiya eyapi kin omakiye cinhan owakihi kta naceca epca.

Hopkins   Wasteinape
hemiye do

Hehan nakaha dena wowapi yawawicawakiya
Maȟpiyatokcadan
Caska
Tahanpiśica
Tiyopa 4

• • • •

I think I can accomplish this if the One they call the Savior helps me, I know I will, probably, be able to do this.

Hopkins   Appears Good
that is me, it is so

Just now, I was able to get these men to read these letters:
Different Cloud
First Born Son
Bad Moccasin
Four Door

MS/AC

1a   Wíyawapi Aug 28th 1864
1b   Month   August 28, 1864

2a   Wakaŋhdiota   Nakaha   aŋpetu De   Ake   Piya   Iĉicoŋze
2b   Many Lightning   just now   day   this   again make new   pledged himself
2c   [Simon] Many Lightning on this day again made a new pledge that

3a   hécen   akeken   Eya   Tohaŋyaŋ Wani Kiŋ hehaŋyaŋ
3b   so/therefore   over again   he said how long I live the so long
3c   as long as he lives, he would quit and never again

4a   Wapiyapi   kiŋ amduŝtan kta   ce
4b   to cure people/to practice traditional medicine   the I quit   shall   when
4c   practice curing people through traditional Indian medicine, that's what

5a   eya   ǵa Hécen Detaŋhaŋ   Kiciksuya   waoŋ kta
5b   to say anything and therefore from now on to recollect for one I am shall
5c   he said.   Therefore, from now on I want to remember this as long

6a   waciŋ   ǵa héoŋ   Wówapi kiŋ de   wakaǵe ye do
6b   I want   and therefore letter   the this I make it is so
6c   as I live.   That's the purpose of this letter I am writing—it is so.

7a   Waŝteinape he miye do
7b   Appears Good, that is me—it is so

16. Waŝteinape, August 28, 1864

Wiyawapi Aug 28th 1864

Wakanhdiota Nakaha anpetu De Ake Piya Içiconze hecen akeken Eya Tohanyan Wani Kin hehanyan Wapiyapi kin amduŝtan kta ce eya qa Hecen Detanhan kiciksuya waon kta wacin qa heon Wowapi kin de wakage ye do

Waŝteinape hemiye do

• • • •

16. Appears Good, August 28, 1864

August 28, 1864

[Simon] Many Lightning on this day again made a new pledge that as long as he lives, he would quit and never again practice curing people through traditional Indian medicine, that's what he said. Therefore, from now on I want to remember this as long as I live. That's the purpose of this letter I am writing—it is so.

Appears Good, that is me—it is so

MS/AC

1a   tamakoce   psiŋhnaketu wi   śákpe   caŋ taŋiŋ   en
1b   His Country   rice harvesting month   six   wood appear   at
1c   His Country, October 6, at Wood Appear

2a   tamakoce   mihuŋka   waŋżi   wayazaŋ   óta   tuka   hinaĥiŋ   taŋyaŋ   waoŋ
2b   His Country   relative   one   sickness   lots   because   as yet   fine   I am
2c   One of my relatives, His Country, there is lots of sickness, yet I am fine.

3a   ḱa   wówapi   kiŋ   de   ciĉu   ye do   Wakaŋtaŋka   cékiyapi   kiŋ   hecedan
3b   and   letter   the   this   give you   it is so.   God   we pray   the   only
3c   And I write this letter to you—it is so.   We only pray to God.

4a   ecuŋkuŋpi   do   wicaśta   kiŋ   ehake   tónana   wówapi wakaŋ   taŋyaŋ   yawa
4b   We do   it is so.   man   the   last   few   Bible   good   read
4c   We do this—it is so.   The last few men cannot read the Bible

5a   okihipi   śni   tuka   owasiŋ   taŋyaŋ   okihipi   kta   oŋ   óhiŋni   wócekiye   nína
5b   they can   not   but   all   good   they can   will   so   always   pray   very
5c   but they all will always pray very good.

6a   oŋkeyapi   do   ḱa   niś   he   ciyaidadapi   kiŋ   oŋ   wócekiye   oŋkeyapi
6b   we say   it is so   and   you   this   can pray   the   so   pray   we say
6c   We say it is so.   And we say you pray for us,

7a   cee   do   detaŋhaŋ   niho   kiŋ   oŋ   tóken   ehe   cinhaŋ   he
7b   always   it is so.   from here   your voice   the   so   how   you say   if   this
7c   always—it is so.   From here, if we hear your voice, and how you think,

8a   awacaŋni   kta   he nayaĥoŋ   kta   miciŋca   mitawiŋ   ko   owasiŋ   taŋyaŋ   oŋpi   keyapi
8b   you think   will   these hear   will   my son   my wife   also   all   fine   they are   they said
8c   my son and my wife will hear, I am also thankful they are fine.

9a   nawaĥoŋ   tuka   tado   yukaŋ   tuka   tuwedaŋ   iwicakihni   śni   kéyapi
9b   I heard   because   meat   there is   because   no one   hunts   not   they said
9c   I heard there is meat, but no one hunts, they said, also

10a   mitawin   wówapi   micaya   henana   epe   kta   mitakuye   nape   ciyuze   do
10b   my   book   bring for me   all   I say   will   my relative   hand   shake   it is so
10c   my wife will take this letter.   That is all I will say.   My relative, I shake your hand—it is so.

11a   Eli Wakiyehdi
11b   Eli Bird Came Back

17. Eli Wakiyehdi, October 6, [1864]

tamakoce psinhnaketuwi śakpe can tan in en

tamakoce mihuka wanji wayazan ota tuka hinarin tanyan waon qa wowapi kin de cicu ye do
Wakantanka cekiyapi kin hecedan ecukupi do wicaśta kin ehake tonana wowapi wakan tanya
yawa okihipi śni tuka owasin tanyan okihipi kta on ohni wocekiye nina onkeyapi do qa niś
he ciyaidadapi kin on wocekiye onkeyapi cee do detanhan niho kin on token ehe cinhan he
awacanni kta henayaron kta micinca mitawin ko owasin tanyan onpikeyapi nawaron tuka tado
yukan tuka tuwedan iwicakihni śni keyapi mitawi wowapi mica ya henana epe kta mitakuye
nape ciyuze do

Eli Wakiyehdi

. . . .

17. Eli Bird Came Back, October 6, [1864]

His Country, October 6, at Wood Appear

One of my relatives, His Country, there is lots of sickness, yet I am fine. And I write this letter to
you—it is so. We only pray to God. We do this—it is so. The last few men cannot read the Bible
but they all will always pray very good. We say it is so. And we say you pray for us, always—it
is so. From here, if we hear your voice, and how you think, my son and my wife will hear, I am
also thankful they are fine. I heard there is meat, but no one hunts, they said, also my wife will
take this letter. That is all I will say. My relative, I shake your hand—it is so.

Eli Bird Came Back

CC/MW

1a
1b

Wíyawapi Oct. 24 1864 Davenport Iowa
Month

2   Mr. S. R. Riggs

3a	Mitakoda	nakaha	wówapi	miyecaǧa	úŋkaŋ	Tóken	oŋyaŋkoŋpi	kiŋ	he
3b	My friend	now	letter	you made for me	and	how	we are	the	that

3c   My friend, you wrote me a letter, and you wanted me to tell you

4a	ake	ociciyake	kta	yaciŋ	eya	ake	nakaha	nína	wayazaŋkapi	tuka
4b	again	to tell you	shall/will	you wanted	Also	again	now	very	they are sick	but

4c   once again how we are doing.   Also, many of the prisoners are very sick, and

5a	ókini	waŋžikži	tápi	kta	naceca	hehan	Ḣeipadaŋ	héciya	wakaŋmani
5b	maybe	some	they die	shall	probably	then	Hillhead	at that place	Walks Sacredly

5c   probably some will die.   Then Walks Sacredly said, there are many persons

6a	wicota	óŋpi	kéyapi	tóhiŋni	mini šoše	ekta
6b	many persons	are there	they said	never	Missouri River	to

6c   up at Hillhead [northern reach of Coteau des Prairies].   They said they will never

7a	hdápi	kte	šni	kéyapi	iho	hehan	hemayakiya	ciǩoŋ	ehake
7b	go home	shall/will	not	they said	yes	then	you said to me	he said	yet

7c   go back to the Missouri River [Crow Creek].   Yes, you then said to me, you will only be there

8a	Wi	2	en	yaoŋ	kta	emayakiye	iho	he	taŋyaŋ	omakiyaka	wo
8b	month	two	at	you to be	shall	said to me	yes	that	well	tell me	to

8c   two more months.   Now tell me in a clear, good way if it's true.

9a	waŋna	winoĥiŋca	awicayapi	kta	keyapi	tuka	ake	wicakapi	kte	šni
9b	now	women	they take	shall/will	they said	but	again	they truthful	shall/will	not

9c   The authorities said they will be taking the women home, but I'm sure they're not telling the truth,

10a	nace	epca	hehan	waniyetu	kiŋ	dehaŋtuke	waŋžigži	cuwita	oŋtapi	kta
10b	probably	I think	Then	this winter	the	just now	some	feeling cold	we die	shall/will

10c   I think.   Then this winter some of us will probably freeze to death,

11a	naceca	oŋkeciŋpi	máza	oceti	kiŋ	hena	taŋkan	eĥpeya po	eyapi	úŋkaŋ
11b	probably	we think	that iron	stoves	the	those	outside	throw away	they said	and

11c   we are thinking.   Throw those iron stoves outside, they said.   And the Dakotas said,

12a	tókeca	uŋkupi	kta	naceca	eyapi	ǫa	owasiŋ	taŋkan	eĥpeyapi
12b	different	give us	shall/will	probably	they said	and	all	outside	they threw out

12c   "Probably they will give us different ones," and they threw out all the stoves,

13a	tuka	osni	oŋkaŋ	ake	owasiŋ	éhdakupi	ǫa	timahen	éuŋhdepi	hehan
13b	but	cold	and	again	all took back		and	back inside	placed inside	then

13c   but it got cold and once again they took the stoves back inside.

>

18. Robert Hopkins, October 24, 1864

Wiyawapi Oct. 24 1864 Davenport Iowa

Mr. S. R. Riggs

Mitakoda nakaha wowapi miyecaga onkan Token onyankonpi kin he ake ociciyake kta yacin eya ake nakaha nina wayazankapi tuka okini wanjikśi ṭapi kta naceca hehan Reipadan heciya wakanmani wicota ompi keyapi tohinni mniśośe ekta hdapi kte śni keyapi iho hehan hemayakiye ciqon ehake Wi 2 en yaon kta emayakiye iho he tanyan omakiyaka wo wanna winoħinca awicayapi kta keyapi tuka ake wicakapi kte śni nace epca hehan waniyetu kin dehantuqe wanzigśi cuwita onṭapi kta naceca onkecinpi maza oceti kin hena tankan eħpeyapo eyapi onkan tokeca onqonpi kta naceca eyapi qa owasin tankan eħpeyapi tuka osni onkan ake owasin ehdakupi qa timahen ehdepi hehan

>

• • • •

18. Robert Hopkins, October 24, 1864

Oct. 24 1864 Davenport Iowa

Mr. S. R. Riggs

My friend, you wrote me a letter, and you wanted me to tell you once again how we are doing. Also, many of the prisoners are very sick, and probably some will die. Then Walks Sacredly said, there are many persons up at Hill Head [northern reach of Coteau des Prairies]. They said they will never go back to the Missouri River [Crow Creek]. Yes, you then said to me, you will only be there two more months. Now tell me in a clear, good way if it's true. The authorities said they will be taking the women home, but I'm sure they're not telling the truth, I think. Then this winter some of us will probably freeze to death, we are thinking. Throw those iron stoves outside, they said. And the Dakotas said, "Probably they will give us different ones," and they threw out all the stoves, but it got cold and once again they took the stoves back inside.

>

14a   ito   iapi   tókeca   iciciye   kta   tóhiŋni Wicaŝta waŋżidaŋ eŝta
14b   well   talk/language   different   say to you   will   never   man   one   although
14c   Well, then I will say something different to you.   I never did say to you,

15a   kiyuŝka po   epe   ŝni Tuka nakaha wicaŝta tóna   táku wakaŋ taŋyaŋ
15b   release from prison   I said not but now men how many Great Spirit well
15c   release from prison one person.   But lately some men who trust and depend upon the Great Spirit,

16a   waciŋyaŋpi hena ociciyakapi   ḳa caże miyecidatapi   kta waciŋ ḳa héoŋ
16b   trusting in those I tell every one and mention their names shall I want and therefore
16c   I will tell you who they are and ask you to mention their names.   Therefore, I want

17a   Rev. Thomas Williamson wówapi yecaǧe   kta   waciŋ Tohaŋ táku waŋżi
17b   Rev. Thomas Williamson letter you write shall/will I want when what one
17c   you to write a letter to Rev. Thomas Williamson.   When I truthfully say

18a   awicakehaŋ eciciyapi kiŋhaŋ ecen   ecamiyecoŋpi kiŋhaŋ sáŋpa iyotaŋ
18b   truly   I say to you if   as it was they do for me if   further greater
18c   something to you, if you can do it for me, it will further inspire me

19a   amiĉiciya   kta   mitakuyepi kiŋ apa   ihamaktapi   ḳa
19b   I make great effort shall/will my relatives the some/a part to obey/follow and
19c   to a greater effort.   I am having a difficult time, along with some of my relatives

20a   dehaŋ om iyotaŋhaŋiyewakiya tuka ito oyakihipi   kiŋhaŋ tóna
20b   now with have great difficulty but well able to accomplish if   how many
20c   who obey and follow me.   I would like you to help me by mentioning the

21a   cażeyate ciŝipi   kiŋhaŋ hena ito   ómayakiyapi iyokipi mayakiyapi
21b   mention by name if   those well/come they help me cause to be pleased
21c   names of my relatives, if you do, it will make me so happy, this is what I want.

22a   kta waciŋ hena eĥpewicaya wahde   kte ciŋ teĥike   wadake
22b   will I want those leave them I go home shall the it would be difficult I think
22c   I would consider it so hard to bear if I have to leave behind these relatives when I go home.

23a   iho   hécen   każepi   dena e epi
23b   See there therefore those names these it is they
23c   Here are the names of those persons.

24a   Waŝteŝte   Ite wakaŋhdi óta
24b   Good-Good   Many Lightning Face

25a   Waŝte inape   Tawamno ho waŝte
25b   Comes Out Good   His Good Voice

26a   Sintomni   Wakiŋyaŋ ǧi
26b   All Over   Brown Thunder

27a   Tinazipe wakaŋ   Peżihuta ska
27b   His Sacred Bow   White Medicine

ito iapi tokeca eciciye kta tohinni Wicaśta wanjidan eśta kiyuśkapo epe śni Tuka nakaha wicaśta tona taku wakan tanyan wacinyanpi hena ociciyakapi qa hena caje miyecidatapi kta wacin qa heon Rev Thos Williamson wowapi yecage kta wacin Tohan taku wanji awicakehan eciciyapi kinhan ecen ecamiyeconpi kinhan sanpa iyotan amiçiciya kta mitakuyepi kin apa ihamaktapi qa dehan om iyotanhan iyewakiya tuka iho oyakihipi kinhan tona cajeyateciśipi kinhan hena ito omayakiyapi iyokipi mayakiyapi kta wacin hena eḣpewicaya wahde kte cin teḣike wadake iho hecen cajepi dena e epi

Waśteśte	Itewakanhdiota
Waśteinape	Tawamnohowaśte
Sintomni	Wakinyangi
Tinazipewakan	Pejihutaska

>

• • • •

Well, then I will say something different to you. I never did say to you, release from prison one person. But lately some men who trust and depend upon the Great Spirit, I will tell you who they are and ask you to mention their names. Therefore, I want you to write a letter to Rev. Thomas Williamson. When I truthfully say something to you, if you can do it for me, it will further inspire me to a greater effort. I am having a difficult time, along with some of my relatives who obey and follow me. I would like you to help me by mentioning the names of my relatives, if you do, it will make me so happy, this is what I want. I would consider it so hard to bear if I have to leave behind these relatives when I go home. Here are the names of those persons.

Good-Good	Many Lightning Face
Comes Out Good	His Good Voice
All Over	Brown Thunder
His Sacred Bow	White Medicine

>

28a   Toŋwaŋbobdumani   Cetaŋ ĥota
28b   Walks and Sees the Blowing Wind   Grey Hawk

29a   Cotaŋka máza   Cápa duta
29b   Iron Flute   Scarlet Beaver

30a   Hepaŋ   Henakeca
30b   Second Son   Plenty

31a   Waŋżiyakiduŝkapi   kiŋhaŋ   pida   mayapi   kta
31b   they free one   if   to be glad   make me   shall/will
31c   If you free one from prison, you will make me glad.

32a   micaŋte   om
32b   my heart   with
32c   With my heart,

33a   Nape   ciyuze   do
33b   hand   take hold of your   it is so
33c   I shake your hand—it is so.

34a   Robert Hopkins

35a   he miye   do
35b   That is me—it is so

Tonwabobdusmani
Cotanka maza
Hepan

Cetanhota
Capaduta
Henakeca

Wanjiyakiduśkapi kinhan pida mayayapi kta
micante om
Nape ciyuze do

Robert Hopkins
he miye do

• • • •

Walks and Sees the Blowing Wind
Iron Flute
Second Son

Grey Hawk
Scarlet Beaver
Plenty

If you free one from prison, you will make me glad.
With my heart,
I shake your hand—it is so.

Robert Hopkins
That is me—it is so

MS/AC

1   Camp McClellan

2   Davenport Iowa

3   Nov. 14th 1864

4   S. R. Riggs

5a   Mitakuye nakaha Wówapi Cícaǧe kta waciŋ Héoŋ Wówapi

5b   My relative now letter make for you will I want therefore letter

5c   My relative, today I write this letter to you, that is the reason why

6a kiŋ de wakaǧe Nahahiŋ Dr. Williamson den hi šni ókini Waŋna aŋpetu

6b the this I make Later Dr. Williamson here he came not perhaps now day

6c I write.   Still, Dr. Williamson, he didn't come, but he may

7a kiŋ de oŋnaci epca Mrs. Williamson den Hi kte ciŋ he Inawaĥni

7b the this he may come Mrs. Williamson here come will the this in a hurry

7c come today.   I am anxious for Mrs. Williamson to come here.

8a Oyate den oŋyakoŋpi kiŋ Wicašta wakaŋ Waŋži kici oŋyakoŋpi kiŋ Héoŋ

8b People here we live here the man holy one with live with us the therefore

8c The people here have a Holy Man [minister] living with us.   It therefore

9a Wicašta owasiŋ waoŋšakapi sececa Hecen oŋ tohaŋ den Waŋži

9b Man all we are stronger it seems thus account of when here one

9c seems all the men are stronger.   Thus, when one of you

10a yaoŋpi kiŋ hécen caŋte Mawašte ece Hehaŋ Nakaha Ĥeipadaŋ heciyataŋhaŋ

10b you live the thus heart my good usually then now Hill head from there

10c comes here, I am very happy.   Also, we have just now news from Hillhead

11a Wótaŋiŋ   óŋkaŋ Waŋna oyate owasiŋ

11b news   and here now people all

11c [northern reach of Coteau des Prairies]. They said, now all the people

12a Wókiyapi ciŋpi kéyapi Waŋna Wambdi oŋpiduta Tipi wikcemna

12b make peace treaty they want they said Now Eagle Tail Red live ten

12c want to make a peace treaty.   Now they have said Redtail Eagle family

13a om Ĥeipa ikiyedan ahdite kéyapi Hena Waŋna Ĥeipa en hdipi

13b amongst Hillhead near arrive/camp they said these now Hillhead they came

13c of ten tipis camped near Hillhead.   I think maybe they have come

14a Nace epca Hehaŋ owapi Hena eš eyake Waŋna owasiŋ aku kéyapi

14b maybe thought then write these them to say now all coming they said

14c to Hillhead.   They say that they are all coming back.

>

19. Elias Ruban Óȟanwayakapi, November 14, 1864

Camp McClellan
Davenport Iowa
Nov. 14th 1864

S. R. Riggs

Mitakoka nakoha Wowapi Cicage kta wacin Heon Wowapi kin de wakage Nahaȟin Dr. Williamson den hi śni okini Wanna anpetu kin den onnaci epca Mrs. Williamson den Hi kte cin he Inawaȟni Oyate den onyakonpi kin Wicaśta wakan Wanji kici onyakonpi kin Heon Wicaśta owasin waonśakapi sececa Hecen on tohan den Wanji yaonpi kin hecen cante Mawaśte ece Hehan Nakaha Reipadan heciyatanhan Wotanin onkan Wanna oyate owasin Wokiyapi cinpi keyapi Wanna Wanmdi onpiduta Tipi wikcemna om Reipa ikiyedan ahdite keyapi Hena Wanna Reipa enhdipi Nace epca Hehan onwapi Hena iś eyake Wanna owasin aku keyapi

>

• • • •

19. Elias Ruban They See His Ways, November 14, 1864

Camp McClellan
Davenport Iowa
Nov. 14th 1864

S. R. Riggs

My relative, today I write this letter to you, that is the reason why I write. Still, Dr. Williamson, he didn't come, but he may come today. I am anxious for Mrs. Williamson to come here. The people here have a Holy Man [minister] living with us. It therefore seems all the men are stronger. Thus, when one of you comes here, I am very happy. Also, we have just now news from Hillhead [northern reach of Coteau des Prairies]. They said, now all the people want to make a peace treaty. Now they have said, Redtail Eagle's family of ten tipis camped near Hillhead. I think maybe they have come to Hillhead. They say that they are all coming back.

>

15a	koŝka	wanżi	Tonwaniteton	takoŝku	Canku	wanżidan	Eciyapi	he
15b	young man	one	Lightning Face	son-in-law	Road	one	they call him	him

15c They have sent home a young man, his name is One Road, he is the son-in-law of

16a	eciyatanhan	Hdi	kéyapi	Hécen	ókini	hena	wicakapi	nace	epca
16b	from there	came home	they said	then	maybe	these	they mean	perhaps	I think

16c Lightning Face. I think possibly they mean these people.

17a	Hehan	Wanna	osni	nakaŝ	Ninahin	oncuwitapi	can	ġa	Nakun
17b	then	now	cold	thus	exceedingly	we are cold	wood	and	also

17c It is cold now, we are very cold. They burn wood and

18a	táku	wanżi	Maka	iyececa	aunpapi	hena	ee	tuka	Imnihan	onḳupi	ŝni
18b	something	one	earth	like	they burn	these	it is	but	enough	we live	not

18c coal. It seems we are always

19a	nakaŝ	osni	tuka	Tehiya	onkonpi	sececa	Eya	Hececaŝta	Wókoyake
19b	indeed	cold	because	terribly	we live	it seems	to say	notwithstanding	clothing

19c in a terrible situation, there is never enough heat. Even though we don't have

20a	coza	onkonpi	onkanŝ	Tanyan	onkonpi	kta	tuka	Hehan	Ptanyetu	kin	de
20b	warm	we are here	and	here good	we are	will	but	then	fall	the	this

20c warm clothing, we are here and we will be fine. Then this fall,

21a	Winuhca	awicayapi	kta	eyapi	tuka	ókini	Wicakapi	kte	ŝni	nace	epca
21b	woman	take them	will	they said	but	maybe	truth	will	not	maybe	I think

21c they said they will take the women. But I think this may not be the truth,

22a	tuka	eŝ	awicayapi	kta	toketu	Sdononyapi	ŝni		Dehan	Iyotan
22b	but	or	take them	will	how	they know	not		at this time	most

22c they may not take them, but they don't know if this will happen. Now it seems

23a	Wóyute	on	tehika	sececa	ŝiceca	ġa	Winuhinca	owasin	Nína	wótektehdapi
23b	food		need	it seems	children	and	women	all	very	they are hungry

23c there is a great need for food, the children and women, they are very hungry.

24a	Hehan	Wówapi wakan	Ożuha	waŝteste	kaġapi	kin	he	Wanżi	Wacin
24b	Then	paper holy	cover	good	they make	the	this	one	I want

24c Then I want you to get me one of those nice Bible covers.

25a	tuka	dehán	Táku on	owakihi	kta	manica	Tuka	Hecicaŝta	ókini	wanżi
25b	but	now	something	I can	will	have none	but	perhaps	an	one

25c But now I have no means to get these. But perhaps maybe

26a	Mduhe	kta	wacin	kta	nace	Henana	epe	kta
26b	I have	will	I want	will	maybe	That is all	I say	will

26c I will have one of these. That is all I will say.

27a		Nape ciyuze	Nitakoda	Wanżi	Miye
27b		handshake	your friend	one	I am

27c I shake your hand, I am your friend.

28a	Elias Ruban	Óhanwayakapi
28b	Elias Ruban	They See His Ways

koṡka wanji Tonwaniteton takoṡku Canku wanjidan Eciyapi he eciyatanhan Hdi keyapi Hecen okini hena wicakapi nace epca Hehan Wanna osni nakaṡ Ninaḣin oncuwitapi can qa Nakun taku wanji Maka iyececa aonpapi hena ee tuka Imnihan onqupi ṡni nakaṡ osni tuka Teḣiyan onkanpi sececa Eya Hicecaṡta Wokoyake coza onhapi onkans Tanyan onkanpi kta tuka Hehan Ptanyetu kin de Winuḣica awicayapi kta eyapi tuka okini Wicakapi kte ṡni nace epca tuka iṡ awicayapi kta toketu Sdononyapi ṡni Dehan Iyotan Woyute onteḣika sececa ṡiceca qa Winuḣica owasin Nina wotektehdapi Hehan Wowapi waken Ojuha waṡteṡte kagapi kin he Wanji Wacin tuka dehan Taku on owakihi kta manica Tuka Hecicaṡta okini wanji Mduhe kta wacin kta nace Henana epe kta

    Nape ciyuze Nitakoda Wanji Miye

Elias Ruban   Oranwayakapi

· · · ·

They have sent home a young man, his name is One Road, he is the son-in-law of Lightning Face. I think possibly they mean these people. It is cold now, we are very cold. They burn wood and coal. It seems we are always in a terrible situation, there is never enough heat. Even though we don't have warm clothing, we are here and we will be fine. Then this fall, they said they will take the women. But I think this may not be the truth, they may not take them, but they don't know if this will happen. Now it seems there is a great need for food, the children and women, they are very hungry. Then I want you to get me one of those nice Bible covers. But now I have no means to get these. But perhaps maybe I will have one of these. That is all I will say.

    I shake your hand, I am your friend.

Elias Ruban   They See His Ways

CC/MW

1a   Tamakoce   mitakoda   Ake   Nakaha   wówapi   cícaġe   ye do
1b   His Country   my friend   again   now   paper/letter   make for you   it is so
1c   My friend His Country, now again, I write this letter to you—it is so.

2a   mniŝoŝe   kiŋ   eciyataŋhaŋ   wówapi   makupi   úŋkaŋ
2b   Missouri River   the   from there   paper/letter   they gave me   and here
2c   They gave me a letter from the Missouri River [Crow Creek], and here

3a   mayakiduŝka   kéyapi   he   imawaŋġapi   kehaŋ   he   wicakapi
3b   you release me   they said   this   they asked me   if so   this   they tell truth
3c   they said you released me, they asked me this, if so, is it true.

4a   tuka   hécen   wakukta   owakihi   ŝni
4b   because   then   come home   I can   not
4c   Because I could not come home.

5a   tuka   tukte   oŋ waku   kta   taŋiŋ   ŝni   epe   ye do
5b   because   where   to come   will   clear   not   I said   it is so
5c   Because where will I live, it is not clear, I said—it is so.

6a   tokaheyaŋ   Akicita   itaŋcaŋ   awanoŋyaŋkapi   kiŋ   he
6b   first   soldier   head   watch us   the   this
6c   The fort commander who watches us,

7a   taŋkan   waoŋ   ecee   kta   kéye   ca   wówapi   waŋ   maku
7b   outside   I am   always   will   he said   so   note/letter   a   gave me
7c   he said I am free, so he gave me a letter.

8a   tuka   hécen   peżihuta   wicaŝta   makakiya   hde
8b   because   then   medicine   man   earth toward   go home
8c   But then Dr. Thomas Williamson took it home for me.

9a   hécen   he   ito   cażedata   waciŋ   ye do
9b   thus   this   well   you named   I want   it is so
9c   Well then, I want you to identify him—it is so.

10a   Iyożaŋżaŋ
10b   Glowing Light

20. Iyożaŋżaŋ, [1864]

Tamakoce mitakoda Ake Nakaha wowapi cicage ye do mnišośe kin eciyatanhan wowapi maqupi onkan mayakidukca keyapi he imawangapi qehan hewicakapi tuka hecen wakukta owakihi śni tuka tukte onwaku kta tanin śni epe ye do tokaheyan Akicita itancan awanonyankapi kin he tankan waon ecee kta keye ca wowapi wan maqu tuka hecen pejihuta wicaśta maka kiya hde hecen he ito cajidata wacin ye do
Iyojanjan

• • • •

20. Glowing Light, [1864]

My friend His Country, now again, I write this letter to you—it is so. They gave me a letter from the Missouri River [Crow Creek], and here they said you released me, they asked me this, if so, is it true. Because I could not come home. Because where will I live, it is not clear, I said—it is so. The fort commander who watches us, he said I am free, so he gave me a letter. But then Dr. Thomas Williamson took it home for me. Well then, I want you to identify him—it is so.
Glowing Light

CC/MW

1a   Tamakoce   mihuŋkawaŋżi
1b   His Country, my brother,

2a   Ito   wówahdake   kte   do   he   Táku teȟika   icaġe   kiŋ en
2b   Well I speak   shall/will it is so that what difficult to do to grow the at
2c   Well, I will speak—it is so.   I was involved in what grew into great difficulty

3a   Ekta waoŋ kiŋ he wake do Iho   Isantaŋka   típi kiŋ en mahażu ahi
3b   at/to to be the that I mean Well Long Knives   lodge the at Mahaju to come
3c   [the war], that is what I mean.   Yes, I was there when they came

4a   kiŋ hen ówape   do   tuka šúŋktaŋka Típi kiŋ Ihukuya hen   Naważin
4b   the there to go with it is so but the horses barn the below   there I stand/stood
4c   to the soldier's lodge—it is so.   But I was standing there below the horse barn—it is so.

5a   tuka ecen   šúŋktaŋka šuŋšuŋna owasiŋ Wakpana kiŋ étkiya iyaya ḋa miš
5b   but as it was horses   mules   all   creek   the toward went and I
5c   But, as it was, all the horses and mules ran towards the creek, and I

6a   wicihakam   imda Mde   ḋa hécen   mázakaŋ Kiŋ bowašdoke šni ecen
6b   followed them to have gone down and therefore gun   the did not shoot so/as it was
6c   followed behind them.   And so I did not shoot my gun, and so

7a   wakiyahde do   ho hécetu   do   hehan ake   Taŋpa wakpana
7b   went home it is so yes as/right it is so   then again Birch Coulee Creek
7c   I then went home—it is so, yes, that is right—it is so. Then, when they came to Birch Coulee Creek,

8a   kiŋ en ahi   kiŋ hen ake   ówape   do   tuka hékta   uŋpi   kiŋ
8b   the in they came the there again I joined it is so but that behind they are the
8c   again I joined them there—it is so.   But those that stayed behind,

9a   héciya   Wauŋ   do   waŋna Eciŋ   wówapi   kiŋ nakaha Wašte e
9b   at that place I was at it is so now today/now book/letter the now   good at
9c   I was with them—it is so.   Now I know about the Bible that it is supposed to be

10a   sdonwaye   do   heciŋ   Hékta ikce wicašta kiŋ ekta Wicohaŋ
10b   have knowledge it is so to think this past Common Man the at/to work/habit
10c   good—it is so.   The Common Man, in the past, had a different custom

11a   tókca   uŋhapi ḋa   uŋkiš   Toiye   wahokoŋ   uŋkiciciyapi
11b   different we had and we ourselves his word counsel/preach to ourselves
11c   or habit.   And now we instruct ourselves in His Word.

>

21. Mázakiŋyaŋhiyaye, [1864]

Tamakoce mihunkawanji
Ito wowahdake kte do he Taku terika icage kin en Ekta waon kin he wakedo Iho Isantanka tipi
kin en maraju ahi kin hen owape do tuka xunktanka Tipi kin Ihukuya hen Nawanjin tuka ecen
xunktankaxuxuna owasin Wakpan kin etkiya iyaya qa mix wicihakam imda Mde qa hecen
mazakan Kin bowaxdokexni ecen wakiyahde do ho hecetu do hehan ake Tanpanwakpanna
kin en ahi kin hen ake owape do tuka hekta onpi kin heciya Waondo wanna Ecin wowapi kin
nakaha Waxte e sdonwayedo hecin Hekta ikcewicaśta kin ekta Wicoran tokca onhapi qa onkiś
Toye wahokon onkiciciyapi

>

• • • •

21. Iron Flyer Flying By, [1864]

His Country, my brother,
Well, I will speak—it is so. I was involved in what grew into great difficulty [the war], that is
what I mean. Yes, I was there when they came to the soldier's lodge—it is so. But I was standing
there below the horse barn—it is so. But, as it was, all the horses and mules ran towards the
creek, and I followed behind them. And so I did not shoot my gun, and so I then went home—it
is so, yes, that is right—it is so. Then, when they came to Birch Coulee Creek, again I joined
them there—it is so. But those that stayed behind, I was with them—it is so. Now I know about
the Bible that it is supposed to be good—it is so. The Common Man, in the past, had a different
custom or habit. And now we instruct ourselves in His Word.

>

12a	ǫa	Hehan	miŝ	waŝicuŋ wakaŋ	Kiŋ	he	wahokoŋ uŋyakiyapi	úŋkaŋ	miye	
12b	and	then	me	minister	the	that	preaches/counsels	and	I/me	

12c And for me, when the white minister preaches to us, I think what the white minister

13a	waŝicuŋ wakaŋ	Kiŋ	iyayapi	kiŋ	hena	hécetu	Tuka	hena	sdonye	ŝni	uŋyaKoŋpi
13b	minister	the	they speak	the	those	right	but	those	know	not	we live together

13c speaks or says is right, because in our life we never knew those things.

14a	ǫa	dehaŋ	uŋkiyepi	uŋ	Taku teȟika	iyahde uŋkiciciyapi	
14b	and	now/at this time	we ourselves	to be	what difficulty	brought upon ourselves	

14c Today, we have brought upon ourselves a terrible difficulty [the war].

15a	ǫa	Hehan	Jehowa	hena	sdonye	uŋkiCiyapi	kehaŋ	hehan	miŝ eya
15b	and	then	The Lord	those	know/knew	we try learn	when	then	I also

15c And now we try to learn the way of the Lord.   And I also blame myself for not

16a	Miĉiba		ǫa	peżihutawicaŝta oiye	He	ǫa	tamakoce	oiye
16b	I blame myself	and	the doctor	his word	that	and	His Country	his word

16c learning sooner.   And I remember the words of the doctor [Williamson] and Rev. Stephen R. Riggs,

17a	kiŋ	hena	Wicaweciksuye	kte	epca	waoŋ	Do
17b	the	those	remember	shall/will	I think	to be/live	it is so

17c and I will think about those every day that I live.

18a	eciŋ	mihuŋkawaŋżi iapi		Kiŋ	hena	hécetu	ce	ecen	ehapi
18b	to think	my brother	talk/language	the	those	so/right	when	so/as it was	they said

18c My brother, those sayings spoken by you are true.

19a	Eciŋ	tuwe	anaġoptan	ŝni	uŋ kta	He	ina	wicawaye	kiŋ	ótapi	ȟiŋce
19b	Today	who	listen	not	to be	that	mother	them have	the	many	very

19c Today, I have many mothers, why would anyone not want to listen.

20a	ǫa	tuwedaŋ	waciŋyapi	ŝni	uŋpi	ǫa	heoŋ	táku wakaŋ	kiŋ
20b	And	no one	depend upon	not	they are	and	therefore	Great Spirit	the

20c And they can't depend upon anyone, but they are very dependent upon the Great Spirit, and

21a	Táku wakaŋ	wacekiye	oŋyakiyapi	kiŋ	he	Caże	mdate	kte	do
21b	Great Spirit	praying	they made us	the	that	name	I mention	shall/will	it is so

21c I will mention that you tell us to pray to the Great Spirit every day—it is so.

22a	he	táku wakaŋ	kiŋ	iŝnana	he	waoŋŝida	ǫa	wacaŋtkiya	ǫa	waŝte
22b	that	Great Spirit	the	only	that	merciful	and	benevolent	and	good

22c The Great Spirit alone is merciful and benevolent and good.

23a	ǫa	hécen	wicotawaCiŋ	waŝte	kiŋ	he	ǫa	Wicotawaciŋ	súta	ǫa
23b	and	therefore	disposition	good	the	that	and	frame of mind	strong	and

23c Therefore many have a good strong mind and disposition and

24a	Táku	waŝte	akitapi	kte	kiŋ	hena	e ece	aiĉiciya po
24b	what	good	search for	shall/will	the	those	it is usually	diligent/make effort

24c shall search for what is good, and usually those persons are very conscious of themselves.

>

qa Hehan miṡ waṡicun wakan Kin he wahokon onyakipi onkan miye waṡicun wakan Kin
iyayapi kin hena hecetu Tuka hena sdoye ṡni onyaKunpi qa dehan onkinyepi on Taku terika
iyahde onkiciyapi qa Hehan Johowa hena sdoye onkiCiyapi qehan hehan miṡ eya Miçiba qa
pejihutawicaṡta oiye He qa tamakoce oiye kin hena Wicaweciksuye kte epca waon Do ecin
mihunkawanji iapi Kin hena hecetu ce ecen ehapi Ecin tuwe anagoptan ṡni onkta He ina
wicawaye kin otapi rince Qa tuwedan wacinyapi ṡni onpi qa heon taku wakan kin Taku wakan
wancekiye onyakiyapi kin he Caje mdate kte do he taku wakan kin ixnana he waonxida qa
wancantkiya qa waxte qa hecen wicotawaCin waxte kin he qa Wicotawacin suta qa Taku waxte
akitapi kte kin hena e ece aiciciyapo

>

• • • •

And for me, when the white minister preaches to us, I think what the white minister speaks
or says is right, because in our life we never knew those things. Today, we have brought upon
ourselves a terrible difficulty [the war]. And now we try to learn the way of the Lord. And I also
blame myself for not learning sooner. And I remember the words of the doctor [Williamson]
and Rev. Stephen R. Riggs, and I will think about those every day that I live. My brother, those
sayings spoken by you are true. Today, I have many mothers, why would anyone not want to
listen. And they can't depend upon anyone, but they are very dependent upon the Great Spirit,
and I will mention that you tell us to pray to the Great Spirit every day—it is so. The Great
Spirit alone is merciful and benevolent and good. Therefore many have a good strong mind
and disposition and shall search for what is good, and usually those persons are very conscious
of themselves.

>

25a   ǫa   Wiconi   oniya   kida po   he iye   táku wakaŋ   iyotaŋ   kéyapi   ce
25b   and   Holy   Spirit   ask for   he himself   Great Spirit   greatest   they said   and
25c   They said, ask only for the Holy Spirit, for the Great Spirit is the greatest.

26a   om   Maŋke   kiŋ   ewicawakiya   úŋkaŋ   ho   ito   táku Wakaŋ   kiŋ   nína
26b   with   I live   the   said to them   and   yes   well   Great Spirit   the   very
26c   And I said to those I live with, pray to the Great Spirit,

27a   ceoŋkiyapi   ǫa   oŋyukcaŋpi   kta   eyapido
27b   we pray   and   we think about   shall/will   they said
27c   and they said, we will think about it, and we will pray to him.

28a   wiconi   oniya   kidapi   kta   kéyapi   do   hécen   miŝ   waŝtewawadake   do
28b   Holy   Spirit   ask for   shall/will   they said   it is so   therefore   I   loved it   it is so.
28c   They said they will ask for the Holy Spirit, and so I loved it—it is so.

29a   Mázakiŋyaŋhiyaye
29b   Iron Flyer Flying By

qa Wiconi oniya kidapo he iye taku wakan iyotan keyapi ce om Manke kin ewicawakiya onkan ho ito taku Wakan kin nina ceonkiyapi qa onkcanpi kta eyapido wiconi oniya kidapi kta keyapido hecen mix waxtewawadakedo
Mazakinyanhiyaye

• • • •

They said, ask only for the Holy Spirit, for the Great Spirit is the greatest. And I said to those I live with, pray to the Great Spirit, and they said, we will think about it, and we will pray to him. They said they will ask for the Holy Spirit, and so I loved it—it is so.
Iron Flyer Flying By

MS/AC

1a Mihuŋka wanżi Tamakoce Ito Ake nakuŋ táku u   wanżi Eciciye
1b My relative one His Country well again also thing coming one   say to you
1c One of my relatives, His Country, when you come again, will you

2a kte do He mihuŋka wanżi he odowaŋ wówapi wake kte Do
2b will it is so that my relative one that song book I mean will it is so
2c bring me—it is so—one of my relatives, I mean that song book—it is so.

3a odowaŋ wówapi he wanżi Waciŋ tuka do he yauŋ kta
3b song book that one I want because it is so that you come will
3c I want one of those song books—it is so.   I heard them say

4a kéyapi nawahuŋ ǫa héoŋ oyakihi kiŋhaŋ Nom mayakau waciŋ do
4b they said I heard and therefore you can if two bring me I want it is so
4c that you are coming, if you can bring me two, I want these—it is so.

5a kaŝpapidaŋ Wanżi kiŋhaŋ kiŋ he etaŋhaŋ wake do Wicaŝta waŋ
5b dime one if the that from I mean it is so man a
5c I mean if they are a dime, we want them—it is so.   I am

6a kici héca oŋ Cíŋpi kiŋ he wecica do hehaŋ Ake táku wanżi
6b with like for reason the that with him it is so then again thing one
6c with a man, it is for that reason—it is so.   Then again I will say

7a eciciye kte do Tuka he mihuŋkawanżi ecen Eca miyecuŋ kta
7b I say to you will it is so because this my relative one then do for me will
7c to you one thing—it is so.   One of my one relatives, I want you to do this

8a waciŋ do he Taŋke maĥpiyapaahdewiŋ   he Tukte en típi
8b I want it is so that sister Takes Cloud Home Woman   that where at they live
8c for me—it is so. I mean my sister, Takes Cloud Home Woman. I want you to go wherever she lives,

9a kiŋhaŋ en yahi kta waciŋ tuka do he Háŋpa ǫa oŋhdohda
9b if at you come will I want because it is so that shoe and coat
9c because I want—it is so—my shoes and coat,

10a eŝta wanżi okihipi kiŋhaŋ makupi kiŋhaŋ Miyecicau waciŋ do
10b even though one they can if they give me if me bring to I want it is so
10c if they can bring them to me, I want this—it is so.

11a hetaŋhaŋ Mdokehaŋ wanmdaka óŋkaŋ Tohan tuwe déciya u kta
11b from there summer last I saw and when who here come will
11c Last summer when I was there, I saw my hide and shoes,

12a úŋkaŋŝ wakeya waŋ háŋpa Kágapi ce wanżi nica u kta Tka eye do
12b and hide a shoe they make so one none come will but him it is so
12c if someone comes here, bring them to me—it is so.

>

22. Zenas Mázakiŋyaŋhiyaye, [1864]

Mihuŋkawaŋji Tamakoce Ito Ake nakun takou wanji Eciciye kte do he mihunkawanji He odowan wowapi wake kte Do odowan wowapi he wanji Wacin tuka do he yaun kta keyapi nawarun qa heon oyakihi kinhan Nom mayaka u wacin do kaxpapidan Wanji kindan kin he etanhan wake do Wicaxta wan kici heca on Cinpi kin he wecica do hehan Ake taku wanji eciciye kte do Tuka he mihunkawanji ecen Eca miyecun kta wacin do he Tanke marpiya pa ahde win he Tukte en tipi kinhan en yahi kta wacin tuka do he Hanpa qa onrdorda exta wanji okihipi kinhan maqupi kinhan Miyecica u wacin do hetanhan Mdokehan wanmdaka onkan Tunhan tuwe deciya u kta onkanx wakeya wan hanpa Kagapi ce wanji nica u kta Tka eye do

>

• • • •

22. Iron Flyer Flying By, [1864]

One of my relatives, His Country, when you come again, will you bring me—it is so—one of my relatives, I mean that song book—it is so. I want one of those song books—it is so. I heard them say that you are coming, if you can bring me two, I want these—it is so. I mean if they are a dime, we want them—it is so. I am with a man, it is for that reason—it is so. Then again I will say to you one thing—it is so. One of my one relatives, I want you to do this for me—it is so. I mean my sister, Takes Cloud Home Woman. I want you to go wherever she lives, because I want—it is so—my shoes and coat, if they can bring them to me, I want this—it is so. Last summer when I was there, I saw my canvas and shoes, if someone comes here, bring them to me—it is so.

>

13a hécen oŋ ito he Típi en yahi wacin do ḳa Hécen
13b thus so well that they live at you come I want it is so and then
13c So you will go to where they live, I want this—it is so—and then

14a ehe kte do mázakiŋyaŋhiyaye he dena hi maŝi ce Waŋżi táku
14b you say will it is so Iron flying by him here come asked so one thing
14c you will say—it is so—Iron Flyer Flying By asked me to come here. So if one

15a oyakihipi kiŋhaŋ yaḳupi kiŋhaŋ wecica Mde kta ce ehe kte do
15b you all can if you give him if I am with him go will you said will it is so
15c of you can give them my items, he will go with me—it is so.

16a iho hécen eca miyecuŋ waciŋ do Henana he eciciya waciŋ
16b well then you do for me I want it is so all that I say to you I want
16c Well, then, I want you to do this for me. That is all I want to say to you,

17a ḳa He eciciye do henana epe kte do
17b and that say to you it is so that's all I say will it is so
17c and I say to you—it is so. That is all I will say to you—it is so.

18a Nape ciyuze do
18b hand shake it is so.
18c I shake your hand—it is so.

19a Zenas Mázakiŋyaŋhiyaye
19b Zenas Iron Flyer Flying By

20a He miye do
20b It is me—it is so

hecen on ito he Tipi en yahi wacin do qa Hecen ehe kte do mazakinyanhiyaye he den hi maxi ce Wanji taku oyakihipi kinhan yaqupi kinhan wecica Mde kta ce ehe kte do iho heEcen eca miyecun wacin do Henana he eciciya wacin qa He eciciye do henana epe kte do Napeciyuze do

Zenas mazakiniyanhiyaye
He miye do

• • • •

So you will go to where they live, I want this—it is so—and then you will say—it is so—Iron Flyer Flying By asked me to come here. So if one of you can give them my items, he will go with me—it is so. Well, then, I want you to do this for me. That is all I want to say to you, and I say to you—it is so. That is all I will say to you—it is so. I shake your hand—it is so.

Zenas Iron Flyer Flying By
It is me—it is so

CC/MW

1   Rev. S. R. Riggs

2a   Mihuŋka   wanżi   nakaha   Wówapi cícaġe   kte wówapi   wakaŋ   cażedata
2b   my relative   one   now   letter   I make for you   will letter   holy   mentioned name
2c   One of my relatives, I write this letter to you.   You mentioned the Holy Bible.

3a   tuka   mázaska   táku   da   mduhe   śni   ąa   héoŋ   wanżi   da   owakihi   śni
3b   because   metal white   thing   this   I have   not   and   thus   one   ask   I can   not
3c   I don't have any money, thus I ask you for this amount.

4a   nakaha   mniśośe   eciyataŋhaŋ   aśkatudaŋ   wówapi   maḳupi
4b   now   water muddy   from   lately   letter   they gave me
4c   I just received word from the Missouri River [Crow Creek].

5a   óŋkaŋ   nína   akihaŋpi   kéye   waniyetu   kiŋ   de   akihaŋ   oŋtapi   kta   nacece
5b   and   very   starving   said   winter   the   this   starve   they died   will   maybe
5c   The people are starving this winter, there they are dying from starvation.

6a   eya   hécen   nina   caŋte   maśice   do   mihuŋka
6b   to say   therefore   very   heart   bad   it is so   my relative
6c   This saddens me very much, my relative.

7a   wanżi   nakaha   táku   wanżi   nawahuŋ   óŋkaŋ   iwaśte   ce   do
7b   one   now   thing   one   I heard   and   good   so   it is so
7c   Recently, there is good news,

8a   maĥpiya   caŋhdeśka   sagdaśiŋ   wicaśta   yatapi   héciya   kéyapi
8b   Cloud   Sacred hoop   French   man   leader   there   they said
8c   the man called Sacred Cloud Hoop, a mixed Frenchman leader, they said

9a   akicita   tukte   duha   hen   eciya   óŋkaŋ   isata   ąa   ekta   kihdace   eya
9b   soldiers   where   you have   there   asked   and   beside   and   at   gone   to say
9c   where are the soldiers, they asked him when he was here, and then he went home.

10a   óŋkaŋ   miyeḳe   ihaŋktoŋwan   amapa   keŝ   ekta   ewatuŋwe   śni
10b   and   me/myself   Yanktons   hit me   even so   at   to tell truth   not
10c   As for myself, even if the Yanktons hit me, I will not be bothered by this.

11a   ece   eya   kéyepi   ite omawapi   waziyata   akiyahdapi   kéyapi
11b   always   to say   they said   They Mark My Face   north   they take him   they said
11c   They said the man they call Paint My Face was taken up north.

12a   Waŝteŝte
12b   Good-Good

23. Waŝteŝte, [1864]

Rev. S. R. Riggs

Mihuka wanji nakaha Wowapi cicage kte wowapi wakan cajedata tuka mazaska taku da
mduhe ŝni qa heon wanji da owakihi ŝni nakaha mniŝoŝe eciyataha aŝka tuka wowapi maqupi
onkan nina akiḣapi keye waniyete kin de akiḣa onṭapi kta nacece eya hecen nina cante maŝice
do mihuka wanji nakaha taku wanji nawaḣu onkan iwaŝte ce do maḣpiya cahdeŝka sadaŝi
wicaŝta yatapi heciya keyapi akicita tukte duha he eciya onkan isata ka ekta kihdace eya onkan
miyeqe ihaktuwana amapa keŝ ekta ewatu we ŝni ece eya keyepi ite omawapi waziyata akiya
hdapi keyapi

Waŝteŝte

• • • •

23. Good-Good, [1864]

Rev. S. R. Riggs

One of my relatives, I write this letter to you. You mentioned the Holy Bible. I don't have any
money, thus I ask you for this amount. I just received word from the Missouri River [Crow
Creek]. The people are starving this winter, there they are dying from starvation. This saddens
me very much, my relative. Recently, there is good news, the man called Sacred Cloud Hoop, a
mixed Frenchman leader, they said where are the soldiers, they asked him when he was here,
and then he went home. As for myself, even if the Yanktons hit me, I will not be bothered by
this. They said the man they call Paint My Face was taken up north.

Good-Good

CC/MW

1a   Tamakoce   mihuŋkawaŋżi   eya   yahi   kiŋ   he   wicaŝta   owasiŋ   waŝtedaka
1b   His Country   one of my relatives   when   you came   the   that   man   all   good   consider
1c   One of my relatives, His Country, when you came, all men were maybe happy,

2a   nace   epce   do   miŝ   yahi   óŋkaŋ   hécen   nínaĥiŋ   waŝte   wadake   tuka
2b   maybe   I thought   it is so   me   you come   and here   then   very   good   I consider   because
2c   I thought—it is so.   Myself, then, when you came, I was very happy, because

3a   táku   wakan   okodakiciye   tawa   eciyataŋtaŋ   caŋte   mawaŝte   ġa   hehaŋ   táku   waŋżi
3b   thing   Sacred   fellowship   my   from   heart   is good   and   then   thing   one
3c   of the sacred fellowship.   From this my heart was good, and then one thing

4a   epe   kte   táku   wakan   oie   oŋyaḳupi   oŋkaŋ   wicaŝta   waŋ   winuĥiŋca   owasiŋ
4b   I said   will   thing   sacred   word   you gave us   and here   man   a   women   all
4c   I will say.   You gave us the Holy Spirit's Word, and here a man

5a   nína   wahokon   wicakiya   óŋkaŋ   hécen   te   wamaŋuŋsa   he   wake   he   eciŋ
5b   very   preach to them   and here   then   died   thief   him   I mean   him   is
5c   preached to all the women, and here then, Always Steals died, he is

6a   toŋkan   waye   nakaŝ   ta   tuka   wéksuye   ca   miŝ   tóken   owakihi   táku   wakan
6b   my father in law   so   died   but   I remember   when   me   how   I can   thing   sacred
6c   my father in law, so he died.   So when I remember this, how I can have the Sacred

7a   oieye   kiŋ   yuha   wówahdake   tuka   eciŋ   mayasapa   en   táku   wakan   oieye
7b   word   the   have   I speak   because   to think   black bank   at   thing   sacred   word
7c   Word but speak, because to think at Black Bank [near Mankato]

8a   oŋyaḳupi   kehaŋ   wicaŝta   owasiŋ   kiŋ   oŋ   taŋiŋyaŋ   wóoŋhdakapi   kiŋ   he
8b   you gave us   when   man   all   the   so   truthful   we speak   the   that
8c   you gave us the Word.   So when all the men, we speak truthful,

9a   wicawaka   nace   epca   waon   óhiŋniyan   táku   wakan   kiŋ   nína   céwakiye
9b   I tell truth   maybe   I think   I am   always   thing   sacred   the   very   I pray
9c   I tell the truth, maybe I think I am always praying very much.

10a   miŝtiŋca   ekta   owasiŋ   céwakiye   haĥaŋna   owasiŋ   céwakiye   óŋkaŋ
10b   rabbit   at   all   I pray   morning   all   I pray   and here
10c   At Rabbit [a place] I pray for all of them all morning.   I pray and here

11a   hécen   óŋŝimada   ġa   makoŝice   óta   tuka   taŋyan   waon   he   etaŋhan   táku   wakan
11b   then   pity me   and   bad lands   alot   but   well   I am   for   there   thing   sacred
11c   God pities me, even through bad situations, but I am doing fine, from there the Holy Spirit

12a   eceyedan   waciŋwaye   ġa   dehan   táku   waŋżi   nakaha   ecuŋpi   tuka   naka
12b   alone   I depend on   and   now   thing   one   now   they did   but   now
12c   alone I depend on.   And now, one thing they have done,

13a   ḳehan   hékta   wau   kiŋ   mini   wakan   kiŋ   he   táku   owasiŋ   ŝicakaġe
13b   when   past   I came   the   water   holy   the   that   thing   all   make bad
13c   and in the past, I used alcohol, all things were bad.

\>

24. Napiŝtaŋyaŋ, [1864]

Tamakoce mihunkawanji eya yahikin he wicaxta owasin waxte daka nace epce do mix yahi
onkan hecen ninarin waxte wadake tuka taku wakan okodakiciye tawa eciyatantan cante
mawaxte qa hehan taku wanji epe kte taku wakan oie onyaqupi onkan wicaxta wan winurinca
owasin nina wahokon wicakiya onkan hecen ṭe wamanunsa he wake he ecin tokan waye
nakax ṭa tuka weksuye ça mix token owakihi taku wakan oieye kin yuha wowahdake tuka ecin
mayasapa en taku wakan oieye onyaqupi qehan wicaxta owasin i on taninyan wo on hdakapi
kin he wicawaka nace epca waon ohiniyan taku wakan kin nina cewakiye mixtince ekta owasin
cewakiye hanranna owasin cewakiye onkan hecen onximada qa makoxice ota tuka tanyan waon
he etanhan taku wakan eceyedan wacin waye qa hehan taku wanji nakaha ecunpi tuka naka
qehan he kta wa u kin mini wakan kin he taku owasin xicakage

>

• • • •

24. Hands That Ruin, [1864]

One of my relatives, His Country, when you came, all men were maybe happy, I thought—it is
so. Myself, then, when you came, I was very happy, because of the sacred fellowship. From this
my heart was good, and then one thing I will say. You gave us the Holy Spirit's Word, and here
a man preached to all the women, and here then, Always Steals died, he is my father in law, so
he died. So when I remember this, how I can have the Sacred Word but speak, because to think
at Black Bank [near Mankato] you gave us the Word. So when all the men, we speak truthful, I
tell the truth, maybe I think I am always praying very much. At Rabbit [a place] I pray for all of
them all morning. I pray and here God pities me, even through bad situations, but I am doing
fine, from there the Holy Spirit alone I depend on. And now, one thing they have done, and in
the past, I used alcohol, all things were bad.

>

14a   hetaŋhaŋ nakaha wówapi wakaŋ yutaŋpi ḳehan miŝ tohaŋyaŋ niwaoŋ kiŋhaŋ
14b   so then now Bible made known when me as long as I live if
14c   So then now the Bible is made known to me, as long as I live,

15a   hehaŋyaŋ oŋġedaŋ mdatke kte ŝni kepce ḍa taku wakan iŋ owakiyake hena he
15b   long any I drink will not I think and thing sacred the I help these this
15c   I will not drink alcohol, I think, and the Holy Spirit can help those who drink.

16a   nayaḣuŋ waciŋ ḍa he óciciyake ḍa hehan wicaŝta tóna huŋkayapi wicayakaġapi
16b   you hear I want and this I tell you and then man some elders they made
16c   These drinkers, I want you to hear, and that is why I tell you, and several men, they made some elders,

17a   kiŋ he tóken yápi kiŋhaŋ he wicihakam waoŋ kta epca caŋte yuswaoŋ
17b   the they where they go if will follow I am will I think heart hold onto
17c   where they go, I will follow, I think I hold them in my heart,

18a   hena he nayaḣun kta epca waoŋ ḍa heoŋ hépe ḍa hehan ito
18b   these those you hear will I thought I am and why I said and then well
18c   these, I thought you will hear, and why I said that.   And

19a   táku waŋżi ociciyake kte koŝka yámni nína wahokoŋ wica wakiye óŋkaŋ waŋna
19b   thing one tell you will young men three very I preached to them and here now
19c   one thing I will tell you, there are three young men I preach to, and here now

20a   táku wakaŋ óŋŝimada ḍa waŋżi taŋkan kiŋhda óŋkaŋ hécen waŝte wadake
20b   thing sacred pity me and one went out and here then good consider
20c   the Holy Spirit pitied me, and one went out, and here I like this,

21a   ḍa imduŝkiŋ num om maŋka tuka nupiŋ mini wakaŋ yatke ŝni
21b   and I am happy two among with sit both water sacred drink not
21c   and I am happy.   I am amongst two of them, both no longer drink alcohol,

22a   wówapi yutaŋpi tuŋwaŋ waŋżidan pa waŝtedan hena waŋs nína wahokoŋ wicawakiye
22b   paper signed arrow one head good these two very preach to them
22c   and signed a paper.   One Arrow, Good Head, these two I really preach to,

23a   táku epe ciŋ owasiŋ anaġoptaŋpi ḍa hécen waŝte wadake
23b   thing I said want all they listen and then good I consider
23c   they listen to all that I say, and I am happy.

24a   henana epe kte mihuŋkawaŋżi jesus eciyataŋhaŋ nape ciyuze
24b   these I say my relative one Jesus from hand I shake
24c   My one relative, this is all I say, from Jesus, I shake your hand.

25a   napiŝtaŋyaŋ he miye do
25b   Hands That Ruin, this is me—it is so.

heetanhan nakaha wowapi wakan yutanpi qehan mix tohanyan niwaon kinhan hehanyan ongedan mdatke kte xni kepe qa taku wakan kin owakiyake hena henayarun wacin qa he ociciyake qa hehan wicaxta tona hunkayapi wicayakagapi kin he token yapi kinhan he wicihakam waon kta epca cante yus waon hena he nayarun kta epca waon qa heon hepe qa hehan ito taku wanji ociciyake kte koxka yamni nina wahokon wica wakiye onkan wanna taku wakan onximada qa wanji tankan kinhda onkan hecen waxte wadake qa imduxkin num om makatuka napin mini wakan yatkexni wowapi yutanpi tunwan wanjidan, pawaxtedan, hena wans nina wahokon wica wakiye tuka taku epe cin owasin anagoptanpi qa hecen waxte wadake henana epekte mihunkawanji jesus eciyatanhan nape ciyuze

napinxtanyan hemiyedo

• • • •

So then now the Bible is made known to me, as long as I live, I will not drink alcohol, I think, and the Holy Spirit can help those who drink. These drinkers, I want you to hear, and that is why I tell you, and several men, they made some elders, where they go, I will follow, I think I hold them in my heart, these, I thought you will hear, and why I said that. And one thing I will tell you, there are three young men I preach to, and here now the Holy Spirit pitied me, and one went out, and here I like this, and I am happy. I am amongst two of them, both no longer drink alcohol, and signed a paper. One Arrow, Good Head, these two I really preach to, they listen to all that I say, and I am happy. My one relative, this is all I say, from Jesus, I shake your hand.

Hands That Ruin, this is me—it is so.

CC/MW

1a Mihaŋkawaŋżi   tamakoce
1b One of my relatives   His Country
1c His Country, one of my relatives

2a Ito tóken caŋte yus waoŋ kiŋ He nayaĥuŋ waciŋ ɋa heoŋ wówapi
2b well how heart hold I am the this you hear I want and thus letter
2c I am writing you this short letter to let you know what is

3a waŋżi cístiŋna ciĉu   he mihuŋkawaŋżi ikce wicaŝta kiŋ táku wóksape
3b one small I give you this my relative one common man the thing wisdom
3c in my heart.   My relative, we Dakota do not have wisdom,

4a oŋnicapi ɋa hécen oŋksapapi ŝni ɋa dehan teĥiya uŋyakuŋpi kiŋ
4b we have not and thus we are wise not and now terrible we are the
4c and so we are suffering.

5a héoŋ   táku wakaŋ oie kiŋ caŋte ocowasiŋ oŋ awacaŋmi
5b therefore spirit holy word the heart whole use I think
5c Therefore, we are thinking about the Holy Spirit and His Word with all our heart.

6a tuka iye táku wakaŋ   ómakiye kta nína icewakiye ɋa hehan
6b but he spirit holy spirit help me will very I pray and then
6c I am always in prayers, so the Holy Spirit will help us.   And

7a mihuŋkawaŋżi tókiya óhiŋniyaŋ waciŋ yeya   waoŋ kiŋ he ociciyake kte
7b my relative one where always depend upon him I am the this I tell you will
7c I always depend on the Holy Spirit, my relative, and I am letting you know that.

8a winuĥica mitawa hokŝiyopa mitawa owasiŋ makiṫapi ɋa héoŋ   miŝnaŋa ni waoŋ
8b my wife mine child/baby my all they died and therefore I alone am alive
8c My wife and all my children have died, and I am alone.

9a tuka hena owasiŋ mini awicakaŝṫaŋpi ɋa hehan ṫápi
9b but these all water baptism and then they died
9c These all have been baptized and died.

10a héoŋ   miŝ tohaŋyaŋ ni waoŋ kiŋhaŋ táku wakaŋ kiŋ heceedaŋ óhiŋniyaŋ waciŋyaŋ
10b therefore I how long I live if spirit holy the alone always I depend on
10c I am thinking that as long as I live, I will depend upon

11a waoŋ kta epca   waoŋ ɋa hehaŋ miŝ tohaŋ táku wakaŋ iye tukten wicuŋte
11b I live will I thought I am and then I when spirit holy him where I die
11c the Holy Spirit.   So then, when my time to die comes, and

12a yuha icaĥmaye ciŋ he   iyehaŋtu hehaŋ mita wiŋ miciŋca
12b have raised me the him   at that time then my female children
12c I will be raised, I will go there also.   Then I will see my wife and daughters.

>

25. Wicaȟiŋca maza, [1864]

Mihuŋkawaŋji tamakoce

Ito token cante yus waon kin He nayarun wacin qa heon wowapi wanji cistinna ciçu he mihunkawanji ikcewicaxta kin taku woksape onnicape qa hecen onksapapi xni qa dehan teriya onyakunpi kin heon taku wakan oie kin cante ocowasin on awacanmi tuka iye taku wakan wakan omakiye kta nina icewakiye qa hehan mihunkawanji tokiya ohiniyan wacin yeya waon kin he ociciyake kte winurinca mitawa hokxiyopa mitawa owasin makiṭapi qa heon mixnana niwaon tuka hena owasin mini awicakaxtanpi qa hehan ṭapi heon mix tohanyan niwaon kinhan taku wakan kin heceedan ohiniyan wacinyan waon kta epca waon qa hehan mix tohan taku wakan iye tukten wicunṭe yuha icar maye cin he iye hanyetu kinhan hehan mita win micinca

>

• • • •

25. Old Iron Man, [1864]

His Country, one of my relatives

I am writing you this short letter to let you know what is in my heart. My relative, we Dakota do not have wisdom, and so we are suffering. Therefore, we are thinking about the Holy Spirit and His Word with all our heart. I am always in prayers, so the Holy Spirit will help us. And I always depend on the Holy Spirit, my relative, and I am letting you know that. My wife and all my children have died, and I am alone. These all have been baptized and died. I am thinking that as long as I live, I will depend upon the Holy Spirit. So then, when my time to die comes, and I will be raised, I will go there also. Then I will see my wife and daughters.

>

13a   hena   owasiŋ   taŋyaŋ   wakaŋtaŋka   hékta   óŋpi   héciŋhaŋ   miŝ   ekta   wai   kta
13b   these   all   well   God   at   live   where   I   at   I go   will
13c   I have preached to all who were alive then,

14a   epca   waoŋ   ɋa   héoŋ   táku   wakaŋ   eceyedaŋ   waciŋ   waye   ɋa   hehaŋ   ito
14b   I think   live   and   therefore   spirit   holy   alone   I depend   upon   and   then   well
14c   and I am depending on the Holy Spirit alone,

15a   mihuŋkawaŋži   táku   waŋži   ociciyake   kte   ĥeyata   tuŋwaŋna
15b   one of my relatives   what something   one   I am telling you   will   back   looking
15c   my relative, and one thing, I am looking back there I have preached very hard, too.

16a   kiŋ   hena   owasiŋ   nína   wahokuŋwicawakiye   tuka   iye   héyapi
16b   the   these   all   very   I preach to/counsel them   because   him   they said that
16c   So I am enabling myself and all of them,

17a   wahokuŋ   oŋyakiyapi   kte   emakiyapi   héoŋ   amiĉiciya   ɋa   waŋna   owasiŋ
17b   preach to us   will/shall   they told me   therefore   I act as I am able   and   now   all
17c   they told me, therefore, I will now transform by the Holy Spirit

18a   táku   wakaŋ   oie   kiŋ   ohna   caŋte   yázapi   óŋkaŋ   hécen   waŝte   wadake
18b   holy   spirit   word   the   in   heart   they hold   and   here   so   good   I consider
18c   to take the Word of God to heart, so I think this is good, and therefore

19a   ɋa   héoŋ   he   ociciyake   tuka   niŝ   eya   waŝteyadake   kta   epca   waoŋ
19b   and   these/some   this   I tell you   because   you   to say   like/good   the   I think   I am
19c   I am telling you, because now I am glad.   I tell you, and maybe you are glad,

20a   ɋa   heoŋ   he   ociciyake   ɋa   hehaŋ   nakaha   táku   waŋžii   wakaŋtaŋka   teĥinda
20b   and   therefore   this   I tell you   And   then   now/today   thing   one   God   cherish
20c   as well.   And now what God values,

21a   waŋži   ecuŋkuŋpi   kte   ŝni   oŋ   ciŋpi   ɋa   wakaŋtaŋka   oŋkokiyakapi
21b   one   we are doing   will/shall   not   they   want   and   God   told them
21c   we are doing, and we have told them, some have been drinking

22a   mini wakaŋ   nína   yatkaŋpi   tuka   he   totaŋhaŋ   komaŝka   kiŋ   he
22b   water holy   very   drink   because   this   from the time   I was younger   the   this
22c   alcohol, and from the time I was a young man, I have not drunk any

23a   taŋhaŋ   he   ecamuŋ   ŝni   kiŋ   he   taŋyaŋ   sdonwakiye   ca   nakuŋ
23b   from   this   I do   not   the   this   good/well   I understand myself   when
23c   alcohol.   I know and understand well, and

24a   wakaŋtaŋka   taŋyaŋ   tóna   sdon   ɋa   epca   waoŋ   ɋa   hehaŋ
24b   God   good/well   some   understand   and   I think   I am   and   then
24c   also God understands well, I think, and then

25a   wicaŝta   wahokoŋ wicawakiye   ciŋ   tóna   mini wakaŋ   yatke   ŝni
25b   man   I preach to/counsel   the   some   water holy   drink   not
25c   I have been preaching to some men not to drink alcohol.

>

hena owasin tanyan wakantanka hekta onpi hecinhan mix ekta wai kta epca waon qa heon taku wakan eceyedan wacin waye qa hehan ito mihunkawanji taku wanji ociciyake kte reyata tunwanna kin hena owasin nina wahokun wica wakiye tuka iye heyapi wahokun onyakiyapi kte e makiyapi heon amiçiciya qa wanna owasin taku wakan oie kin ohna cante yuzapi onkan hecen waxte wadake qa heon he ociciyake tuka nix eya waxte yadake kta epca waon qa heon he ociciyake qa hehan nakaha taku wanjii wakantanka terinda wanji ecunkunpi kte xni on cinpi qa wakantanka onkokiyakapi mini wakan nina yatkanpi tuka he totanhan komaxka kin he tanhan he ecamun xni kin he tanyan sdonwakiye ça nakun wakantanka tanyan sdon ca epca waon qa hehan wicaxta tona wahokon wicawakiye cin tona mini wakan yatke xni

>

• • • •

I have preached to all who were alive then, and I am depending on the Holy Spirit alone, my relative, and one thing, I am looking back there I have preached very hard, too. So I am enabling myself and all of them, they told me, therefore, I will now transform by the Holy Spirit to take the Word of God to heart, so I think this is good, and therefore I am telling you, because now I am glad. I tell you, and maybe you are glad, as well. And now what God values, we are doing, and we have told them, some have been drinking alcohol, and from the time I was a young man, I have not drunk any alcohol. I know and understand well, and also God understands well, I think, and then I have been preaching to some men not to drink alcohol.

>

26a   wówapi   yutaŋpi   kiŋ   he   ociciyake   kte   tate yuha mani,
26b   paper   they signed   the   this   I tell you   will/shall   Wind Holds As He Walks
26c   They all signed a paper that they will not drink, they are Walks With the Wind,

27a   otiŋiyape   maḣpiya aihduhomni,   kaḣboke,   tuŋwaŋ wakiŋyaŋ,
27b   To Dwell and To Breathe   Makes the Cloud Go Around Him   Drifting/Floating   Thunder Arrow
27c   Let Him Live, Brings the Cloud Around Him, Drifting, Thunder Arrow,

28a   áŋpaohdinażẏŋ,   wakiŋyaŋġi,   heḣakamaza,   mázawamnuha,
28b   Arrives at Day-Break   Brown Thunder   Iron Elk   Iron Pumpkin Shell
28c   Arrives at Daybreak, Brown Thunder, Iron Elk, Iron Pumpkin Shell,

29a   mazayeyamani,   huŋka, hena   om   wówapi   wakaŋ   mdutaŋ   ḋa   hehaŋ   iyuḣpa
29b   Walking Throwing Iron   Root   these   amongst   paper   holy   revealed   and   then   further
29c   Walking Throwing Iron, Root, these I have revealed the Bible to.   Then further,

30a   táku   wakaŋ   idowaŋpi   kiŋ   iyuškiŋpi   héoŋ   miš imduškiŋ   waoŋ   tuka   ito
30b   spirit   holy   they sang   the   they are happy   therefore   I am happy   I am   because   well
30c   they are singing joyfully about the Holy Spirit.   So then I am happy, because from here on

31a   detaŋhaŋ   tokata   tóken   camuŋ   ḋa   owotaŋna   ḋa   wašte   kta   idukcaŋ   kiŋhaŋ
31b   from here   forward   what   to do   and   straight   and   good   will   think for myself   if
31c   I am doing good.   If you think I am doing fine,

32a   he   nawaḣuŋ   waciŋ   do   mihuŋkaważẏ   jesus   eciyataŋhaŋ   nape   ciyuze
32b   the   I hear   I want   this is so   one of my relatives   Jesus   from him   hand   I shake
32c   I want to hear this, so this is all.   One of my relatives, I shake your hand through Jesus.

33a   wicaḣiŋca máza   he miye
33b   Old Man Iron, this is me

wowapi yutanpi kin he ociciyake kte tate yuhmani, otiniyape, marpiyaaihduhomni, karboke, tunwanwakinyan, anpaohidinaji, wakinyangi, herakamaza, mazawamnuha, mazayeyamani, huntka, hena om wowapi wakan mdutan qa hehan iyurpa taku wakan idowanpi kin iyuxkinpi heon mix imduxkin waon tuka ito detanhan tokata token camun qa owotanna qa waxte kta idukcan kinhan he nawarun wacin do mihunkawanji jesus eciyatanhan nape ciyuze

Wicarincamaza he miye

• • • •

They all signed a paper that they will not drink, they are Walks With the Wind, Let Him Live, Brings the Cloud Around Him, Drifting, Thunder Arrow, Arrives at Daybreak, Brown Thunder, Iron Elk, Iron Pumpkin Shell, Walking Throwing Iron, Root, these I have revealed the Bible to. Then further, they are singing joyfully about the Holy Spirit. So then I am happy, because from here on I am doing good. If you think I am doing fine, I want to hear this, so this is all. One of my relatives, I shake your hand through Jesus.

Old Man Iron, this is me

CC/MW

1a Mihunka   wanżi Tamakoce   anpetu kiŋ de   wówapi cicaġe   kte
1b My relative one   His Country day   the this letter   give you   will
1c His Country one of my relatives, this day I will give you a letter.

2a takomni   eya   hécen epe   kta iyecece nakaŝ héoŋ   anpetu
2b Nevertheless to say then I say will right   so   therefore   day
2c Nevertheless, I will say the right thing today.

3a he   táku   wanżi wanna uŋ   miŝ imiyeciye kta Waciŋ do.
3b There something one   now   for me say for me will I want it is so
3c Now there is one thing I want you to say for me, it is so.

4a he   Oyate matokca Nakaŝ héoŋ   tuwedaŋ uŋŝimada ŝni ąa dehaŋyaŋ
4b I am tribe different so   therefore no one   pity   not and so far
4c I am of a different tribe, so therefore no one pities me, and so far

5a uŋ iyotaŋhaŋ iyewakiye ho eya   waŝicuŋ wakaŋ kiŋ Ikce wicaŝta kiŋ he
5b we greatly   suffering   so to say minister   the common man   the this
5c we the common men are greatly suffering, so to say.

6a Waciŋuŋniyaŋpi Nakaŝ Niŝ tohaŋ uŋkeyeciyapi Owasiŋ Nauŋĥuŋpi tuka
6b we need your help so   you   when   speak for us   all   they hear us but
6c We need your help, so when you speak for all of us, they hear us, but

7a he eciŋ   hépa iyecece do
7b so suppose I say right   it is so
7c so suppose it is right, I say—it is so.

8a Mihuŋka   wanżi Nape ciyuza ye do.
8b My relative one   hand shake it is so.
8c One of my relatives, I shake your hand—it is so.

9a   Hotaŋke
9b   Ho-Chunk

10a Makainape   He miye Do
10b Comes Out of the Earth   it is me—it is so

26. Makainape, [1864]

Mihunka wanji Tamakoce anpetu kin de wowapi ciçu kte takomni eya hecen epa kta iyecece
nakax heon anpetu he taku wanji wanna un mix imiyeciye kta Wacin do he Oyate matokca
Nakax heon tuwedan unximada xni qa dehanyan un iyotanhan iyewakiye ho eya waxicun
wakan kin Ikce wicaxta kin he wacinunniyapi Nakax Nix tohan unkeyeciyapi Owasin
Naunrunpi tuka he ecin hepa iyecece do
Mihunka wanjin Nape ciyuza ye do

       Hotanke
     Makainape He miye Do

• • • •

26. Comes Out of the Earth, [1864]

His Country one of my relatives, this day I will give you a letter. Nevertheless, I will say the right
thing today. Now there is one thing I want you to say for me, it is so. I am of a different tribe, so
therefore no one pities me, and so far we the common men are greatly suffering, so to say. We
need your help, so when you speak for all of us, they hear us, but so suppose it is right, I say—
it is so.
One of my relatives, I shake your hand—it is so.

       Ho-Chunk
     Comes Out of the Earth it is me—it is so

CC/MW

1a	tamakoce	Mihuŋka waŋżi	nakaha	wówapi	cícaġe	kta	waciŋ	tuka	uŋmaspe
1b	His Country	my relative one	now	letter	make	will	I want	but	know
1c	One of my relatives, His Country, I don't know how to write you a letter, but

2a	śni	wehaŋna	wahdi	tuka	hécen	waŋna	mihiŋhna kiŋ	ṫe haŋ	wahdi
2b	not	last spring	I came home	but	then	now	husband the	died	I came home
2c	now last spring I came home [to Redwood], but then now my husband died, I came home.

3a	nakaśin	tuwedaŋ	táku	óŋśimakiyap kiŋ	naka kiŋ	tehiya	waoŋ	hécen
3b	and	no one	thing	pitied me the	and the	terrible	I am	then
3c	And then no one takes pity on me, and I am suffering terribly.

4a	oŋ	niśnana	waciŋciye	ĥiŋ	ce	tuka	téhaŋyaŋ	naka kiŋ	waŋciyake
4b	because	you alone	I depend	very	so	but	far	you are the	see you
4c	I depend on you alone very much, but you are too far away.							To see you

5a	kta	owakihi kiŋ	eya	táku waŋżi	epe	eciciye	kta	waciŋ	tuka	owakihi śni
5b	will	I can the	to say	thing one	say	to you	will	I want	but	I can not
5c	I can, I will say one thing to you, I want to but I cannot.

6a	mihiŋhna kiŋ	he	típi kiŋ	táku	ohnaka kiŋ	owasiŋ	każużupi	kta	e
6b	husband the	this	dwelling the	thing	put in the	all	payed for	will	so
6c	My husband, they paid for all his belongings in his dwelling, so

7a	okiwapi kiŋ	he	wake	he ṫe kiŋ	econpi	ca	he	ciŋhaŋ
7b	they wrote the	this	I mean	this died the	they did	so	this	if
7c	if they wrote this is when he died,

8a	he	nínaĥiŋ	oŋ	waciŋciye	ómayakiye	kta	waciŋ	ecin	hokśiyopa kiŋ
8b	this	very	because	I depend on you	help me	will	I want	because	infant the
8c	I depend on you very much, I want you to help me because of the infant,

9a	uŋma	eṫe kiŋ	nituka	ecin	kici	táku	waciŋwaye	kta	iye	cece śni
9b	other	that the	live	because so	both	thing	I depend on you	will	he	like not
9c	so the other can live, both of us should not depend on you.

10a	wókoyake	ḳa	wóyute	ko	owasiŋ	ĥiŋ	oŋ	tehiya	waoŋ
10b	clothing	and	food	both	all	very	thus	terrible	I am
10c	I am suffering for the lack of food and clothing.

11a	ce	hécen	mázaska kiŋ	he	icu	oyakipi	úŋkan kiŋ	iyacu
11b	so	then	metal white the	this	give	they said	and the	you took
11c	So then they said you took the money,

12a	ḳa	heciŋ	miye	ḳu	kiŋhaŋ	pidamayaye	kta	tuka	epca	caŋśayapi
12b	and	thus	me	give	if	I thank you	will	but	I thought	wood red
12c	and if you can give me back my money, I will thank you, but I thought, at Redwood

13a	hnaya	ko	upi	kiŋ den	ówape	ecin	eya	waziyata	imdamde	kta
13b	these	all	are coming	here	I am amongst them	so	to say	west	I am going	will
13c	I am amongst all those are coming here, I will be going west.

>

27. Makaahewiŋ, [1864]

tamakoce Mihunka wanji nakaha wowapi cicage kta wacin tuka umaspe xni wehanna wahdi tuka hecen wana mihinhna kin te han wahdi nakaxin tuwedan taku onsimakiyap xin naka xin teriya waon hecen on nixnana wacinciye rin ce tuka tehanyan naka xin waciyake kta owakihi xni eya taku wanji epe eciciye kta wacin tuka owakihi xni mihinhna kin he tipi kin taku ohnaka kin owasin kajujupi kta e okiwapi kin he wakac e he te kin econpi ca he cinhan he ninarin on wacinciye omayakiye kta wacin ecin hokxiyopa kin uma eqe xin nituka ecin kici taku wacinwaye kta iye cece xni wokoyake qa woyute ko owasin rin on teriya waon ce hecen mazaska kin he icu oyakipi unkan xin iyacu qa hecin miye cu kinhan pidamayaye kta tuka epca canxayakis hnaya ko upi kin din owape ecin eya waziyata imda mde kta

>

• • • •

27. Stands on Earth Woman, [1864]

One of my relatives, His Country, I don't know how to write you a letter, but now last spring I came home [to Redwood], but then now my husband died, I came home. And then no one takes pity on me, and I am suffering terribly. I depend on you alone very much, but you are too far away. To see you I can, I will say one thing to you, I want to but I cannot. My husband, they paid for all his belongings in his dwelling, so if they wrote this is when he died, I depend on you very much, I want you to help me because of the infant, so the other can live, both of us should not depend on you. I am suffering for the lack of food and clothing. So then they said you took the money, and if you can give me back my money, I will thank you, but I thought, at Redwood I am amongst all those are coming here, I will be going west.

>

14a iyecece śni tuka ecin miye cin ḳa śni ḑa dehan teȟiya ȟin
14b seems not because to think I decided not and now terrible very
14c It does not seem right, and now I am suffering very much.

15a wahdi ecin heciya tanhan waku kte kinhan owapi epe kin
15b came home thus this from coming will if they write them the
15c If I will be coming from there, I will write a letter,

16a tuka hehan naȟun an wahdiyaku naka kin hánpa ḑa táku yútapi ko
16b but then heard so I came back now the shoe and thing they eat both
16c but they hear I came back now, I need shoes and something to eat.

17a on iyotanhan iyewakiye ȟinca wahdi tuka hécen mihihna ehanna ta
17b because of suffering very I came home but then my husband long ago died
17c I am suffering very much, I came home, but then they said my husband died long ago,

18a kéyapi tuka ecin sdonwakiye śni naka kin wanunyaka kta nace epca
18b they said because so remember not now the see us will maybe I thought
18c because I don't remember now, maybe he will see us,

19a tuka hécen wamdake śni naka kin teȟiye ȟin ca
19b because then I saw not now the terrible very so
19c because I did not see him then. Now it is very terrible.

20a mitakuyepi owasin nape ciyuzapi hécen óhinni miye ksuyapi kta
20b my relatives all hand shake so always me remember will
20c All my relatives, I shake your hands, so you will always remember me.

21a wacin nitakuyepi wanżi miye
21b I want your relative one I am
21c I want you to remember me, I am one of your relatives,

22a makaahewin
22b Stands on Earth Woman

iyecece xni tuka ecin miye cin ka xni qa deha teriya rin wahdi ecin he ciyatanha waku kte cinhan owapi epe xin tuka hehan narun an wahdiyaku naka xin hanpa qa taku yutapi ko on iyotanhan iyewakiye rinca wahdi tuka hecen mihecuhana ehanna ta keyapi tuka ecin sdowakiye xni naka xin wamdake kta nace epca tuka hecen wamdake xni naka xin teriye rin ca mitakuyepi owasin nape ciyuzapi hecen ohini miye ksuyapi kta wacin nitakuyepi wanji miye

makaahewiŋ

• • • •

It does not seem right, and now I am suffering very much. If I will be coming from there, I will write a letter, but they hear I came back now, I need shoes and something to eat. I am suffering very much, I came home, but then they said my husband died long ago, because I don't remember now, maybe he will see us, because I did not see him then. Now it is very terrible. All my relatives, I shake your hands, so you will always remember me. I want you to remember me, I am one of your relatives,

Stands on Earth Woman

CC/MW

1a tamakoce mihuŋkawaŋži ito taku waŋzi epe kta totaŋhaŋ makaŝkapi
1b His Country my brother well what one I say will ever since put me in prison
1c Mr. S. R. Riggs, my brother. Well, there is one thing I will say. Since they put me in prison,

2a kiŋ hetaŋhaŋ aŋpetu owasiŋ ninahiŋ caŋtemaŝice táku uŋ
2b the from that time day all exceedingly sorrowful what to be
2c from that time, I am very sad every day. You will hear

3a caŋtemaŝice kiŋ he nayahoŋ kte makoce mayasapa eciyapi kiŋ hen
3b sorrowful the that you hear will country Black Bank called the there
3c about what saddens me. At the place called Black Bank [near Mankato]

4a misuŋka waŋži makite ḳa nakuŋ taŋhaŋŝiwaya waŋži hen
4b my younger brother one one's own died and also my cousin one there
4c one of my younger brothers died. There they also hung one of my cousins

5a nakuŋ pa makiyuksapi dakota ciŋca yámni hen wicaktepi
5b also head cut off friends children three there they killed
5c by breaking his head off. Also at the same place they killed three Dakota children,

6a kiŋ hen ope hehan ĥaĥamdote kiŋ en
6b the there join then the confluence of Mississippi-Minnesota Rivers the at
6c he was present there. Then at the mouth of the Minnesota River,

7a miciŋca waŋži makite ḳa hehaŋ makoce kiŋ den uŋhipi kiŋ hetaŋhaŋ
7b a child one own died and then country the here we came the from that time
7c a child of mine died. And from the time we came to this land,

8a ciŋye maĥpiyaoicaĥmani makite ḳa dekŝi waya waŋži nakuŋ
8b older brother Walks Among the Clouds one's own died and uncle my one also
8c my older brother, Walks Among the Clouds, died. And one of my uncles also

9a makite ate waya he suŋkaku ḳa nakuŋ miye taŋhaŋwaya waŋži
9b one's own died father my that brother and also me/I brother-in-law one
9c died. My father's brother and also my brother-in-law

10a makite wakiŋya wicakte eciyapi hena yámni den tápi
10b one's own died Thunder Kills his name Those three here died they
10c died, his name was Kills Thunder. Those three relatives of mine died here,

11a takuwicawaya kiŋ ŝákpe makitapi do mihuŋkawaŋži ehake mihuŋkawaŋžidaŋ
11b my relatives the six one's own died it is so my brother last one my only brother
11c also six more relatives died—it is so. My brother, I am alive here with only one brother,

12a kici den ni wauŋ hécen hena en aŋpetu owasiŋ
12b with here living are/to be so/therefore those at/in day all/everyone
12c therefore, every day my heart is

13a nína caŋtemaŝica tuka niye yakaǵapi ḳa wakaŋtaŋka oie kiŋ mayaḳupi
13b very my heart sad but you they made and Great Spirit word the gave me
13c very sorrowful. But you brought the Great Spirit's Word and gave it to me.

28. Ȟewaŋke [1864 or 1865]

tamakoce mihunkawanji ito taku wanji epe kta totanhan makaśkapi kin hetanhan anpetu
owasin ninaȟin cantemaśice taku un cantemaśice kin he nayaȟun kte makoce mayasapa eciyapi
kin hen misunka wanjin makiṭe qa nakun tahanśiwaya wanji hen nakun pa makiyuksapi dakota
cinca yamni hen wicaktepi kin hen ope hehan ȟaȟamdote kin en micinca wanji makiṭe qa
hehan makoce kin den onhipi kin hetanhan cinye maȟpiyaoicaȟmani makiṭe qa dekśi waya
wanji nakun makiṭe ate maya he sunkaku qa nakun miye tanhanwaya wanji makiṭe wakinya
wicakte eciyapi hena yamni den ṭapi takuwicawaya kin śakpe makiṭapi do mihunkawanji ehake
mihunkawanjidan kici den ni waun hecen hena en anpetu owasin nina cantemaśica tuka niye
yakagapi qa wakantanka oie kin mayaqupi

>

• • • •

28. Frost, [1864 or 1865]

Mr. S. R. Riggs, my brother. Well, there is one thing I will say. Since they put me in prison, from
that time, I am very sad every day. You will hear about what saddens me. At the place called
Black Bank [near Mankato] one of my younger brothers died. There they also hung one of my
cousins by breaking his head off. Also at the same place they killed three Dakota children, he
was present there. Then at the mouth of the Minnesota River, a child of mine died. And from
the time we came to this land, my older brother, Walks Among the Clouds, died. And one of
my uncles also died. My father's brother and also my brother-in-law died, his name was Kills
Thunder. Those three relatives of mine died here, also six more relatives died—it is so. My
brother, I am alive here with only one brother, therefore, every day my heart is very sorrowful.
But you brought the Great Spirit's Word and gave it to me.

>

14a ɋa hécen caŋte suta mayakaġapi héceŝ wakaŋtaŋka dehaŋ
14b and therefore heart strong made me that's why Great Spirit now
14c Therefore, you made my heart strong. Now I think that's why the Great Spirit

15a óŋŝimada kta epca nína aŋpetu owasiŋ céwakiye tuka miŝ ito
15b pity/mercy on me will I think very day all I pray but I well
15c will have mercy on me. Well, I pray every day, but

16a mihuŋkawaŋźi ómayakiye kta waciŋ wicaŝta kŝápa wohdakapi kiŋ hena
16b my brother help me will want Man wise you see the those
16c my brother will help me, I want you to. In you, those people see a wise man speaking,

17a owasin en oyapa hecen tóken owahdakapi kiŋ hena taŋyaŋ nayahuŋ
17b all at you joined therefore how they talk about it the those well you listen
17c because you joined them, therefore what they talked about, you heard those things, and you listen

18a ɋa taŋyaŋ sdoyaye maka akan detaŋhan wakaŋtaŋka oie kiŋ
18b the well to know earth upon from now on Great Spirit his word the
18c well and are very knowledgeable. While on this earth, I think from now on, when I am released

19a yuha taŋkan mde keŝ epca wauŋ tuka do
19b with out side I go although I think to be but it is so
19c I will take the Great Spirit's Word with me, although I am now confined—it is so.

20a mihunkawanźi waŋna henana epe kte do nape ciyuze do
20b my brother now so much I say will it is so hand I take hold of your it is so
20c My brother, that is all I will say for now—it is so. I shake your hand—it is so.

21a Ḣewanke miye do
21b Frost, that is me—it is so.

qa hecen cante suta mayakagapi heces wakantanka dehan onśimada kta epca nina anpetu owasin cewakiye tuka miś ito mihunkawanji omayakiye kta wacin wicaśta ksapa wahdakapi kin hena owasin en oyapa hecen token owohdakapi kin hena tanyan nayahun qa tanyan sdoyaye maka akan detanhan wakantanka oie kin yuha tankan mde qeś epca waun tuka do mihunkawanji wanna henana epe kte do nape ciyuze do

Rewanke miye do

• • • •

Therefore, you made my heart strong. Now I think that's why the Great Spirit will have mercy on me. Well, I pray every day, but my brother will help me, I want you to. In you, those people see a wise man speaking, because you joined them, therefore what they talked about, you heard those things, and you listen well and are very knowledgeable. While on this earth, I think from now on, when I am released I will take the Great Spirit's Word with me, although I am now confined—it is so. My brother, that is all I will say for now—it is so. I shake your hand—it is so.

Frost, that is me—it is so.

MS/AC

1a	Tamakoce	mihuŋka	waŋżi	ito	ake	táku	waŋżi	epe	kte	yedo	damakota
1b	His Country	relative	one	well	again	thing	one	I say	will	it is so	I am Dakota

1c One of my relatives, His Country, well again one thing I want to say.   I am Dakota,

2a	ģa	hécen	dakota	wicohaŋ	tawapi	kiŋ	owasiŋ	ĥiŋ	sdonwaye	tuka	dehan
2b	and	then	Dakota	ways/work	their	the	all		very knowledgeable	but	now

2c and all these Dakota ways, I am very knowledgeable about, but now

3a	hena	waŋna	amduśtaŋ	kta	keciye	kiŋ	he	óhiŋniyaŋ	kiksuya	wauŋ	eciŋ
3b	these	now	I quit	will	to tell you	the	this	always	remember	I am	because

3c I will quit these now, I tell you that I am always remembering because

4a	hena	oŋ	matakuni śni	kiŋ	nakaha	sdonwakiye	hécen	detaŋhan	wicohaŋ
4b	these are	I am nothing	the	now	now myself	then	from here	ways-work

4c these are nothing to me.   Now I realize, from here onwards

5a	kiŋ	he	ĥeyata	iyewaye	kta	epca	wauŋ	wakaŋtaŋka	hena	ohimáye	kiŋhaŋ
5b	the	this	past	behind	will	I thought	I am	God		these	won me	if

5c these are behind me.   In the past, I thought, if God won me

6a	hena	hécetu	kte	hehan	wicohaŋ	mayaķupi	kiŋ	he	ito	cażemdate	kte
6b	these	right	will	then	ways-work	you all gave me	the	this	well	I named	will

6c these ways you all gave me, well, I will remember.

7a	wakaŋtaŋka	oieye	mayaķupi	ģa	hécen	oŋ	waditake	mayaśipi
7b	God	words	you all gave me	and	then	are	brave	you all told me to do

7c You all told me to be brave, and you all gave me God's Word.

8a	ģa	he	ecamuŋ	kta	óhiŋniyaŋ	epca	waoŋ	detaŋhan	wakaŋśica	kici weciza
8b	and	this	I do	will	always	I thought	I am	from here	Devil	fight

8c And I will always do this.   I thought, from here onward I will fight

9a	kta	epca	waoŋ	eciŋ	hécen	ecuŋ	mayaśipi	nakaś óhiŋni
9b	will	I thought	I am	because	then	do	you all told me to do	I surely

9c the Devil.   I thought, I am to do, because you all told me to do, surely

10a	ecamuŋ	kta	epca	waoŋ	tuwedan	iapi	śíca	oŋ	makte	kte	śni
10b	do	will	I thought	I am	no one	speaking	bad	with	kill me	will	not

10c I will do.   I thought, maybe no one will kill me with bad words,

11a	nace	epca	waoŋ	héoŋ	táku	epe	kta	eca	taŋiŋyaŋ	epa	ece
11b	maybe	I thought	I am	thus	thing	I say	will	so	clearly	say	so

11c thus, clearly I will say,

12a	homakśidaŋ	ģa	wóksape	śni	tuka	tohaŋyan	maka	akaŋ	ni	waoŋ
12b	as a boy	and	wisdom	not	thing	from	earth	upon	live	I am

12c as a young boy, I have no wisdom as long as I live on earth.

>

29. Ĥewaŋke, [1864]

Tamakoce mihunka wanji ito ake taku wanji epe kte yedo damakota qa hecen dakota wicoran
tawapi kin owasin rin sdonwaye tuka dehan hena wanna amduxtan kta keciciye kin he ohiniyan
kiksuya waun ecin hena on matakunixni kin nakaha sdonwakiye hecen detanhan wicoran kin
he reyata iyewaye kta epca waun wakantanka hena ohihimaye kinhan hena hecetu kte hehan
wicoran mayaqupi kin he ito cajemdate kte wakantanka oieye mayaqupi qa hecen on waditake
mayaśipi qa he ecamu kta ohiniyan epca waon detanhan wakanśica kiciwecize kta epca waon
ecin hecen ecun mayaśipi nakaśohini ecamu kta epca waon tuwedan iapi śica on makte kte
xni nace epca waon heon taku epe kta eca taniyan epa ece homakśidan qa waksape śni tuka
tohanyan maka akan ni waon

>

• • • •

29. Frost, [1864]

One of my relatives, His Country, well again one thing I want to say. I am Dakota, and all these
Dakota ways, I am very knowledgeable about, but now I will quit these now, I tell you that I am
always remembering because these are nothing to me. Now I realize, from here onwards these
are behind me. In the past, I thought, if God won me these ways you all gave me, well, I will
remember. You all told me to be brave, and you all gave me God's Word. And I will always do
this. I thought, from here onward I will fight the Devil. I thought, I am to do, because you all
told me to do, surely I will do. I thought, maybe no one will kill me with bad words, thus, clearly
I will say, as a young boy, I have no wisdom as long as I live on earth.

>

13a   kiŋhaŋ hehaŋyaŋ táku   waŝte kiŋ oŋ   óciciyapi kta képa   micicuŋze kiŋ he
13b   if   from   thing good the use   help you   will I say promise   the this
13c   If I am alive, this good source I will help you, I promise

14a   óhiŋni kiksuya   waoŋ   wakaŋtaŋka tuwe cékiye kiŋhaŋ ni   kta   kéhapi
14b   always remember I am   God   who pray   if   live will you all said
14c   to always remember.   If someone prays to God he will live, you all said,

15a   kiŋ héoŋ amiĉiciya   wakaŋtaŋka cékiya waoŋ ḳa   wanna   wakaŋtaŋka
15b   the thus dedicate myself God   pray   I am and now   God
15c   thus I dedicate myself.   I am praying to God, and now God

16a   óŋŝimada ḳa iye oiye   kiŋ yuha cúŋkaŝke kiŋ detaŋhaŋ taŋkan amaye ḳeŝ
16b   pity me   and his word the have prison   the from   release me   even so
16c   pity me with His Words.   I thought from this prison I am getting better.   Even so,

17a   epca   tuka táku waŋżi ecanuŋpi kta eca   oyakihipi   e ce hécen
17b   I thought but thing one   you can do will truly you all can do also thus
17c   there is one thing you can do.   Truly you can all do this, thus,

18a   ito micaże   kiŋ he cażedatapi   waciŋ tuka do   mihuŋkawaŋżi
18b   well my name the this name them   I want but it is so relative one
18c   well, mention my name, you will mention their names.   I want you to do this, my relative,

19a   ito henana epe kte ye do
19b   well that's all I say will it is so
19c   that is all I will say to you—it is so.

20a   nape ciyuze   do
20b   hand your shake it is so
20c   I shake your hand—it is so.

21a   Ĥewaŋke miye ye do
21b   Frost, it is me—it is so

kinhan hehanyan taku waśte kin on ociciyapi kta kepa micicunze kin he ohini kiksuya waon
wakantanka tuwe cekiye kinhan ni kta kehapi kin heon amiçicya wakantanka cekiya waon qa
wanna wakantanka onśimada qa iye oiye kin yuha cunkaśke kin detanhan tankan amaye qeś
epca tuka takuwanji ecanupi kta eca oyakihipi ece hecen ito micaje kin he cajedatapi kta wacin
tuka do mihunkawanji ito ehenana epe kte ye yedo
nape ciyuze do

        Rewanke miye ye do

· · · ·

If I am alive, this good source I will help you, I promise to always remember. If someone prays
to God he will live, you all said, thus I dedicate myself. I am praying to God, and now God pity
me with His Words. I thought from this prison I am getting better. Even so, there is one thing
you can do. Truly you can all do this, thus, well, mention my name, you will mention their
names. I want you to do this, my relative, that is all I will say to you—it is so.
I shake your hand—it is so.

        Frost, it is me—it is so

CC/MW

1a Tamakoce   mihuŋka   wanżi   táku   wanżi   epe   kte   do   táku   wanżi
1b His Country   relative   one   thing   one   say   will   it is so   something   one
1c One of my relatives His Country, one thing I will say, it is so.   I am

2a uŋ   waciŋciya   wauŋ   he   owahdake   kte   do   nakaha   ĥaĥambdte   héciyataŋhaŋ
2b so   help me   I am   this   tell you   will   it is so   recently   waterfalls   from there
2c going to tell you what I need your help for, it is so.   Recently, I heard them

3a iyapi   wanżi   nawaĥuŋ   Mihuŋka   wan   hen   kaśka   ahdihnakapi
3b they say   one   I heard   my relative   a   at   jailed   they brought him
3c say one thing from Waterfalls [Fort Snelling].   They have captured my relative and brought him there,

4a he   wake   do   Mihuŋka   kiŋ   he   waśicu   wanżi   kte   ꞯa   hécen   iś
4b him   I mean   it is so   my relative   the   him   white man   one   kill   and   then   he
4c I mean him, it is so.   My relative, they say he has killed a white man and he will

5a hécen   teĥiya   kakiżapi   eśta   eś   hécen   ꞯa   hécen   econ   epce   mihuŋka
5b then   terrible   suffer   even so   if so   then   and   then   do   I think   my relative
5c suffer terribly, even so.   I think, my relative,

6a kiŋ   waśicu   wanżidan   kte   śni   tka   Mihuŋka   dehan   teĥiya   kuwapi   kte
6b the   white man   one   kill   not   but   my relative   now   terrible   treatment   will
6c he did not kill a white man.   So now they will make him suffer terribly,

7a wicaśta   táku   śica   econ   ca   teĥiya   kuwapi   tuka   héya   táku   śica   ica
7b men   thing   bad   do   so   terrible   treatment   because   he said   thing   bad   occur
7c bad men who do this will be terribly punished, because my relative said,

8a ꞯehan   mihuŋka   kiŋ   kici   waśicu   óta   niwicayapi   mihuŋka   kiŋ   hehan
8b when   my relative   the   with   whiteman   a lot   saved   my relative   the   then
8c when bad things occurred, he saved a lot of white people.   My relative was then

9a makośica   uŋ   iśtayazaŋ   ꞯa   wamaza   wakaŋ   econ   okihi   śni   do   waśicu
9b badlands   at   sore eyes   and   iron   holy   do   can   not   it is so   white man
9c in the badlands with sore eyes and could not shoot any gun—it is so.   If I could

10a wówapi   wicoĥan   táwa   kiŋ   wanżi   icu   waŋmdake   kiŋhaŋ   ecen   taŋyan   omdake   kta
10b newspaper   ways   theirs   the   one   take   view   if   then   good   tell   will
10c tell my story in a white man's newspaper, I will tell this,

11a tuka   do   Eś   nína   wakaŋtaŋka   eciyataŋhaŋ   ómakiye   do   Kośkadan
11b but   it is so   even so   very   God   from   help me   it is so   young men
11c because it is so.   God is very good, he helps me—it is so.   The young men

12a wicamduhe   kiŋ   wanżidan   wakaŋśica   makikte   śni   wacin   ꞯa   nína   wicihdukśan   waon
12b I have   the   none   Devil   kill mine   not   I want   and   very   protection   I am
12c I have, I don't want the Devil to kill none of my young men, and I am protecting them very much.

13a aŋpetu wanżi   ake   owasiŋ   wicaweco   ꞯa   ake   iwicamuŋǵa   ece   eca   ake   téhaŋyan
13b one day   again   all   invite   and   again   question   always   so   again   good
13c One day I would like to invite all of them, and again question them good.

>

30. Ĥewaŋke, [1864-1865]

Tamakoce mihunka wanji taku wanji epe kte do taku wanji un wacinciya waun he owahdake kte
do nakaha rarambote heciyatanhan iyapi wanji nawarun Mihunka wan hen kaśka ahdihnakapi
he wake do Mihunka kin he waśicu wanji kte qa hecen iś hecen teriya kakijipi eśta eś hecen qa
hecen econ epce mihunka kin waśicu wanijan kte śni tka Mihunka dehan teriya kuwaqpi kte
wicaśta taku śica econ ca teriya kuwapi tuka heya taku śica ica qahan mihunka kin kici waśicu
ota niwicayapi mihunka kin hehan makośica un iśtayazan qa wamaza wakan econ okihi śni do
waśicu wowapi wicoran tawa kin wanji icu wanmdake kinhan ecen tanyan omdake kta tuka
do iś nina wakantanka eciyatanhan omakiye do hokśidan wicamduhe kin wanjidan wakanśica
makikte śni wacin qa nina wicihdukśan waon anpetu wanji ake owasin wicaweco qa ake
wicamuga ece eca ake tohanyan

>

• • • •

30. Frost, [1864-1865]

One of my relatives His Country, one thing I will say, it is so. I am going to tell you what I need
your help for, it is so. Recently, I heard them say one thing from Waterfalls [Fort Snelling]. They
have captured my relative and brought him there, I mean him, it is so. My relative, they say he
has killed a white man and he will suffer terribly, even so. I think, my relative, he did not kill
a white man. So now they will make him suffer terribly, bad men who do this will be terribly
punished, because my relative said, when bad things occurred, he saved a lot of white people.
My relative was then in the badlands with sore eyes and could not shoot any gun—it is so. If I
could tell my story in a white man's newspaper, I will tell this, because it is so. God is very good,
he helps me, it is so. The young men I have, I don't want the Devil to kill none of my young
men, and I am protecting them very much. One day I would like to invite all of them, and again
question them good.

>

14a maka akan ni oŋpi kiŋhaŋ hehaŋyaŋ wakaŋtaŋka ecedaŋ wiciyanoŋpi kta

14b earth upon they live if that long God alone be with them will

14c If they live that long, God alone will be with them, upon Mother Earth,

15a kéyapi koda ece eca hépa ece wicayakapi he epa eca ho eyapi ece

15b they said friend if so I said so you tell truth this I said so this they said so

15c they said. If what you told us is true, I said so, they said so—

16a ye do mihuŋka waŋżi héoŋ wakaŋtaŋka óŋśiwicada do ķeŝ epca waoŋ

16b it is so relative one for reason God pities it is so so I thought I am

16c it is so. One of my relatives, God pities them, and for this reason, if it so, I am in thought.

17a tuka do Koda dena hécetu ḳa héoŋ ociciyake ye do

17b because it is so friend these are true and for this I tell you it is so

17c These things I tell you are true, for this reason I tell you, it is true.

18a ito henana epe kta Tamakoce mihuŋka waŋżi nape ciyuze do

18b well that's all I say will His Country my relative one hand shake it is so

18c That is all I will say. One of my relatives His Country, I shake your hand—it is so.

19a Ĥewaŋke he miye do

19b Frost, this is me—it is so.

maka akan nionpi kinhan hehanyan wakantanka ecedan wiciyanonpi kta keyapi koda ece eca hepa ece wicayakapi he epa eca ho eyapi ece ye do mihunka wanji heon wakantanka onśiwica do qeś epca waon tuka do koda dena hecetu qa heon ociciyake ye do ito henana epe kta tamakoce mihunka wanji nape ciyuze do

Rewanke he miye yedo

• • • •

If they live that long, God alone will be with them, upon Mother Earth, they said. If what you told us is true, I said so, this said so—it is so. One of my relatives, God pities them, and for this reason, if it so, I am in thought. These things I tell you are true, for this reason I tell you, it is true. That is all I will say. One of my relatives His Country, I shake your hand—it is so.

Frost, this is me—it is so.

CC/MW

1a Tamaȟpiyaȟotedaŋ ḳa Mazakoyaginape ḳa Tuŋkaŋaputagmani
1b His Cloud Grey Little and Iron wears comes out and Stone Touches Walks
1c His Little Grey Cloud and Comes Out Wearing Iron and Touches Stone As He Walks

2a ḳa Ŝuŋkaȟdo ḳa Oyoposmani ḳa ȟdayamani ḳa Kaŋpeska ḳa
2b and Dog Growl and Gathers as He Walks and Rattles Walks and Shell white and
2c and Growling Dog and Gathers As He Walks and Rattles As He Walks and White Shell and

3a Tateohnaiŋyaŋkedaŋ ḳa Mazawakiŋyaŋna ḳa Okoŋze wakaŋna iho dena wikcemna
3b Wind upon Running and Iron Thunder little and Prophecy Holy well these ten
3c Little Wind Running and Little Iron Thunder and Little Holy Prophet, these ten

4a cuŋkaŝke kiŋ den mahen awaŋwicamdake kiŋ éepi hécen ito tóken ohaŋpi kiŋ
4b prison the here inside take care of the I said then well how we do the
4c in prison, I take care of them inside here. I said how we do things,

5a he nayaȟuŋ kte eya mihuŋkawaŋżi hokŝipidaŋ ece nakaŝ táku waŋżi
5b this you hear will to say relative one Boys alone thus thing one
5c I want you to hear. I tell you, one of my relatives, these boys alone, one thing

6a ewicawakiya eca kohaŋna ecunpi ece iho hécen waŋna núǧe kiŋ
6b say to them so soon they do so well then now ear the
6c I say to them, so as soon as we do this, then now our ears

7a hduȟdokapi nace epca waoŋ eciŋ waŋżidaŋ wakaŋŝica taokiye kiŋ
7b They open maybe I thought I am thus one Devil Disciple the
7c maybe are opened, I thought no one will be the Devil's Disciples.

8a hécapi ŝni kiŋ héoŋ hépe do mihuŋkawaŋżi waŋżidaŋ wakaŋŝica taokiye
8b they are not the thus I said it is so relative one one Devil Disciple
8c They are not, that's what I said, it is so. My one relative, there is one Devil's Disciple.

9a kiŋ héca tuka mayasapa en tóken ičicuŋze kiŋ hetaŋhaŋ
9b the he is because Bank Black at how decided the from
9c He is at Black Bank [near Mankato], he decided from here

10a dakota wicoȟaŋ tawa kiŋ waŋżidaŋ icuŝni do
10b Dakota ways his the one take not it is so
10c his Dakota ways he did not do, it is so.

11a [Ȟewaŋke]
11b [Frost]

31. [Ȟewaŋke, 1864 or 1865]

Tamarpiyarotedan qa mazakoyaginape qa Tunkanaputagmani qa Ṡunkardo qa Oyoposmani qa rdayamani qa kanpeska qa Tateohnaiyankedan qa mazawakinyanna qa okonze wakanna iho dena wikcemna cunkoṡke kin den mahen awanwicamdake kin eepi hecen ito token oranpi kin he nayarun kte eya mihunkawanji hokṡipidan ece nakaṡ taku wanji ewica wakiya eca kohanna ecencunpi ece iho hecen wanna nuge kin hdurdokapi nace epca waon ecin wanjidan wakanṡica taokiye kin hecapi ṡni kin heon hepe do mihunkawanji. wanjidan wakanṡica taokiye kin heca tuka mayasapa en token içicunze kin hetanhan dakota wicoran tawa kin wanjidan icuṡni do

[Rewanke]

• • • •

31. [Frost, 1864 or 1865]

His Little Grey Cloud and Comes Out Wearing Iron and Touches Stone As He Walks and Growling Dog and Gathers As He Walks and Rattles As He Walks and White Shell and Little Wind Running and Little Iron Thunder and Little Holy Prophet, these ten in prison, I take care of them inside here. I said how we do things, I want you to hear. I tell you, one of my relatives, these boys alone, one thing I say to them, so as soon as we do this, then now our ears maybe are opened, I thought no one will be the Devil's Disciples. They are not, that's what I said, it is so. My one relative, there is one Devil's Disciple. He is at Black Bank [near Mankato], he decided from here his Dakota ways he did not do, it is so.

[Frost]

CC/MW

1a   Tamakoce   mihuŋkawaŋżi
1b   His Country   my brother
1c   Rev. Stephen R. Riggs   my brother

2a   nakaha   ake   wówapi   cícaǧe   kte   nakaha   wicohaŋ   waŋ   ouŋpapi   kiŋ
2b   now/today   again   letter   I make   will   now/today   work   a   are part of   the
2c   Today, I will again write you a letter.   Today I will write you a

3a   heciyataŋhaŋ   táku   yámni   uŋ   wówapi   cícaǧe   kte   uŋkihuŋkakepi   kiŋ   wicohaŋ
3b   from that place   what   three   to be   letter   I make   shall   our ancestors   the   work
3c   letter telling you three things about the work we are involved in.   Our ancestors had some

4a   yuhapi   kiŋ   śiceca   dehaŋ   uŋ   tehiya   uŋyankoŋpi   tuka   waŋna   hena
4b   they had   the   children   now   to be   with difficulty   live with it   but   now   those
4c   bad habits, and now we and our children have to live with these bad habits.   But now those

5a   owihaŋke   epca   wauŋ   caskada   he   tokaheya   cażemdate   kta
5b   the end of anything   I thought   I am/be   First Son   that   first   mention by name   shall
5c   bad habits are coming to an end, I think.   I will mention Robert Hopkins's name first.

6a   waniyetu   óta   dakota   wauŋspeyakiyapi   tuka   oyakihipi   śni
6b   winters   many   Dakota language   you have taught them   but   cannot/you could   not
6c   You have taught the Dakota for many years now, but you couldn't teach them.

7a   tuka   caske   táku wakaŋ   óŋśida   ḣa   uŋ   wicoicaǧe
7b   but   First Son   Great Spirit   he pitied him   and   to be   a generation
7c   But the Great Spirit had compassion upon Robert Hopkins, and so a new generation

8a   tókeca   icaǧe   kte   he   waśtewadake   do   táku wakaŋ   taokiye   yaoŋpi
8b   different   grow   shall/will   that   I love/like   that   it is so   Great Spirit   his disciples   you are
8c   will grow up differently, and I love that very much—it is so.   You are like the Great Spirit's disciples,

9a   kiŋ   he   iyecen   oŋyecicaǧapi   kta   waciŋ   do   caże   kiŋ   waŋna   daotaniŋpi
9b   the   that   like   make us like that   shall   I want   it is so   name   the   now   they announce
9c   and I want you to make us like that—it is so.   Now I want you to announce his

10a   waciŋ   do   detaŋhaŋ   tókidaŋ   ye   śni   eŝta   tawicu   ḣa   ciŋca
10b   I want   it is so   from this place   nowhere   go   not   although   wife   and   children
10c   name—it is so.   Even if he doesn't go nowhere, I would like you to take care of his wife and children,

11a   kiŋ   he   hena   en   ewicayatuŋwaŋpi   kta   epe   e   do   táku   yámni   uŋ
11b   the   that   those   at   look after them   shall   I said   it   it is so   what   three   for/of
11c   I say this because it's right to do so—it is so.   I said there were three

12a   wówapi   cícaǧe   kta   epe   cikoŋ   waŋżi   he   wake   do   hehan   mihuŋkawaŋżi
12b   letter   I make   shall   I said   of time   one   that   I mean   it is so   then   my brother
12c   things why I wrote this letter, that was the first thing that I meant—it is so.   Then, my brother,

13a   táku   waŋżi   epe   kta   tuka   he   emicetu   kta   waciŋ   do
13b   what   one   I say   shall   but   that   be accomplished   will   I want   it is so
13c   there is one thing I will say, but I want this to be fulfilled for me—it is so.

>

32. Tomas Waŝteŝte, [1864]

Tamakoce mihunkawanji

nakaha ake wowapi cicage kte nakaha wicoran wan onpapi kin heciyatanhan taku yamni on wowapi cicage kta onkihukakepi kin wicoran yuhapi kin siceça dehan on teriya onyakupi tuka wana hena owihanke epca waon caskada he tokaheya caje mdate kta waniyetu ota dakota waonspeyakiyapi tuka oyakihipi xni tuka caske taku wakan onxida qa on wicoicage tokeca icaga kte he waxtewadake do taku wakan taokiye yaonpi kin he iyecen onyecicagapi kta wacin do caje kin wana daotaipi wacin do detanhan tokida ye xni xta tawicu qa cinca kin he hena en ewicayatuwipi kta epe e do taku yamni on wowapi cicage kta epe ciqu wanji he wakedo hehan mihukawanji taku wanji epe kta tuka he emicetu kta wacindo

>

• • • •

32. Thomas Good-Good, [1864]

Rev. Stephen R. Riggs my brother

Today, I will again write you a letter. Today I will write you a letter telling you three things about the work we are involved in. Our ancestors had some bad habits, and now we and our children have to live with these bad habits. But now those bad habits are coming to an end, I think. I will mention Robert Hopkins's name first. You have taught the Dakota for many years now, but you couldn't teach them. But the Great Spirit had compassion upon Robert Hopkins, and so a new generation will grow up differently, and I love that very much—it is so. You are like the Great Spirit's disciples, and I want you to make us like that—it is so. Now I want you to announce his name—it is so. Even if he doesn't go nowhere, I would like you to take care of his wife and children, I say this because it's right to do so—it is so. I said there were three things why I wrote this letter, that was the first thing that I meant—it is so. Then, my brother, there is one thing I will say, but I want this to be fulfilled for me—it is so.

>

14a nakaha wicoicaġe tókeca awaoŋciŋpi he waŋna onŋipi kta epe śni
14b now/today generation different to think about that now they will live shall I say not
14c Today, I don't think the next generation is different, and I did not say they will not live.

15a tuka mniĥuhawiyokiyedaŋ waŋżi taŋka waŋżi uŋyakupi kta waciŋ do
15b but cloth flag one large one give us shall I want it is so
15c I want you to give us one large cloth flag—it is so.

16a oyate kaśkauŋpi kiŋ dena owihaŋke eśta uŋkiciŋcapi he yuha wicoicage
16b people imprisoned the those end of anything although our children that have generation
16c Although those persons imprisoned here come to an end, our next generation of children will look for

17a tókeca akitapi kta epce do táku wakaŋ taokiye yaoŋpi kiŋ he
17b different look for shall I think it is so Great Spirit his disciples you are the that
17c something different, that's what I think—it is so. You are the Great Spirit's helpers,

18a oyakihipi kta waciŋ do taku wakaŋ aŋpetu tawa heehan
18b able to accomplish shall I want it is so Great Spirit day his at that time
18c and you can accomplish what I want—it is so. At that time on the Great Spirit's day

19a ipica taniŋya he kta waciŋ do hehan mihuŋkawaŋżi táku waŋżi
19b can go openly that shall I want it is so then my brother what one
19c I want to go openly—it is so. Then, my brother, there's one thing

20a idukcaŋ kta waciŋ do peżihuta wicaśta mdokehaŋ huŋkayapi kaĥapapi
20b you think about shall I want it is so doctor last summer the elders they drove off
20c I want you to think about—it is so. Last summer, Dr. Williamson told the elders when they were

21a kehaŋ táku waŋżi e ye he kiksuya uŋyakupi wanakaża huŋkayapi kaĥapapi
21b when what one he said that remember you gave us long ago elders they drove off
21c driven away from their homeland a long time ago, that was one thing they needed to remember,

22a úŋkaŋ he uŋkokiyakapi úŋkaŋ en táku waŋżi he eya tokata wicaśtayatapi
22b and that they told us and at something one that said future chief
22c is what he told us. He said, there is one thing you should remember, you will choose a chief

23a níĉicaġapi kta eye he kiksuya en yakupi do iho
23b they make/chose shall he said that remember at coming back it is so come/see there
23c in the future, and you're coming back to do that—it is so. So that is

24a he tóketu kiŋ he idukcaŋ kta waciŋ do hécetu héciŋhaŋ idukcaŋ
24b that how is it the that think/decide shall I want it is so so/well if it is so to think/decided
24c how I want you to think about it—it is so. Well, if that is so, I want you to think

25a kta waciŋ do waŋna káġapi kta idukcaŋ kiŋhaŋ oŋkoyakidakapi kta
25b shall I want it is so now they made shall remember if you tell us shall
25c about it—it is so. If they have now done this, I want you to think about it and tell us.

26a wahpetuŋwaŋ en núnpa ʠa waŋżi he uŋmatukte he ohna oŋciŋpi kta naceca
26b Wahpeton at two and one that either one that in/into we want shall probably
26c Among the Wahpeton there are two leaders, and for us we would select either one.

>

nakaha wicoicage tokeca awaoncipi he wana onŋipi kta epe xni tuka mniruhawiyokiyeda wanji tanka wanji onyaqupi kta wacindo oyate kaxkaonpi kin dena owihanke exta onkicicapi he yuha wicoicage tokeca akitapi kta epce do taku wakan taokiye yaonpi kin he oyakihipi kta wacindo taku wakan anpetu tawa he ehan ipica taiya he kta wancin do hehan mihukawanji taku wanji idukcan kta wacindo pejihuwa wicaxta mdokehan hukayapi karapi qehan taku wanji e ye he kiksuya onyakupi wanakaja hukayapi karapi onkan he onkokiyakapi onkan en taku wanji he eya tokata wicaxtayatapi niçicagapi kta e ye he kiksuya on yakupi do iho he toketu kin he idukca kta wacin do hecetu hecinhan idukca kta wacin do wana kagapi kta idukca kihan onkoyakidakapi kta warpetuwana en nunpa qa wanji he onmatukte he ohna oncinpi kta naceca

>

• • • •

Today, I don't think the next generation is different, and I did not say they will not live. I want you to give us one large cloth flag—it is so. Although those persons imprisoned here come to an end, our next generation of children will look for something different, that's what I think—it is so. You are the Great Spirit's helpers, and you can accomplish what I want—it is so. At that time on the Great Spirit's day I want to go openly—it is so. Then, my brother, there's one thing I want you to think about—it is so. Last summer, Dr. Williamson told the elders when they were driven away from their homeland a long time ago, that was one thing they needed to remember, is what he told us. He said, there is one thing you should remember, you will choose a chief in the future, and you're coming back to do that—it is so. So that is how I want you to think about it—it is so. Well, if that is so, I want you to think about it—it is so. If they have now done this, I want you to think about it and tell us. Among the Wahpeton there are two leaders, and for us we would select either one.

>

27a   waŋna   wicaŝtayatapi waŋna hena owihaŋke hena ŝíce ca   héoŋ   dehaŋ
27b   Now   chief   now   those end   those   children   therefore now
27c   Now days, these chiefs are like little children, that's why it ended like it did.   Therefore, we are now

28a   teȟiya   oŋyakuŋpi   nakaha táku epe ciŋ de waŝte kta oŋkeyapi
28b   badly/with difficulty are in a place lately/today what I said the this good will we said
28c   living with great difficulty.   What I have said will be good, and we

29a   waȟpetuŋwaŋna hécen   oŋciŋpi táku wakaŋ maȟpiya ekta naŋke ciŋ
29b   Wahpetons   so/therefore we want Great Spirit heaven at/in sit/be the
29c   Wahpeton said we want it this way.   Great Spirit in heaven, from where you are at,

30a   maka akan   táku onciŋpi owasiŋ okihioŋyaŋpi nuŋwe
30b   earth on/upon what we want all   help us to do may it be so/amen
30c   when there is anything we want on earth, we know you will help us to do all things—may it be so.

31a   mitakoda nakaha   ake   wówapi oŋ   nape oŋniyuzapi   do
31b   my friend now/today again letter   with hand we hold your it is so
31c   Today, my friend, with this letter we shake your hand—it is so.

32a   Tomas Waŝteŝte   he miye
32b   Thomas Good-Good, that is me

33a   Waŝte Inape he miye do
33b   Appears Good, it is me—it is so

34a   Iyożaŋżaŋ he miye
34b   Glowing Light, it is me

35a   Tinazipe wakaŋ he miye do
35b   His Sacred Bow, it is me—it is so

36a   Wówapi kiŋ de yawamaŝipi   hécen   micaże   en   yaŋke   kta
36b   letter   this told me to read so/therefore my name at/to to be/exist shall
36c   They asked me to read this letter, so my name will appear on this letter.

37a   Robert Hopkins

38a   Itewakaŋhdióta
38b   Many Lightning Face

wana wicaxtayatapi wana hena owihanke hena xice ca heon dehan teriya onyakupi nakaha taku
epe cin de waxte kta onkeyapi warpetuwana hecen oncinpi taku wakan marpiya ekta nake cin
maka akan taku en cinpi owasin okihionyapi nunwe mitakoda nakaha ake wowapi on nape
onniyuzapi do

Tomas Wasteste he miye
Wasteinape he miye do
iyojanjan he miye
Tinazipewakan he miye do

Wowapi kinde yawamasipi hecen micaje en yanke kta
Robert Hopkins

itewakanhdiota

• • • •

Now days, these chiefs are like little children, that's why it ended like it did. Therefore, we are
now living with great difficulty. What I have said will be good, and we Wahpeton said we want
it this way. Great Spirit in heaven, from where you are at, when there is anything we want on
earth, we know you will help us to do all things—may it be so. Today, my friend, with this letter
we shake your hand—it is so.

Thomas Good-Good, that is me
Appears Good, it is me—it is so
Glowing Light, it is me
His Sacred Bow, it is me—it is so

They asked me to read this letter, so my name will appear on this letter.
Robert Hopkins

Many Lightning Face

MS/AC

1   Camp Indian Jan 21st 1865

2a Tamakoce   mihuŋka   wanżi   nakaha   Wówapi   cícaġa   tuka   he   tóken   Waoŋ
2b His Country my relative one   now   letter   make for you because   this   how   I am
2c One of my relatives, His Country, now I write this letter to you, because of how I am.

3a kiŋ   he   ociciyake   kta   Waciŋ   ḋa   Wówapi   kiŋ   de   cícaġe   do
3b the   this tell you   will   I want   and   letter   the   this   make for you   it is so
3c I want to tell you, and I write this letter to you.

4a eya   nína   Wamayazaŋka   tuka   Wakaŋtaŋka   óŋŝimada   ḋa   hécen
4b to say very   I am sick   but   God   pity me   and   thus
4c I want to tell you I am very sick, but God pitied me, and

5a taŋyaŋ   Amakiŝni   do   hécen   miŝ   mihuŋka   Wanżi   de   Wówapi   kiŋ   de
5b fine   I am well   it is so thus   I   my relative one   this   letter   the   this
5c I am well—it is so.   Thus, one of my relatives, this letter

6a iyecen   taŋyaŋ   naŋke   kta   en   nii   kta   Wakaŋtaŋka   iceWakiye   do
6b right   good   sit   will   at   reach you   will   God   I pray to   it is so.
6c will reach you in a good way, I pray to God, it is so.

7a hehan   mihuŋka   wanżi   táku   on   Waciŋciye   ḋa   Wówapi   kiŋ
7b then   my relative one   thing   so   I depend on you   and   letter   the
7c Then one of my relatives, I write this letter to depend on you for something,

8a de   oŋ   ociciyake   kte   do   eciŋ   he   mihuŋka   wanżi   Wicaŝta   Wanżi
8b this so   I tell you   will   it is so   reason this   my relative one   man   one
8c so this is the reason I tell you.   My relative, this one man [myself]

9a Waoŋŝida   kiŋ   he   ŝíca   nakaŝ   miŝnana   Waciŋciye   do
9b compassionate   the   this bad   thus   I alone   I depend on you it is so
9c is both compassionate and bad, so I alone always depend on you—it is so.

10a ḋa   hehan   maya wakaŋ   kiŋ   en   Amainapi   ḳehaŋ   en   yaoŋ   ḋa
10b and then   bank sacred   the   at   I hid   then   at   you are   and
10c And then I hid at the sacred bank [near Mankato], when you were there, and

11a wanżi taŋyaŋ   sdonyaye   do   hécen   táku   ŝíca   ecamoŋ   kiŋ   tuwedaŋ   sdonye   ŝni
11b good   you know   it is so thus   thing bad   I do   the   no one   knows   not
11c you know this good, it is so.   Thus no one knows if I did something bad.

>

33. Joseph Godfrey, January 21, 1865

Camp Indian Jan 21th 1865

Tamakoce mihunka wanji nakaha Wowapi cicaga tuka he token Waon kin he ociciyake kta Wacin qa Wowapi kin de cicage do eya nina Wamayazanka tuka Wakantanka onximada qa hecen tanyan Amasni do hecen mix mihunka Wanji de Wowapi kin de iyecen tanyan nake kta en nii kta Wakantanka ice Wakiye do hehan mihunka wanji taku on Wacinciye qa Wowapi kin de on ociciyake kte do ecin he mihunka wanji Wicaxta Wanji Waonxida kin he xica nakax nixnana Wacinciye do qa hehan maya wakan kin en Amainapi qehan en yaon qa tanyan sdonyaye do hecen taku xica ecamon kin tuwedan sdonye xni

>

• • • •

33. Joseph Godfrey, January 21, 1865

Camp Indian Jan 21st 1865

One of my relatives, His Country, now I write this letter to you, because of how I am. I want to tell you, and I write this letter to you. I want to tell you I am very sick, but God pitied me, and I am well—it is so. Thus, one of my relatives, this letter will reach you in a good way, I pray to God, it is so. Then one of my relatives, I write this letter to depend on you for something, so this is the reason I tell you. My relative, this one man [myself] is both compassionate and bad, so I alone always depend on you—it is so. And then I hid at the sacred bank [near Mankato], when you were there, and you know this good, it is so. Thus no one knows if I did something bad.

>

12a   tuka   Wakaŋtaŋka   eceyedaŋ   taŋyaŋ   sdonya   tuka   tákudaŋ   ŝíca   ecamoŋ   kiŋ
12b   but   God   alone   good   knows   but   nothing   bad   I did   the
12c   God alone knows I have not done anything bad,

13a   taŋyaŋ   sdonye   ḳa   nakoŋ   nakaha   iwaye   ciŋ   nakoŋ   namahoŋ   ḳa
13b   good   know   and   also   now   I speak   the   also   hears   and
13c   God knows good, and also now he hears as I speak,

14a   owotaŋna   iwaye   ciŋ   taŋyaŋ   namahon   do   héoŋ   etaŋhan   niŝ   mihuŋka   waŋżi
14b   straight   I speak   the   good   hear   it is so   thus   from   you   relative   one
14c   I speak straight, he hears the good, it is so.   For this reason, you, one of my relatives,

15a   ómayakiye   kta   Waciŋ   ḳa   nína   Waciŋciye   do   hécen   mihuŋka   Waŋżi
15b   help me   will   I want   and   very   depend on you   it is so   thus   my relative   one
15c   I want you to help me, I depend upon you very much, it is so.   Thus maybe

16a   óŋŝimayada   kta   nacece   ecin   Waoŋŝida   nakaŝ   nína   Waciŋciye   do
16b   pity me   will   maybe   because   compassionate   also   very   depend on you   it is so
16c   you will pity me, my relative, because you are very compassionate.   I depend on you, it is so.

17a   hécen   mihuŋka   Waŋżi   niŝ   tóken   Waciŋ   duze   ciŋ   namahuŋ   kta   Waciŋ   do
17b   Thus   my relative   one   you   how   your   thought   the   hear me   will   I want   it is so
17c   Thus, one of my relatives, I depend on what you think about this.   I want you to hear me,

18a   hécen   mihuŋka   Waŋżi   henana   eciciye   kte   do   Nape   ciyuze   do
18b   thus   my relative   one   all   say to you   will   it is so   hand   shake   it is so
18c   one of my relatives, this is all I will say—it is so.   I shake your hand—it is so.

19a   nitakuye
19b   your relative

20a   Joseph Godferyy
20b   Joseph Godfrey

21a   he miye   do
21b   It is me—it is so.

tuka Wakantanka eceyedan tanyan sdonya tuka takudan xica ecamon kin tanyan sdonye qa
nakon nakaha iwaye cin nakon namaron qa owotanna iwaye cin tanyan namarun do heon
etanhan nix mihunka wanji omayakiye kta Wacin qa nina Wacinciye do hecen mihunka Wanji
onximayada kta nacece ecin Waonxida nakux nina Wacinciye do hecen mihunka Wanji nix
token Wacinduze cin namarun kta Wacin do hecen mihunka Wanji henana eciciye kte do Nape
ciyuze do
nitakuye

      Joseph Godferyy
         he miye do

• • • •

God alone knows I have not done anything bad, God knows good, and also now he hears as
I speak, I speak straight, he hears the good, it is so. For this reason, you, one of my relatives, I
want you to help me, I depend upon you very much, it is so. Thus maybe you will pity me, my
relative, because you are very compassionate. I depend on you, it is so. Thus, one of my relatives,
I depend on what you think about this. I want you to hear me, one of my relatives, this is all I
will say—it is so. I shake your hand—it is so.
Your relative

      Joseph Godfrey
         It is me—it is so.

CC/MW

1   Davenport Iowa

2   March th 6, 1865

3a   Tamakoce   Mitakuye   Ito   Nakaha   wówapi wanżi cícaǧe   kta   ǫa
3b   His Country   my relative   well   now   letter one   I make for you   will   and
3c   My relative, His Country, I will write a letter to you now, and

4a   táku   wanżi   epe   kta   mitakuye   wówapi wanżi   mayaku   kta   epca
4b   thing   one   say   will   my relative letter one   give me will   I thought
4c   I will say one thing.   My relative, I thought you will write me a letter,

5a   ǫa   héon   de   cícaǧe   do   táku   wake   cin   ociciyake   kta
5b   and   thus   this   I make for you   it is so something I mean the   I tell you   will
5c   and this is why I write to you, it is so.   I will tell you what I mean.

6a   wayawapi   onspaye   miċiciye   kta   epca   tuka   hécen   tanyan   onmaspe   śni
6b   reading   teach   myself   will   I thought because   thus   well   I learn   not
6c   I thought about teaching myself how to read, because I don't know how to read well.

7a   hécen   wanżi   miyecaǧe   kta   wacin   ǫa   heon   deci   caǧe   tóken   yawapi
7b   thus   one   make for me   will   I want and   thus   here   make   how   they read
7c   Thus, I want you to write me a letter.   And therefore I write how they read,

8a   kin   owasin   ecen   maza   on   miyecaǧe   kta   ǫa   mayaku   kta   epca
8b   the   all   so   metal   thus   make for me   will   and   give me will   I thought
8c   they are all reading, so write me with metal, and I will give you my thoughts.

9a   wayawapi   kektopawinǧe   wóyawatanka   hena   keca   yawapi   ǫa   máza
9b   reading   thousand   writing big   these   amount   they read   and   metal
9c   Reading and writing a thousand words, this amount using metal

10a   on   miyecaǧe   ǫa   mayaku   kta   wacin   do
10b   of   make for me   and   give me will   I want it is so
10c   you can write for me, and I want you to give me—it is so.

11a   tóken   on   yawapi   kin   owasin   ecin   máza   on   miyecaǧe   kta
11b   how   why   they read   the   all   think   metal use   make me   will
11c   How all the writing can be done by metal, I want you to write to me.

12a   wacin   tóken   on   yakażużu   kin   omayakidake   kta   hécen   miś   ecen   cicażużu   kta
12b   I want how   use   you pay   the   you tell me   will   thus/so   me   therefore   I pay you   will
12c   I want to know how much it will cost you, therefore I will pay you.

13a   Mitakuye   hécen   wacin   ǫa   héon   de   cícaǧe   do
13b   my relative   thus/so   I want   and   therefore   this   I make for you it is so
13c   My relative I want this, therefore, I write this letter to you—it is so.

>

34. John Kaȟapa, March 6, 1865

Davenport Iowa

March th 6. 1865.

Tamakoce Mitakuye Ito Nakaha wowapi wanji cicage kta qa taku wanji epe kta mitakuye wowapi wanji mayaqu kta epca qa heon de cicage do taku wake cin ociciyake kta wayawapi onspe miçiye kta epca tuka hecen tanyan onmaspi xni hecen wanji miyecage kta wacin qa heon deci cage token yawapi kin owasin ecen maza on miyecage kta qa mayaqu kta epca wayawapi kektopawige woyawatanka hena keca yawapi qa maza on miyecage qa mayaqu kta wacin do token on yawapi kin owasin ecin maza on miyecage kta wacin token on yakajuju kin omayakidake kta hecen mix ecen cicajuju kta mitakuye hecen wacin qa heon de cicage do

>

. . . .

34. John Driver, March 6, 1865

Davenport Iowa

March 6, 1865

My relative, His Country, I will write a letter to you now, and I will say one thing. My relative, I thought you will write me a letter, and this is why I write to you, it is so. I will tell you what I mean. I thought about teaching myself how to read, because I don't know how to read well. Thus, I want you to write me a letter. And therefore I write how they read, they are all reading, so write me with metal, and I will give you my thoughts. Reading and writing a thousand words, this amount using metal you can write for me, and I want you to give me—it is so. How all the writing can be done by metal, I want you to write to me. I want to know how much it will cost you, therefore I will pay you. My relative I want this, therefore, I write this letter to you—it is so.

>

14a   hécen   tohaŋ   oŋkaŋpi   kiŋ   ekta   de   kta   héciŋhaŋ   hehaŋ   mayakai   kta
14b   thus/so   when   where we are   the   at   go   will   if so   then   bring me   will
14c   So whenever you will come to where we live, you will bring this letter

15a   epca   maŋke   kta
15b   I think   I sit   will
15c   to me.

16a   hena   oŋ   wówapi   cícaǧe   do
16b   that   is   letter   make you   it is so
16c   That is why I write this letter to you—it is so.

17a   henana   epe   kta
17b   all   say   will
17c   That is all I will say.

18a   wówapi   de   oŋ   Nape   ciyuza   táku   wakaŋ   kiŋ   nici nuŋwe
18b   letter   this   with   hand   shake your   something   sacred   the   be with you
18c   With this letter I shake your hand, may the Holy Spirit be with you.

19a   John Kaĥapa
19b   John Driver

20a   miye   do
20b   It is me—it is so.

hecen tohan onkanpi kin ekta de kta hecinhan hehan mayaka i kta epca make kta
hena on wowapi cicage do
henana epe kta
wowapi de on Nape ciyuza taku wakan kin Nici onwe

John Icarape
miye do

• • • •

So whenever you will come to where we live, you will bring this letter to me. That is why I write this letter to you—it is so.
That is all I will say.
With this letter I shake your hand, may the Holy Spirit be with you.

John Driver
It is me—it is so.

CC/MW

1   Davenport, Iowa
2   April 1th 1865

3   S. R. Riggs

4a   Mitakuye
4b   My relative

5a Ȟtánihaŋ   Wówapi   waŋ   miye   caġe   ciŋ   he   Ȟtánihaŋ   waŋmdake   do
5b Yesterday letter   one   me   wrote   the   that   yesterday   I saw/seen   it is so
5c Yesterday, I saw the letter you wrote to me—it is so.

6a mitakuye   táku   emayakiye   ciŋ   hena   wašte   wadake   makiyuškapi   ayakitake
6b my relative   what   you said to me   the   those   good   I like   release me   seek for
6c I like what you said to me, that you would attempt to have me released, that

7a héciŋhaŋ   he   nínaȟin   wašte   wadake   do
7b if it is so   that   exceedingly   good   I like   it is so
7c is especially good, I like that—it is so.

8a   Iyotaŋ   Táku wakaŋ   nínaȟin   Wópida   ewakiye   do
8b   Great   Great Spirit   exceedingly   thanks   I give   it is so
8c   Most of all, I give great thanks to that which is sacred, the Great Spirit—it is so.

9a maka   akan   ake   takuwicawaya   ciŋ   wawicamdake   kta   epca   héoŋ
9b Earth   upon   again   my relatives   the   I see them   shall/will   I think   therefore
9c When I think about seeing my earthly relatives again,

10a Táku wakaŋ   wópida   ewakiye
10b Great Spirit   thanks   I give/say
10c I give thanks to the Great Spirit.

11a   Hehan   Den   wicašta   taŋ nina   ni   oŋyakoŋpi   kiŋ   he   caže pi   kiŋ   owasiŋ
11b   Then   here   men   old/oldest   live   living here   the   that   their names   the   all
11c   I gave you all the names of the oldest men living here,

12a ake   ciču   do   ġa   Hehan   tápi   cažepi   ciču   kiŋ   Iyohakam   ake
12b again   I gave   it is so   and   then   died   name their   I gave   the   afterwards   again
12c then afterwards, I gave you the names of those who died, and again

13a honȟ   tápi   do   tuka   tohaŋya   ciču   kiŋ   awektonže   do
13b some more   died they   it is so   But   how many   I gave   the   I forgot   it is so
13c some more men died—it is so.   But I forgot how many I gave you—it is so.

14a Tašuŋkawakaŋ
14b His Sacred Horse

15a Maȟpiya wakaŋhdi
15b Lightning Cloud

>

35. Elias Ruban Óȟaŋwayakapi, April 1, 1865

Davenport, Iowa
April 1th 1865

S. R. Riggs
Mitakuye

Ṙtanihan Wowapi wan miye cage cin he Ṙtanihan wanmdake do mitakuye taku emayakiye cin hena waśte wadake makiyuśkapi ayakitake hecin he ninaȟin waśte wadake do

Iyotan Taku wakan ninaȟin Wopida ewakiye do maka akan ake takuwicawaye cin wawicamdake kta epca heon Taku wakan wopida ewakiye

Hehan Den wicaśta tan nina ni onyakonpi kin he caje pi kin owasin ake ciçu do qa Hehan ṭapi cajepi ciçu kin Iyohakam ake honȟ ṭapi do tuka tohanya ciçu kin awektonje do

Taśonkawakan
Maȟpiya wakanhdi

>

• • • •

35. Elias Ruban They See His Ways, April 1, 1865

Davenport, Iowa
April 1th 1865

S. R. Riggs
My relative

Yesterday, I saw the letter you wrote to me—it is so. I like what you said to me, that you would attempt to have me released, that is especially good, I like that—it is so.

Most of all, I give great thanks to that which is sacred, the Great Spirit—it is so. When I think about seeing my earthly relatives again, I give thanks to the Great Spirit.

I gave you all the names of the oldest men living here, then afterwards, I gave you the names of those who died, and again some more men died—it is so. But I forgot how many I gave you—it is so.

His Sacred Horse
Lightning Cloud

>

16a	Wicota máza
16b	Many Irons

17a	Ipaĥte
17b	The Bridle

18a	Cápaduta
18b	Scarlet Beaver

19a	Tawahiŋkpemaza
19b	His Iron Arrow

20a	Hokŝidaŋduta
20b	Scarlet Boy

21a	Wakiŋyaŋwakute
21b	He Shoots the Thunder

22a	Ĥupahu tókca
22b	Different Wing

23a	Dowaŋwaŋki
23b	The Singer

24a	Iyapos máni
24b	Walks Close

25a dena waŋ honĥ ciĉu naceca tuka tohaŋyaŋ ciĉu kiŋ
25b these a some more I gave perhaps/probably but how many I gave the
25c These are probably some of the names I gave you but how many I gave you I

26a awektonże tuka wicacaże tápi kiŋ de waŋna honĥ ciĉu
26b I forgot but men's names they died the this now some more I gave
26c don't remember, but now here are some more names.

27a héciŋhaŋ waŋdake ca honĥ eĥpeyaye kta do Nitakuye
27b if it is so you see and some more throw away shall/will it is so Your relative
27c If you have already seen these names, you can just throw them away—it is so. Your relative

28a	Elias Óĥaŋwayakapi
28b	Elias They See His Ways

Wicota maza
Ipaḣte
Capaduta
Tawahinkpemaze
Hokṡidanduta
Wakinyanwakute
Ḣupahu tokca
Dowanwanki
Iyapos mani

dena wan honḣ ciçu naceca tuka tohanyan ciçu kin awektonje tuka wicacaje tapi kin de wanna honḣ ciçu hecinhan wandake ca honḣ aḣpeyaye kta do Nitakuye

Elias Oḣanwayakapi

• • • •

Many Irons
The Bridle
Scarlet Beaver
His Iron Arrow
Scarlet Boy
He Shoots the Thunder
Different Wing
The Singer
Walks Close

These are probably some of the names I gave you but how many I gave you I don't remember, but now here are some more names. If you have already seen these names, you can just throw them away—it is so. Your relative

Elias They See His Ways

MS/AC

1   April 7th 1865

2a   Tamakoce
2b   His Country
2c   Rev. Stephen R. Riggs

3a   mitakuye   wówapi   cícaġe   kte   waciŋ   ḳa
3b   my relative letter   I make you shall   I want   and
3c   My relative, I wanted to write this letter to you and so,

4a   héoŋ   de cícaġe   yedo   waŋna   hahaŋna   héciya   Peżihuta wicaṡta
4b   Therefore this I make   it is so now   tomorrow   there   root doctor
4c   I'm writing this letter—it is so.   Dr. Williamson will be going home tomorrow, so

5a   hde   kta   e   wówapi   kiŋ   den   Ahde   waṡi
5b   to go home   shall   at/to letter   the   here   to take home   told him
5c   I told him to take this letter home with him.

6a   táku   tókiyataŋhaŋ   ociciyake kta   wanica   tuka   waŋna   uŋkiṡnana
6b   what   where/from that place I tell you shall   none   but   now   we two alone
6c   I have nothing to tell you from anyone or anywhere.   But now we two will be

7a   uŋyankoŋpi   kta   uŋkaŋṡ héoŋ   caŋte maṡica   yedo   eya   keṡ
7b   we are in a place   shall   if   therefore I am sad   it is so also   although
7c   left here alone, if so, it makes me sad—it is so.   They had

8a   téhaŋ   ihauŋktapi   tuka   hécen   tóken owakihi   kiŋ   hécen
8b   a long time ago to have regard for but   therefore how   to be able to the   so
8c   great concern for us for a long time, now I should make a personal diligent effort—

9a   amiċiciya   kta   nacece   eya   táku   oyakapi   taŋyaŋ   uŋmaspe
9b   I am diligent shall probably   also   what   they tell/told well   I have learned
9c   that's the best I can do.   I know that the things they tell us,

10a   ṡni   sdonwakiya   tuka   tóken   ecoŋ oŋyaṡipi   kiŋ   hena   awaciŋ
10b   not   to know one's own except   how   gave us orders the   those   think/thought
10c   I don't understand very well, except I think about and try to carry out the orders

11a   waoŋ   ḳa   dehaŋyaŋ aiċiciya   waoŋ   hécen   dehaŋ   iyotaŋ
11b   to be   and   so far   to be diligent   to be   therefore   now   most
11c   you gave us to do, and up to now I try to persevere in what I do.   So now, my thought

12a   nína   amiċiciya   waoŋ kta   sececa   epca   yedo   Hehan
12b   very   I make effort to be   shall it seems as if I thought it is so   Then
12c   seems to be to make the greatest effort in everything I shall do while I am here.   Then,

13a   Wanihaŋ wówapi mayaḳu   úŋkaŋ   wicaṡta   ṡákpe   wicakeya   ṡkáŋpi
13b   Winter   letter   you gave me and   man/men   six   truthfully   they do
       last winter you wrote me a letter and told there were six men, truthfully, doing their work.

>

36. Mowis Itewakaŋhdióta, April 7, 1865

April 7th 1865

Tamakoce

mitakuye wowapi cicage kta wacin qa heon decicage yedo wanna hahanna heciya Pejihuta wicaśta hde kta e wowapi kin den Ahde waśi taku tokiyatanhan ociciyake kta wanica tuka wana onkiśnana onyakonpi kta onkans heon cante maśice yedo eya qeś tehan ihaonktapi tuka hecen token owakihi kin hecen amiçiciya kta nacece eya taku oyakapi tanyan onmaspe śni sdonwakiya tuka token econ onyaśipi kin hena awacin waon qa dehanyan aiçiciya waon hecen dehan iyotan nina amiçiciya waon kta sececa epce yedo Hehan Wanihan wowapi mayaqu onkan wicaśta śakpe wicakiya skanpi

>

• • • •

36. Moses Many Lightning Face, April 7, 1865

April 7th 1865

Rev. Stephen R. Riggs

My relative, I wanted to write this letter to you and so, I'm writing this letter—it is so. Dr. Williamson will be going home tomorrow, so I told him to take this letter home with him. I have nothing to tell you from anyone or anywhere. But now we two will be left here alone, if so, it makes me sad—it is so. They had great concern for us for a long time, now I should make a personal diligent effort—that's the best I can do. I know that the things they tell us, I don't understand very well, except I think about and try to carry out the orders you gave us to do, and up to now I try to persevere in what I do. So now, my thought seems to be to make the greatest effort in everything I shall do while I am here. Then, last winter you wrote me a letter and told there were six men, truthfully, doing their work.

>

14a ota e Wópeton hánska wówapi yutaŋ e okini ecetu kte ehe cikoŋ
14b many Long buyer letter signed perhaps/possibly fulfilled shall you said
14c You said, if General H. H. Sibley signed the document, it shall be possible many can go home,

15a Nahaŋĥiŋ ecetu   ŝni inawaĥni ḉa taŋyaŋ ecamuŋ ŝni
15b yet   accomplished/fulfilled not I am in a hurry and well I did not
15c but nothing hasn't been done yet.   I was in a hurry and didn't do it well.

16a Henana   epe
16b Only so much/none I say
16c That is all I say.

17a Napeciyuze
17b I hold your hand
17c I shake your hand,

18a   mitakuye
18b   my relative
18c   my relative.

19a Miye do
19b This is me—it is so

20a Mowis Itewakaŋhdióta
20b Moses Many Lightning Face

ota e Wopeton hanska wowapi yutan e okini ecetu kte eheciqun Nahanhin ecetu śni inawaḣni
qa tanyan ecamu śni Henana epe
Napeciyuze
          mitakuye

Miye do
Mowis Itewakanhdiota

• • • •

You said, if General H. H. Sibley signed the document, it shall be possible many can go home,
but nothing hasn't been done yet. I was in a hurry and didn't do it well. That is all I say.
I shake your hand,
          my relative.

This is me—it is so
Moses Many Lightning Face

MS/AC

1   Davenport, Iowa April 17, 1865

2   S. R. Riggs

3a   Mitakuye   Ito   wówapi   cícaġe   kta   waciŋ   Nakaha   wótaŋiŋ
3b   My relative well   paper   I give to you will I want   now   news
3c   Well, my relative, I wish to write you a letter, we have heard

4a   Naoŋȟoŋpi   Toŋkaŋśidaŋ   ktepi   kéyapi   Tuka   hécen   tuwe
4b   we heard   grandfather   they killed they said   But   then   someone
4c   news.   They have said that the President [Abraham Lincoln] was killed.   But someone

5a   táku   taŋyaŋ oŋkokiyakapi kta iyecece   śni heoŋ mitakuye   wówapi ciĉu
5b   something   good   tell us   will right/correct not thus my relative paper   I give you
5c   of authority should tell us if this is not true.   Thus, my relative, I write to you this letter.

6a   eya táku waŋžikži nawaȟoŋ   waciŋ ġa   heoŋ den wówapi kiŋ cicaġe   yedo
6b   also several rumors I have heard I want and thus here letter the I make for you it is so
6c   Also, I have heard several rumors, therefore, I want to write you this letter—it is so.

7a   Toŋkaŋśidaŋ   he óŋśioŋdapi   ġa   dehaŋyaŋ ni oŋyakoŋpi tuka hécen Nakaha
7b   grandfather   had compassion for us and so far   we are still alive but   then   now
7c   The President has compassion for us, as so far we are still alive, but now they

8a   ktépi   kéyapi   héoŋ   caŋte óŋśicapi   tóna oŋkiyukcaŋpi héciŋhaŋ   hena
8b   they killed him they said therefore our hearts are sad some we think   if this is so we are
8c   told us he was killed, and we are saddened.   Those of us here think if this is so, we are

9a   caŋte óŋśicapi hehaŋ hécen isaŋtaŋka kiŋ hécen tóken caŋte oŋkiyuzapi kta   naceca
9b   heartbroken   then   this   big knives the thus   how   heart hold us   will   maybe
9c   heartbroken.   Perhaps the attitude of the cavalry soldiers may change toward us.

10a   idukcaŋ   héciŋhaŋ omayakidaka waciŋ ġa   héoŋ   wówapi cícaġe   ye do
10b   what you think if   you tell me   I want and therefore paper   I make for you it is so
10c   Tell me what your thoughts are, I want to know, that's why I write to you.

11a   hehaŋ Toŋkaŋśidaŋ tóken ktepi   héciŋhaŋ he   taŋyaŋ nawaȟoŋ kta   waciŋ   yedo
11b   then   grandfather   how   they killed when   that well   I hear   will   I want   it is so
11c   Then I wish to hear exactly how they killed the President.

12a   hehaŋ eya   aŋpetu wakaŋ eca   tokeŋ owakihi   heceŋ wahokuŋ wicawakiye
12b   then   to say day   holy   when   how   I am able thus   I preach to them
12c   Then, also on Sundays when I am able, I do the preaching to them.

13a   henana   epe   kta owasin nape ciyuzapi
13b   that is all I say will all   hand   they shake
13c   This is all I'm going to say, I shake all your hands.

14a   Mowis Itewakaŋhdióta   he miye
14b   Moses Many Lightning Face   This is me

37. Mowis Itewakaŋhdióta, April 17, 1865

Davenport, Iowa April 17, 1865

S. R. Riggs

Mitakuye Ito wowapi cicage kta wacin Nakaha wotanin Naonȟonpi Tonkanśidon ktepi keyapi tuka hecen tuwe taku tanyan onkokiyakapi kta iyecece śni heon mitakuye wowapi ciçu eya taku wanjikji nawaȟon wacin qa heon den wowapi kin cicage yedo Tonkanśidan he onśiondapi qa dehanyan nionyakonpi tuka hecen Nakaha ktepi keyapi heon cante onśicapi tona onkiyukcanpi hecinhan hena cante onśicapi hehan hecen isantanka kin hecen token cante onkiyuzapi kta naceca idukcan hecinhan omayakidaka wacin qa heon wowapi cicage ye do hehan Tonkanśidan token ktepi hecinhan he tanyan nawaȟon kta wacin yedo hehan eya Anpetu wakan eca token owakihi hecen wahokun wicawakiye Henana epe kte owasin Nape ciyuzapi

Mowis Itewakanhdiota   he miye

• • • •

37. Moses Many Lightning Face, April 17, 1865

Davenport, Iowa April 17, 1865

S. R. Riggs

Well, my relative, I wish to write you a letter, we have heard news. They have said that the President [Abraham Lincoln] was killed. But someone of authority should tell us if this is not true. Thus, my relative, I write to you this letter. Also, I have heard several rumors, therefore, I want to write you this letter—it is so. The President has compassion for us, as so far we are still alive, but now they told us he was killed, and we are saddened. Those of us here think if this is so, we are heartbroken. Perhaps the attitude of the cavalry soldiers may change toward us. Tell me what your thoughts are, I want to know, that's why I write to you. Then I wish to hear exactly how they killed the President. Then, also on Sundays when I am able, I do the preaching to them. This is all I'm going to say, I shake all your hands.

Moses Many Lightning Face   This is me

CC/MW

| 1a | | | | | | Wíyawapi | April 24 1865 |
| 1b | | | | | | Month | April 24 1865 |

2   Rev. S. R. Riggs

3a	Mitakoda	ake	wówapi	Mayaǥu	úŋkaŋ	hécen	tóken	Táku	uŋ
3b	My friend	again	letter	you gave me	and	therefore	how	what	be/is
3c	My friend, you wrote me a letter again, and you said to me								

4a	wani	kta	iyececa	šni	emayakiya	ḋa	nína	caŋte Mašica
4b	I live	shall/will	like/such as	not	you said to me	and	very	to be sorrowful/sad
4c	that I don't have anything to live for, and so it made me very sad.							

5a	tuka	táku	waŋżi	uŋ	Iyotaŋ	nína	caŋtemašica	Misuŋka
5b	but	what	one	be/is	great/most	very	to be sad/sorrowful	younger brother
5c	But what makes me especially sad, is when will they release my younger brother							

6a	waŋna	héoŋ	Caŋtemašica	he	kiyušǩapi	Kiŋhaŋ	ninahiŋ
6b	now	therefore	to be sad/sorrowful	that	release from prison	if	especially
6c	from prison, when they do I will						

7a	piwada	kta	kecin	wauŋ		tuka	e	hi	ito
7b	thankful for	shall/will	to think that	to be		but	to/at	came	well
7c	be so thankful, I've been thinking about this as I sit here.				The Rev. Dr. Thomas Williamson			

8a	Maka	kiŋ	dehaŋ	Thos. Williamson	Kiyušǩe		yaši	kta	waciŋ
8b	earth	the	now	Thomas Williamson	to release from prison		tell him	shall	I want
8c	came here to this part of the country, and I want you to tell him to seek his release.								

9a	Eya	óhiŋniyan	ómayakiyapi	Kiŋ	he	sdonwakiya	tuka	he	Iyotaŋ	kici
9b	also/too	always	you help me	if		I know	but	that	great/most	with
9c	I know you always help me, but the greatest thing I want most									

10a	wauŋ	kta	Nínahiŋ	waciŋ	hehan	Wakaŋtaŋka	oie	kiŋ	héoŋ
10b	to be	shall	especially	I want	then	Great Spirit	his word	the	therefore
10c	is to be with my younger brother. Then, as I was coming home, from place to place,								

11a	Oyate	iyaza	waku		kiŋ	eŋ	Wahokoŋwicakiya	wauŋ	do
11b	people	one after another	to come toward home		the	at	counsel/preach	to be	it is so
11c	I preached the Great Spirit's Word—it is so.								

12a	He	óhiŋniyan	epe	kta	kepca	hécen	tohaŋyan	wani
12b	That	always	I say	shall/will	I thought that	so/therefore	how long	I live
12c	I said, I think I will always say that.			Therefore, as long as I live,				

13a	kiŋhaŋ	Wakaŋtaŋka	każeya	wauŋ	kta	Kepca	ce
13b	if/when	Great Spirit	in the name of	to be	shall	I thought	that
13c	I think I will always proclaim the name of the Great Spirit.						

>

38. Robert Hopkins, April 24, 1865

Wiyawapi April 24 1865

Rev. S. R. Rigagas

Mitakoda ake wowapi mayaqu onkan hecen token Taku on wani kta iyececa śni emayakiya qa nina cante Maśica tuka taku wanji on Iyotan nina cantemaśica Misunka wanna heon Cantemaśica he kiyuśkapi kinhan ninahin piwada kta kecin waun tuka e hi ito maka kin dehan Thos Williamson kinyuśke yaśi kta wacin Eya ohinniyan omayakiyapi kinhe sdonwakiya tuka he Iyotan kici waon kta Ninahin wacin hehan Wakantanka oie kin heon Oyate iyaza waku kin on Wahokonwicakiya waon do He ohinniyan epe kta kepa hecen tohanyan wani kinhan Wakantanka cajeya waon kta Kepca ce

>

• • • •

38. Robert Hopkins, April 24, 1865

Month April 24 1865

Rev. S. R. Rigagas

My friend, you wrote me a letter again, and you said to me that I don't have anything to live for, and so it made me very sad. But what makes me especially sad, is when will they release my younger brother from prison, when they do I will be so thankful, I've been thinking about this as I sit here. The Rev. Dr. Thomas Williamson came here to this part of the country, and I want you to tell him to seek his release. I know you always help me, but the greatest thing I want most is to be with my younger brother. Then, as I was coming home, from place to place, I preached the Great Spirit's Word—it is so. I said, I think I will always say that. Therefore, as long as I live, I think I will always proclaim the name of the Great Spirit.

>

14a hehan nakaha   Wayoźudaŋ en   tipi   10   hdípi   do   hehan tohaŋ
14b then   now/today Wayojudan at/in live/home ten came home it is so Then   when
14c Then, just now ten persons came back to Wayojudan, where they live—it is so.   Then, when

15a mitawiŋ hi   kiŋhaŋ wayaźuźu ti   kiŋ héciya   wahokoŋ wicakiye mde kta
15b my wife comes if   Wayajuju lives the over there counsel/preach to I go shall/will
15c my wife comes, I am going to Wayajuju, and there I will preach to them.

16a Thos. Williamson   he   ye maśi   hécen   ekta wai   kta
16b Thomas Williamson that told me to go so/therefore at/to to have gone to shall/will
16c Reverend Thomas Williamson told me to go there, so this is what

17a waciŋ   hehan Dakota 10   wicaśta wokcaŋ   hécapi
17b I want   then   Dakota 10   men   prophet/missionary they are such
17c I want to do.   Then you said that ten Dakota men will become missionaries,

18a kta   kéheciŋ he   waśte Wadake   do   hehan wahokoŋ Wicakiye mde
18b shall/will you said that I like/love that it is so then   counsel/preach I go
18c when you said that, I really liked that—it is so.   When I go to preach to them,

19a ciŋhaŋ   ate   kici mde kta   waciŋ yedo   E he   ociciyake
19b if/when father with I go shall/will I want it is so You say I am telling you
19c I want to go with my father—it is so.   I am telling what you said—

20a yedo   hehan ehake   wi   wanźi mitawiŋ akipe   maŋke   kta
20b it is so then   lastly/finally month one   my wife wait for sit here shall/will
20c it is so.   Finally, I have to wait one more month for my wife before she gets here—

21a yedo   hehan mitakoda wókoyake Uŋ   teĥiya   wauŋ yedo
21b it is so then   my friend clothes   for/on account of with difficulty I am   it is so
21c it is so.   Then, my friend, I am in great need of clothing, I hardly have anything—it is so.

22a iho   mitawiŋ wócekiye eniciye   do
22b always/be it so my wife prayer   she says for you it is so
22c My wife said she is constantly praying for you—it is so.

23   Robert Hopkins

24a   he miye do
24b   that is me—it is so

hehan nakaha Wayojudan en tipi 10 hdipi do hehan tohan mitawin hi kinhan wayajuju ti kin heciya wohokon wicakiye mde kta Thos Williamson he yemaśi hecen ekta wai kta wacin hehan Dakota 10 wicaśta wokcan hecapi kta kehe cin he waśte Wadake do hehan wahokon Wicakiye mde cinhan ate kici mde kta wacin yedo E he ociciyake yedo hehan Ehake wi wanji mitawin akipe make kte yedo hehan mitakoda wokoyake On teḣiya waon yedo iho mitawin wocekiye eniciye do

Robert Hopkins
hemiyedo

• • • •

Then, just now ten persons came back to Wayojudan, where they live—it is so. Then, when my wife comes, I am going to Wayajuju, and there I will preach to them. Reverend Thomas Williamson told me to go there, so this is what I want to do. Then you said that ten Dakota men will become missionaries, when you said that, I really liked that—it is so. When I go to preach to them, I want to go with my father—it is so. I am telling what you said—it is so. Finally, I have to wait one more month for my wife before she gets here—it is so. Then, my friend, I am in great need of clothing, I hardly have anything—it is so. My wife said she is constantly praying for you—it is so.

Robert Hopkins
that is me—it is so

MS/AC

1   Davenport Iowa

2   Apr 30 1865

3   S. R. Riggs

4a   Mitakoda   Nakaha   Ake   wówapi   cícaǧe   kta   wacin ǫa
4b   My friend just now again paper   I make for you shall/will I want and
4c   My friend, once again, I now want to write you a letter, and that's why I'm

5a   héon   óhinni   cícaǧe   yedo   mitakoda ito   wicaŝta den   unpi
5b   therefore always I make for you it is so my friend well men   here they are
5c   constantly writing to you—it is so.   Well, my friend, I want to tell you about

6a   kin he tóken cante yuzapi ǫa   tóken tawacinpi kin hena
6b   the that how heart they hold and how their mind the those
6c   the men that are here, how they're thinking and feeling, that's what

7a   ociciyake kte   yedo   wanna Anpetu wakan 4 wicaŝta wakan tuwedan
7b   I tell you shall it is so   now   Sunday   4 minister   no one/nobody
7c   I want to tell you—it is so.   No minister hasn't preached to the men for four Sundays

8a   wahokon wicakiyapi ŝni héon etanhan tóken ohanyanpi   kin hena   wanna
8b   they preach to them not therefore   how their behaviors the those now
8c   now.   I have a good understanding of what the men are doing,

9a   tanyan iwicamdukcan   héon   owasin ecen   tanyan ociciyake
9b   well   have understanding of them therefore all   so/thus well   to tell anything
9c   therefore, I want to tell you everything that affects

10a   kte   wacin dehan iŝnana únpi   únkan hécen   wicaŝta otoiyohi
10b   shall/will I want now   alone they are and   therefore man   each one
10c   them.   Now that every man has time alone,

11a   nína aičiciyapi   yedo   ĥtayetu ǫa
11b   very they are diligent it is so   evening and
11c   they're making every effort to take a look at themselves—it is so. In the evening and

12a   hanĥanna hena owasina nína wahokon ičiciyapi   hehan Anpetu nakun
12b   morning those all   very counsel themselves then   day   also
12c   morning, they're very diligent in counseling themselves. Then, it is true every day

13a   eca wica ǫa wínyan ko owasin wítaya céunkiyapi hécetu yedo
13b   when men and women too all   together we pray   as/right it is so
13c   all the men and women too pray together—it is so.

14a   hécen dehanyan   wanna sutaya   awacinpi sdonwaya
14b   so   so far/so long now   firmly/hard they think I know/knew
14c   Therefore, I know they are very solid in their thinking.

\>

39. Moses Itewakaŋhdióta, April 30, 1865

Davenport Iowa
Apr 30 1865

S. R. Riggs

Mitakoda Nakaha Ake wowapi cicage kta wacin qa heon ohni cicage yedo mitakoda ito wicaśta den onpi kin he token cante yuzapi qa token tawacinpi kin hena ociciyake kte yedo wanna Anpetu wakan tom 4 wicaśta wakan tuwedan wahokon wicakiyapi śni heonetanhan token ohanyanpi kin hena wanna tanyan iwicamdukcan heon owasin ecen tanyan ociciyake kte wacin dehan iśnana onpi onkan hecen wicaśta otoiyohi nina aiçiciyapi yedo htayetu qa hanhanna hena owasina nina wahokon içiciyapi hehan Anpetu nakun eca wica qa winyan ko owasin witaya ceonkiyapi hecetu yedo hecen dehanyan wanna sutaya awacinpi sdonwaya

>

• • • •

39. Moses Many Lightning Face, April 30, 1865

Davenport Iowa
Apr 30 1865

S. R. Riggs

My friend, once again, I now want to write you a letter, and that's why I'm constantly writing to you—it is so. Well, my friend, I want to tell you about the men that are here, how they're thinking and feeling, that's what I want to tell you—it is so. No minister hasn't preached to the men for four Sundays now. I have a good understanding of what the men are doing, therefore, I want to tell you everything that affects them. Now that every man has time alone, they're making every effort to take a look at themselves—it is so. In the evening and morning, they're very diligent in counseling themselves. Then, it is true every day all the men and women too pray together—it is so. Therefore, I know they are very solid in their thinking.

>

15a héoŋ   detaŋhaŋ   óhiŋniyaŋ   caŋtemawašte wauŋ   hehan hepca   wauŋ
15b therefore   from this time always   to make glad   I am   then   I think that   to be/I am
15c Now, therefore, I am always happy.   Then I am thinking,

16a táku wakaŋ kiŋ óŋšiwicakida   qa   maka akan   décen   uŋpi
16b Great Spirit the   has pity/compassion and   on this earth after this manner   they are
16c in my opinion, the Great Spirit has compassion on those living in this way on this earth,

17a keš   epca   wauŋ   iye káeš   waŋna tókiya ipi
17b although   I thought that   I am   even he   now   where/in what place
17c and no matter what, they probably will never fall

18a ešta   waŋna ayuštaŋpi   kte   šni   naceca   wadake   yedo   tuka
18b even if now   they cease from shall/will   not   probably   in my opinion it is so   but
18c away from the Great Spirit—it is so.   But

19a táku waŋzi ociciyake kte   Aŋpetu wakaŋ icuhaŋ   wicohtani   econpi   ece e
19b what one   I tell you   shall   Sunday   during   labor/work they do   usually they
19c there is one thing I will tell you.   During Sunday they usually do work,

20a tuka hena Wakaŋtaŋka nína kiksuyapi   tuka   hécen   iyeciŋka
20b but   those Great Spirit   very they remember   what   therefore of one's self
20c but are very diligent in remembering the Great Spirit.   I want them to do this on their own,

21a econpi waciŋ isaŋtaŋka hécoŋ   wicašipi   iho   hécetu   hehan táku
21b they do I want long knives   to do that   told them   always as/well   then
21c without advice.   The soldiers told them, too, so that's the way it is.   Then there's

22a waŋži iniciye mašipi   winohiŋca den   úŋpi   kiŋ hena   kinapa
22b what   one   to say something to you women   here   they are the   those to come out of
22c one thing they told me to say to you, the women that are here are getting out

23a waŋna makoce   tókeca ekta   uŋyakoŋpi   kta   uŋciŋpi eyapi
23b now   earth/land different at/to   we are/place to be   shall   we want   they said
23c and going home, and they said, we want to be at a different place, and that's what

24a qa   he   ociciyake mašipi   iho   hécen   he   wicakapi
24b and   that   I tell you   they told me come/see there therefore   that   they speak the truth
24c they told me to tell you.   Therefore, I think they speak

25a epca   heoŋ   tóken eyapi   kiŋ ecen ociciyake yedo
25b I think therefore how   they said the   so   I tell you   it is so
25c the truth.   I'm telling you just as they said—it is so.

26a hécen   hena   ekeš   dehan tokan   iyayapi   kta
26b therefore those that which/even that now   in another place they will go   shall/will
26c So it seems like they should go now to where they want to go.

>

heon detanhan ohiniyan cantemawaśte waon hehan hepca waon taku wakan kin onśiwicakida qa maka akan dencen onpi qeś epca waon iyaqeś wanna tokiyaipi eśta wanna ayuśtanpi kte śni naceca wadake yedo tuka taku wanji ociciyake kte Anpetu wakan icuhan wicoḣtani econpi ece e tuka hena Wakantanka nina kiksuyapi taku hecen iyecinka econpi wacin Wakantanka hecon wicaśipi iho hecetu hehan taku wanji iniciyemaśipi winoḣinca den onpi kin hena kinapa wanna makoce tokeca ekta onyakonpi kta oncinpi eyapi qa he ociciyake maśipi iho hecen he wicakapi epca heon token eyapi kin ecen ociciyake yedo hecen hena eqeś dehan tokan iyayapi kta

>

· · · ·

Now, therefore, I am always happy. Then I am thinking, in my opinion, the Great Spirit has compassion on those living in this way on this earth, and no matter what, they probably will never fall away from the Great Spirit—it is so. But there is one thing I will tell you. During Sunday they usually do work, but are very diligent in remembering the Great Spirit. I want them to do this on their own, without advice. The soldiers told them, too, so that's the way it is. Then there's one thing they told me to say to you, the women that are here are getting out and going home, and they said, we want to be at a different place, and that's what they told me to tell you. Therefore, I think they speak the truth. I'm telling you just as they said—it is so. So it seems like they should go now to where they want to go.

>

27a iyececa   hehan uŋkiš   waŋna dehaŋyaŋ kaška uŋpi   om   waŋna
27b like/such as then we ourselves now   so long   we imprisoned with   now
27c Then those of us imprisoned up to now

28a atakunipi   šni yedo hehan eya   ake   déciya yahi
28b to come to nothing not it is so then also/too again here   you come to
28c are being forgotten—it is so.   Then, if you're coming here again,

29a kta   hécinhaŋ itokam nahoŋ unyakiyapi   kta   waciŋ yedo
29b shall if/if it is so before to cause to hear/make us hear shall I want it is so
29c if you would let us know beforehand, it would be good, that's what I want—it is so.

30a Pežihuta wicašta kiŋȟde   ciŋ iyohakam wica yámni tápi   ḋa
30b Doctor   to have gone home the afterwards men three they died and
30c After Dr. Williamson left and went home, three men and

31a winohiŋca waŋzidaŋ ta   yedo   henakeca tápi   do
31b woman   one   died it is so so many they died it is so
31c one woman died—it is so.   That many died—it is so.

32a henana   epe   kte   yedo   Nape ciyuze
32b only so much I will say shall it is so Hand take hold of
32c That is all I will say—it is so.   I shake your hand.

33a   Moses Ite wakaŋhdióta
33b   Moses Many Lightning Face

34a   he miye
34b   that is me

iyececa hehan onkinś wanna dehanyan kaśkaonpi om wanna antakunipi śni yedo hehan eya ake deciya yahi kta hecinhan itokam nahon onyakiyapi kta wacin yedo Pejihutawicaśta kinhde cin yohakam wica yamni ṭapi qa winohinca wanjidan ṭa yedo henakeca ṭapi do henana ipe kte yedo Nape ciyuze

Moses Itewakanhdiota
    hemiye

• • • •

Then those of us imprisoned up to now are being forgotten—it is so. Then, if you're coming here again, if you would let us know beforehand, it would be good, that's what I want—it is so. After Dr. Williamson left and went home, three men and one woman died—it is so. That many died— it is so. That is all I will say—it is so. I shake your hand.

Moses Many Lightning Face
    that is me

MS/AC

1   Camp Kearney

2   Davenport Iowa

3   June 1.

4a Hehan mitakuye Ito wówapi kiŋ De Oŋ Táku waŋżi iciwaŋġe kta

4b then my relative well letter the this so thing one ask you will

4c Well then, my relative, with this letter, I thought of not asking you this question.

5a Epca ꞯa Héoŋ Wówapi kiŋ de cícaġe do

5b I thought and thus letter the this make for you it is so

5c Thus I thought, and I write you this letter, it is so.

6a Dehaŋyaŋ kaśka waoŋ kta Epca śni óŋkaŋ Hécen Waŋna

6b This long imprisoned I am will I thought not and then now

6c How long will I be in prison, I have been terribly imprisoned

7a waniyetu yámni Teȟiya kaśka waoŋ kiŋ Héoŋ Hepe do

7b year three terrible prison I am the therefore I said it is so

7c here for three years, that's what I said—it is so.

8a Eciŋ Isaŋtaŋka waŋżi mázakaŋ Awapazo śni ꞯa Hehan Isaŋtaŋka tawaȟpaya

8b Thus long knife one gun point not and then long knife belongings

8c So I did not point a gun at the soldiers, and did not take the soldiers' belongings.

9a Waŋżidaŋ iwacu śni Héoŋ Isaŋtaŋka etkiya waꞰu ꞯa óŋkaŋ Hécen

9b one take not therefore long knife towards give and and here thus

9c I did not take one, I gave them to the soldier, and here I am

10a Dehan om kaśka waoŋ kiŋ He Tóken oŋ Décin waoŋ kiŋ He ito

10b now among prison I am the this why here I am the this well

10c in prison here, and that is why

11a Omiyecidake kta waciŋ ꞯa Héoŋ Hépe Do iho Hena Hécetu do

11b you speak for me will I want and therefore I said it is so well these right it is so

11c I want you to speak for me. And therefore I said this, well this is true, it is so.

12a Henana epe kte do

12b all I say will it is so

12c This is all I will say—it is so.

13a Mr. Henry Waŋna

13b Mr. Henry Now

14a Miye do

14b It is me—it is so.

40. Henry Waŋna, June 1, [1865]

Camp Kearney
Davenport Iowa
June 1.

Hehan mitakuye Ito wowapi kin De On Taku wanji iciwange kta Epca qa Heon Wowapi kin
De cicage do Dehanyan kaśka waon kta Epca śni onkan Hecen Wanna waniyetu yamni Teriya
kaśka waon kin Heon Hepe do Ecin Isantanka wanji mazakan Awapazo śni qa Hehan Isantanka
tawarpaye Wanjidan iwaco śni Heon Isantanka etkiya waku qa onkan Hecen Dehan om kaśka
waon kin He Token on Decin waon kin He ito Omiye cidake kta wacin qa Heon Hepe Do iho
Hena Hecetu do Henana epe kte do

Mr. Henry Wanna
miye do

• • • •

40. Henry Now, June 1, [1865]

Camp Kearney
Davenport Iowa
June 1.

Well then, my relative, with this letter, I thought of not asking you this question. Thus I thought,
and I write you this letter, it is so. How long will I be in prison, I have been terribly imprisoned
here for three years, that's what I said—it is so. So I did not point a gun at the soldiers, and did
not take the soldiers' belongings. I did not take one, I gave them to the soldier, and here I am
in prison here, and that is why I want you to speak for me. And therefore I said this, well this is
true, it is so. This is all I will say—it is so.

Mr. Henry Now
It is me—it is so.

CC/MW

1   Davenport Iowa June 2, 1865

2a   Mr. S. R. Riggs   tamakoce
2b   His Country

3a   Mitakuye   ito   wówapi Waŋżi cícaǧe   kte   ǫa   taku   waŋżi eciciye
3b   My relative well letter   one   make you shall and what   one   I say to you
3c   My relative, I will write you a letter, and there is one thing I will

4a   kte   Wicaṡta óta   wicakaṡkapi úŋkan en táku wakaŋ oie   kiŋ   en áyaipi
4b   shall/will Men   many   imprisoned and   at Great Spirit word the   at   you took
4c   say to you.   There were many men imprisoned, and you took the Word of God to them,

5a   ǫa   dakota   wauŋspeyakiyapi etaŋhaŋ wicaṡta tona   mdewakaŋtoŋwaŋ oyate   ocowasiŋ
5b   and   Dakota   you taught them   from   men   some   Mdewakaŋtoŋwaŋ people   all together
5c   and you taught them.   You told us to teach all of the men from the Mdewakantonwan people,

6a   wauŋspekiye onyaṡipi ǫa   ecen ecuŋkunpi ǫa   uŋkiyepi iapi   uŋkitawapi
6b   taught them   told us to and so   we did it   and us   language our
6c   and we did as you told us to.   It was through our teaching God's Word

7a   uŋ   oyate   kiŋ Wakaŋtaŋka oie   kiŋ onspepi heoŋ   kiyepice   epca
7b   for   people the Great Spirit [his] Word the learned therefore it's worth saying I think
7c   that these men learned God's Words and teachings, I think it's worth mentioning.

8a   Hopkins caskedaŋ   ǫa   tahoḣpi wakaŋ   ǫa   tateṡica   ǫa   Tapetataŋka
8b   Hopkins First Born Son and His Nest Sacred and Wind Bad and Fire His Big
8c   Robert Hopkins First Born Son and His Sacred Nest and Bad Wind and His Big Fire

9a   ǫa   itewakaŋhdióta   ǫa   icaḣape ǫa   Wakiyehdi   tuka he   ta
9b   and   Face Lightning Many and Driver   and Bird Came Back but   that and
9c   and Many Lightning Face and Driver and Bird Came Back, but he died,

10a   James hepaŋ   ǫa   miye hena 10 mdewakaŋtoŋwaŋ oyate   waoŋspekiye
10b   James Second Born Son and me   those 10 mdewakaŋtoŋwaŋ people teach them
10c   James Second Born Son and me are the ten that you told to teach the Mdewakantonwan people,

11a   onyaṡipi ǫa   ecoŋkupi   ǫa   waŋna owasiŋ wówapi onspepi
11b   told us to and we did   and now   all   letter   know how
11c   and we did that.   You [Rev. Stephen R. Riggs and Rev. Thomas S. Williamson]

12a   hena niye ecaŋupi kta   tuka uŋkiyepi econonyasipi
12b   those you you did shall/will but we   you told us to do
12c   were supposed to do this, but instead you asked us to do it,

13a   ǫa   waŋna owasin uŋṡtanpi   iyececa okini   niye ecaŋupi
13b   and now   all   we finished is like   maybe you   you did
13c   so now we're finished.

                                                                                                >

41. Mr. Sagyekituŋ, June 2, 1865

Davenport june 2th 1865

Mr. S. R. Riggs tamakoce

Mitakuye ito wowapi Wanji cicage kte qa taku wanji eciciye kte Wicaxta ota wicakaxkapi onkan en taku wakan oie kin en ayaipi qa dakota waunspeyakiyapi Etanhan wicaxta tona mdewakantunwan oyate ocowasin waunspekiye onyaxipi qa ecen ecunqunpi qa onkiyepi iapi onkitawapi on oyate kin Wakantanka oie kin onspepi heon kiyepice epca Hopkins caskeda qa tahorpi wakan qa tatexica qa Tapetatanka qa itewakanhdiota qa icarape qa Wakiyehdi tuka he ṭa James hepan qa miye hena 10 mdewakantunwan oyate waonspekiye onyaxipi qa econqunpi qa wanna owasin wowapi onspepi henaniye ecanupi kta tuka onkiyepi econonyaxipi qa wanna owasin onxtanpi iyececa okini niye ecanapi

>

• • • •

41. Mr. Uses a Cane, June 2, 1865

Davenport Iowa June 2, 1865

Mr. S. R. Riggs His Country

My relative, I will write you a letter, and there is one thing I will say to you. There were many men imprisoned, and you took the Word of God to them, and you taught them. You told us to teach all of the men from the Mdewakantonwan people, and we did as you told us to. It was through our teaching God's Word that these men learned God's Words and teachings, I think it's worth mentioning. Robert Hopkins First Born Son and His Sacred Nest and Bad Wind and His Big Fire and Many Lightning Face and Driver and Bird Came Back, but he died, James Second Born Son and me are the ten that you told to teach the Mdewakantonwan people, and we did that. You [Rev. Stephen R. Riggs and Rev. Thomas S. Williamson] were supposed to do this, but instead you asked us to do it, so now we're finished.

>

14a   šta   Téhaŋhaŋ   den   yahipi   šni   heoŋ   henaĥin   óta   wówapi

14b   although far/long   here you came not   therefore yet not   many   letters

14c   Although you were supposed to do this you did not come for a long time,

15a   oŋspepi   kte   šni   tka   nače   epca   waoŋ   tuka   waŋna   waoŋspekiyapi

15b   they know shall/will not but maybe I think I am   but   now   teachers

15c   I think, many did not learn to read or write.   All the teachers

16a   owasin kiŋ hdápi   qa   he   ehake icaĥape suŋkaku   kici   qa

16b   all   the went home and that last   Driver younger brother with and

16c   are going home at this time, and the last two that will be here are Driver and his younger brother

17a   miye henaoz   den   onyaŋkoŋpi he   ito   taku   waŋži iwaŋdake

17b   I/me those two here we sit here   that   well what one   you examine

17c   and me.   Well, there is one thing we want you to take a look at

18a   qa idukcan   qa   ito   henaoz óuŋyakiyapi kta   uŋciŋpi do

18b   and to think/decide and well those two you help us shall/will we want it is so.

18c   and think about it.   The three of us want you to help us—it is so.

19a   ómaka   kiŋ   de   onkiyohanpi tóken owayaŋke ciŋ he   waka   he

19b   this year the this open for us how   written   the that I mean that

19c   This year is open, and we think it can be done, whatever is written about us, I want

20a   iwaŋdake   qa idukcan   kta   táku   yakuwapi   ca

20b   take a look at and think about it shall/will what you pursue when

20c   you to look and think about it.   Whenever you pursue something,

21a   wakaŋtaŋka óniciyapi nakaeš owasin ecen   oyakihipi cée

21b   Great Spirit helps you truly   all   thus/so you are able so

21c   the Great Spirit always helps you.   For sure, that is why you're able to accomplish it.

22a   héoŋ   mihuŋkawaŋži ito   óuŋyakiyapi kta   uŋciŋpi   do

22b   therefore my brother   well help us   shall/will we want it is so

22c   For that reason, we wish that you will help us—it is so.

23a   waŋna oŋkiš   uŋkitakuyapi wanwicoŋhdakapi   uŋciŋpi qa uŋ   he   iapi

23b   now   ourselves our relatives we want to see them we want and to be that talk

23c   We are writing this letter seeking your help, my relative, we want to see our relatives, and we

24a   óuŋyakiyapi kta   uŋ   de   wówapi de   uŋnicaǧapi   Eya wakaŋtaŋka

24b   you help us shall/will to be this letter   this make for you Also Great Spirit

24c   need your help to talk for us, that's the purpose of our letter.   Also, if the Great Spirit

25a   oŋšiuŋdapi   uŋkaŋš ecadan uŋkitakuyapi wanwicaŋhdakapi kta   tka epca

25b   have pity on us if   soon   our relatives we see them   shall/will but I think

25c   will have compassion on us, we will soon see our relatives, I think.

>

xta Tehanhan den yahipi xni heon hinarin ota wowapi onspepi kte xni tka nace epca waon
tuka wanna waonspekiyapi owasin kin hdapi qa he ehake icarape sonkaku kici qa miye henaoz
den onyankunpi he ito taku wanji iwandake qa idukcan qa ito henaoz ounyakiyapi kta oncinpi
do omaka kin de onkiyoranpi token owayanke cin he waka he iwandake qa idukcan kta taku
yakuwapi ca wakantanka oniciyapi nakaex owasin ecen oyakihipi cee heon mihonkawanji ito
oonyakiyapi kta oncinpi do wanna onkix onkitakuyepi wanwiconhdakapi oncinpi qa on he
iapi oonyakiyapi kta on de wowapi de onnicagapi Eya wakantanka onxinondapi onkanx ecada
onkitakuyepi wanwicunhdakapi kta tka epca

>

. . . .

Although you were supposed to do this you did not come for a long time, I think, many did not
learn to read or write. All the teachers are going home at this time, and the last two that will be
here are Driver and his younger brother and me. Well, there is one thing we want you to take a
look at and think about it. The three of us want you to help us—it is so. This year is open, and
we think it can be done, whatever is written about us, I want you to look and think about it.
Whenever you pursue something, the Great Spirit always helps you. For sure, that is why you're
able to accomplish it. For that reason, we wish that you will help us—it is so. We are writing this
letter seeking your help, my relative, we want to see our relatives, and we need your help to talk
for us, that's the purpose of our letter. Also, if the Great Spirit will have compassion on us, we
will soon see our relatives, I think.

>

26a   héoŋ   uŋkiŝ   uŋkiyepi   nína   céuŋkiyapi   waŋna   Wakaŋtaŋka   oie   kiŋ   uŋ
26b   therefore   we   ourselves   very   pray to   now   Great Spirit   his word   the   to be
26c   Therefore, we ourselves now pray to the Great Spirit, and many men among us

27a   Wicaŝta   óta   yuha tápi   apa   uŋkis   nakuŋ   maka   Akan   uŋnipi   ꝗa
27b   man   many   have died with   some   ourselves   also   earth   upon   we live   and
27c   have died holding on to God's Word.   Also, those of us who live on this earth, and

28a   Taku Wakaŋ   oie   maka   akan   Caźeuŋyantapi   eŝta   uŋkiŝ   eya   wicaŝta   óta
28b   Great Spirit   his word   earth   upon   mention by name   although   we   also   men/man   many
28c   although we proclaim His Word, we are still the object of evil intention against us

29a   uŋ   wócaŋtahde   oŋyaŋpi   kta   naceca   tuka   he   ito   maka   akan
29b   to be   evil intention against   they make us   shall/will   maybe   but   that   come   earth   upon
29c   as we travel upon this earth, and we will need your help so we can go on living.   Life on earth

30a   wiconi   ptécedaŋ   en   óuŋyakiyapi   kta   iyececa   uŋciŋpi   He   den   nakaha
30b   life   short   at   you help us   shall/will   like as/such as   we want   that   here   now
30c   is brief, this is why you should help us, this is what we want.   Recently, my friend

31a   John   makoda   McCullough   hi   úŋkaŋ   iye   Hécen   ecuŋoŋŝipi   uŋ   de
31b   John   my friend   McCullough   came   and   him/he   therefore   told us to do   us   this
31c   John McCullough came and told us to do this.

32a   oŋnicaĝapi   hécen   eya   hena   waoŋspekiya   niŝipi   tókeca   ce   waŋna
32b   we write/make   therefore   also   those   teach them   told you to   different   when   now
32c   In this way, we would give back your efforts that you made.   Now

33a   wówapi   wicakupo   óniciyapi   kta   ce   eya   iye   hécen   ecuŋniŝipi
33b   letter   gave them   help you   shall/will   when   to say anything   he/him   so   told you to do
33c   a letter was written saying we will help you, the letter told us to do this,

34a   ꝗa   dehan   waŋna   oyate   ocowasin   wówapi   uŋspepi   hena   niye   yakiĝapi
34b   and   today   now   people   all   letter   they know   those   you   they made
34c   as a result, the entire nation of people know how to read and write letters, so your efforts paid off.

35a   nakuŋ   Tuŋkaŋŝidayapi   e   eŝta   he   Wicohaŋ   waŋ   wauŋspeyakiyapi   he   iwaŋyake
35b   also   grandfather   at   although   that   custom   a   you taught them   that   observe
35c   If the President saw the new program you have enacted, he would be thankful and

36a   cinhaŋ   taŋyaŋ   ecanupidake   kta   iyececa   ce   Waŋna   tamakoce
36b   if/when   well   consider it done well   shall/will   like   when   now   His Country
36c   say you did a good job, and he would commend you for your work.   Now

37a   wówapi   ku   po   óniciyapi   kta   ce   eya   heoŋ   de   onniciĝapi
37b   letter   give him   help they   shall/will   when   he said   therefore   this   we write you
37c   you can give Rev. S. R. Riggs a letter, that is why we are writing this letter.

\>

heon onkix onkiyepi nina Ceunkiyapi wanna Wakantanka oie kin on Wicaxta ota yuhaṭapi opa onkix nakun maka Akan onnipi qa taku wakan oie maka akan Cajeonyantapi exta onkix eya wicaxta ota un wocantahde onyanpi kta i yececa oncinpi He den nakaha John makoda McCullough hi onkan iye Hecen ecunonxipi on de onnicagapi hecen eya hena waonspekiya nixipi tokeca ce wanna wowapi wicaqupo oniciyapi kta ce eya iye hecen ecunnixipi qa dehan wanna oyate ocowasin wowapi onspepi hena niye yakigapi nakun tunkanxidayapi e exta he Wicoran wan waunspeyakiyapi he iwanyake cinhan tanyan ecanupidake kta iyececa ce Wanna tamakoce wowapiqupo oniciyapi kta ce eya heon de onnicigapi

>

· · · ·

Therefore, we ourselves now pray to the Great Spirit, and many men among us have died holding on to God's Word. Also, those of us who live on this earth, and although we proclaim His Word, we are still the object of evil intention against us as we travel upon this earth, and we will need your help so we can go on living. Life on earth is brief, this is why you should help us, this is what we want. Recently, my friend John McCullough came and told us to do this. In this way, we would give back your efforts that you made. A letter was written saying we will help you, the letter told us to do this, as a result, the entire nation of people know how to read and write letters, so your efforts paid off. If the President saw the new program you have enacted, he would be thankful and say you did a good job, and he would commend you for your work. Now you can give Rev. S. R. Riggs a letter, that is why we are writing this letter.   >

38a   hehan   onkohaŋpi   he   iwaŋyakapo   ḋa   iyukcanwo   epe   ciŋ
38b   then   our actions   that   look at   shall/will   think about it   I said   the
38c   Then we want you to look at our actions and think about it.

39a   Takomni   tóken   onkohaŋpi   owasin   owayanka
39b   nevertheless   how   our actions   all   written down
39c   Although our actions have taken place, they're all written down.

40a   kiŋ   hena   woitonśŋi   on   hécen   owa   eonhnakapi   nace   epca
40b   the   those   lie/lied   for   therefore   written   we put down   perhaps   I think
40c   There can be no lies about what we did, because it's all written down.

41a   heoŋ   Ito   hena   iwandake   kta   onciŋpi   ḋa   de   oŋnicaǧapi   iho
41b   therefore   well   those   to look at   shall/will   we want   and   this   we write you   be it so
41c   Therefore, we're asking you to consider what we've done, that's why we write to you.

42a   mitakuye   henana   epe   kte   owasin   nape   onniyuzpi
42b   My relative   this is all   I say   shall/will   all   hand   we shake
42c   My relative this is all I will say.   All of us shake your hand.

43a   Nitakuye
43b   Your relative

44a   Mr. Sagyekituŋ
44b   Mr. Uses a Cane

45a   He miye   do
45b   That is me—it is so

hehan onkoranpi he iwanyakapo qa iyukcanwo epe cin Takomni token onkoranpi owasin
owayanka kin hena woitonxni on hecen owa eonhnakapi nace epca heon ito hena iwandake kta
oncinpi qa de onnicagapi iho

    Mitakuye henana epe kte owasin nape onniyuzapi

    Nitakuye

Mr. Sagyekitun
    Hemiyedo

• • • •

Then we want you to look at our actions and think about it. Although our actions have taken
place, they're all written down. There can be no lies about what we did, because it's all written
down. Therefore, we're asking you to consider what we've done, that's why we write to you.

    My relative this is all I will say. All of us shake your hand.

        Your relative

Mr. Uses a Cane
    That is me—it is so

                        MS/AC

1   Davenport

2   July 7th 1865

3a   Mihuŋka waŋżi tamakoce ito Wakaŋtaŋka itokam tóken caŋte yus   wauŋ
3b   My brother one His Country well Great Spirit before how heart take hold of I am
3c   My brother Rev. Stephen R. Riggs, well, I will tell you before the Great Spirit how I hold Him

4a   kiŋ ociciyake ḋa Idukcaŋ   kta   taku   wakan oie
4b   the I tell you and have an understanding of shall/will something sacred a word
4c   in my heart, and I want you to think about it.   From the time

5a   nawaĥoŋ kiŋ hetaŋhaŋ   táku tóken waciŋwaye   kta   owakihi   śni
5b   I heard   the from that time what how I depend upon shall/will able to accomplish not
5c   I heard the Great Spirit's Word I haven't been able to depend upon anything or anyone else.

6a   wakaŋtaŋka waciŋwaye Iye iśnana waoŋśida iye   iśnana ksapa owotaŋna
6b   Great Spirit I depend upon he/she alone merciful he/she he/she wise   straight
6c   I depend upon the Great Spirit, He alone is merciful, He alone is wise and good,

7a   miye mitawaciŋ kiŋ hee   śni Tuka iye   tawaciŋ uŋ   ksapa
7b   I   my mind the that is it not But he/she mind to be wise
7c   this is not my mind saying this.   But with my mind I pray He

8a   makaġe kta   Cewakiya óŋśimada   kiŋhaŋ iye   tacaŋKu owotaŋna
8b   made me shall/will I pray Have mercy on me if   he/she his road straight
8c   will make me wise.   I pray He will have mercy on me and help me

9a   omani   maye   ḋa mate eśta   Maĥpiya ekta wiconi owihaŋkewanica
9b   to walk in he makes and if I die although heaven at life   everlasting
9c   to walk in His straight path, and even though I may die, He

10a ópa maye   kta   ĥtayetu haŋhaŋna owasiŋ Cewakiye do
10b join he make shall/will   Evening morning all   I pray   it is so
10c will let me enter into everlasting life. I pray every morning and evening—it is so.

11a ḋa hécetu śni śta   iye   oie   kiŋ yuha maka akan iyaya   maye
11b and so/right not although he/she a word the with earth upon to have gone he make
11c Although it might not be right, but by His Word, if He would place me upon earth,

12a kiŋhaŋ Winuĥiŋca hokśiyopa wicaśta owasiŋ Tóken owakihi   okodakiciya
12b if   women children men all   how I am able to church
12c if it is possible, I would bring all women, children, and men into His church,

13a kiŋ en awicawau kta   ecin   waun ce   hehan waśicun Wakaŋ yauŋpi
13b the at I bring them towards to think to be when then   white ministers they are
13c this is what I am thinking.   Then you that are white ministers,

14a kiŋ tóken wahokoŋ uŋyakiyapi   kiŋ micaŋte ekta yuha   waun epca Ce
14b the how   they counseled/preached the my heart at   have with to be I think when
14c when you preached to us, I think I have kept all in my heart.

>

42. Peżiĥota, July 7, 1865

Davenport
July 7th 1865

Mihunka wanji tamakoce ito Wakantanka itokam token cante yus waun kin ociciyake qa
Idukcan kta tuka wakan oie nawarun kin hetanhan taku token wacinwaye kta owakihi xni
wakantanka wacinwaye Iye ixnana waunxida iye ixnana ksapa owotanna miye mitawacin
kin hee xni Tuka iye tawacin un ksapa makage kta Cewakiya unximada kinhan iye tacanKu
owotanna omani maye qa maṭe exta Marpiya ekta wiconi owihankewanica ope maye kta ĥtayetu
hinĥanna owasin Cewakiyedo qa hecetu xni xta iye oie kin yuha maka akan iyaya maye kinhan
Winuĥinca hokśiyopa wicaxta owasin Token owakihi okodakiciya kin en awicaWaukta ecin
waun ce hehan waxicun Wakan yaunpikin token wahokon unyaKiyapi kin micante ekta yuha
waun epca Ce

>

• • • •

42. Sage, July 7, 1865

Davenport
July 7th 1865

My brother Rev. Stephen R. Riggs, well, I will tell you before the Great Spirit how I hold Him
in my heart, and I want you to think about it. From the time I heard the Great Spirit's Word
I haven't been able to depend upon anything or anyone else. I depend upon the Great Spirit,
He alone is merciful, He alone is wise and good, this is not my mind saying this. But with my
mind I pray He will make me wise. I pray He will have mercy on me and help me to walk in His
straight path, and even though I may die, He will let me enter into everlasting life. I pray every
morning and evening—it is so. Although it might not be right, but by His Word, if He would
place me upon earth, if it is possible, I would bring all women, children, and men into His
church, this is what I am thinking. Then you that are white ministers, when you preached to us,
I think I have kept all in my heart.

>

15a   wópe   kiŋ de   makaowaŋcaya   yuhapi   ḳa   Wicowaśte   wicowaĥbadaŋ
15b   law   the this   all over the earth   owned/held   and   goodness   gentleness
15c   This commandment is respected all over the earth, so goodness and compassion

16a   kohaŋna   icaġe Kta   ciŋpi   kiŋ   he   miś   nínaĥiŋ   waciŋ   ce
16b   very soon   grow   shall   they want   the   that   I myself   very   I want   when
16c   will grow very soon.   This is what's wanted, and I want that very much, too.

17a   owasiŋ   okpaza   ehna   oŋyakoŋpi   tka   wakaŋtaŋka   iyoyamuŋyaŋpi   kiŋ   héoŋ
17b   All   darkness   in   we are in a place   but   Great Spirit   to enlighten us   the   therefore
17c   We are all living in darkness, but the Great Spirit enlightens us, therefore

18a   nína   Iyuśkiŋyaŋ   céuŋkiyapi   kta   waciŋ   ce   Mihuŋka waŋzi   hena   hécen
18b   very   gladly   we pray   shall/will   I want   when   my brother one   those   so/therefore
18c   we shall gladly pray to him, this is what I want.   My brother,

19a   caŋte   yus   Wauŋ   ḳa   nayahoŋ   kta   waciŋ   ḳa   de   cícaġe
19b   heart   take hold of   to be   and   you hear   shall/will   I want   and   this   I make
19c   I hold those in my heart, therefore, I want you to hear this, so I write this letter to you.

20a   Peżiĥota   miye do
20b   Sage, it is I—it is so

wope kin de makaowancaya yuhapi qa Wicowaxte wicowarbadan kohanna icage Kta cinpi kin
he mix ninaḣin wacin ce owasin otpaza ehna unyakunpi tka wakantanka iyoyamunyapi kin
heon nina Iyuxkinyan ceunkiyapi kta wacin ce Mihunka wanji hena hecen cante yus Waun qa
nayaḣon kta wacin qa de cicage

Pejiḣota miye do

. . . .

This commandment is respected all over the earth, so goodness and compassion will grow very
soon. This is what's wanted, and I want that very much, too. We are all living in darkness, but
the Great Spirit enlightens us, therefore we shall gladly pray to him, this is what I want. My
brother, I hold those in my heart, therefore, I want you to hear this, so I write this letter to you.

Sage, it is I—it is so

MS/AC

1   Camp Kearney

2   Davenport Iowa

3   Nove 16th 1865

4   Rev. S. R. Riggs

5a	Mitakuye	ake	Ito	Wówapi	cícaǧe	kta	waciŋ
5b	My relative	again	well/come	Letter	to make	shall/will	I want

5c My relative, once again I want to write you a letter.

6a	Mitakuye	eya	óhiŋni	makiyuŝkapi		kta	Ayakite	ciŋ	he
6b	My relative	also/too	always	to release me from prison		shall/will	to seek for	the	that

6c My relative, I know you are making every effort to free me from prison,

7a	sdoŋwaye	tuka	Dehaŋyaŋ	Oyakihi ŝni	tuka	eya	Héceca eŝta	Dehaŋyaŋ	tokeŋ
7b	I know	but	up to now	you can not	but	also/too	although	up to now	how

7c but you haven't been successful.   Although you were not successful,

8a	Oyakihi	Hécen	Ayakita	kta	nace	epca	Waŋna	Waŋiyetu	yamni
8b	you are able to	so	search for	shall/will	perhaps	I think	now	winters	three

8c I think you will search for, so you will succeed.   This is what I am thinking.   Now it has been

9a	Hehaŋyaŋ	Kaŝka	Waoŋ	tuka	eya	tukteŋ kteŋ		Iyomakiŝica
9b	so far	imprisoned	to be	but	also/too	sometimes/once in a while		to be sad/grieved

9c three years that I have been imprisoned.   Also, I am usually sad

10a	ece	tuka	nakaha	Aŋpetu Iyohi	Caŋtemaŝica	ciŋ	he	niŝ	eyahi	sdoŋyaye
10b	usually	but	now	day	every	to be sad	the	that	you	also/too	to know of

10c once in a while, but lately, I'm always sad, every day.   You also know that.

11a	Mitawiŋaĥtiŋ	ǫa	Ina	ǫa	miciŋca	hena	oŋ	Aŋpetu Iyohi	oŋ
11b	my very (dear) wife	and	mother	and	my child	those	for	every day	for

11c My dear wife, mother, and my child, because of them, I am very sad

12a	CaŋteMasica	ĥiŋca	Taŋhaŋ	Kawaŋke	nioŋ	kiŋhaŋ	Hena	wicayuha	oŋ
12b	sorrowful	very	brother-in-law	Knocks Down	alive	if/when	those	have them	for

12c every day.   When my brother-in-law Knocks Down was alive, he would keep them.

13a	nakaŝ	makaŝkapi	eŝta	óhiŋni	Caŋte mawaŝte	dehan
13b	indeed/truly	they imprisoned me	although	always	I am happy/glad	at this time/right now

13c Although I am imprisoned, I am always happy for that.   Right now,

14a	tuwedaŋ	Wicayuha	oŋ ŝni	kéyapi	óŋkaŋ	nína	Caŋte Maŝica
14b	nobody	to have them/own	to be/we/us not	they said	and	very	sad/sorrowful

14c they said nobody is taking care of them and it makes me very sad.

>

43. Elias Ruban Óȟaŋwayakapi, November 16, 1865

Camp Kearney
Davenport Iowa
Nove 16th 1865

Rev. S. R. Riggs

Mitakuye ake Ito Wowapi cicage kta wacin Mitakuye eya ohinni makiyuśkapi kta Ayakitecin he sdonwaye tuka Dehanyan Oyakihi śni tuka eya Hececa eśta Dehanyan token Oyakihi Hecen Ayakita kta nace epca Wanna Waniyetu yamni Hehanyan Kaśka Waon tuka eya tukten kten Iyomakiśica ece tuka nakaha Anpetu Iyohi Cante maśica cin he niś eyahi sdonyaye Mitawinaȟtin qa Ina qa micinca hena on Anpetu Iyohi on Cante Masica ȟin ce Tanhan Kawanke nion qehan Hena wicayuha on nakaś makaśkapi eśta ohinni Cante mawaśte dehan tuwedan Wicayuha onśni keyapi onkan nina Cante Maxica

>

• • • •

43. Elias Ruban They See His Ways, November 16, 1865

Camp Kearney
Davenport Iowa
Nove 16th 1865

Rev. S. R. Riggs

My relative, once again I want to write you a letter. My relative, I know you are making every effort to free me from prison, but you haven't been successful. Although you were not successful, I think you will search for, so you will succeed. This is what I am thinking. Now it has been three years that I have been imprisoned. Also, I am usually sad once in a while, but lately, I'm always sad, every day. You also know that. My dear wife, mother, and my child, because of them, I am very sad every day. If my brother-in-law Knocks Down was alive, he would keep them. Although I am imprisoned, I am always happy for that. Right now, they said nobody is taking care of them and it makes me very sad.

>

15a		hécen	Wétu kiŋhaŋ	tókeŋ	Oyakihi			Omayakiye
15b		So	spring	if how	able to accomplish/to be able			help me
15c		So this spring if you are able to help me,						

16a	ċa	mitawiŋahtiŋ	kiŋ hena	Wicaduha	waoŋ	kta	waciŋ	do
16b	and	my very (dear) wife	the those	to have/own you	you/to be	shall/will	I want	it is so
16c	I want you to take care of my very dear wife and family—it is so.							

17a	Eya	hena	dehan	tuwedan	Wicayuha un	ŝni	kiŋ	hena	niŝ		Sdoŋyaye
17b	also/too	those	now	nobody	to have them	not	the	those	you/yourself		you know
17c	Also, you know that no one is caring for my family right now.										

18a		Iho		Hena	hécetu	Hehaŋ	Fort Thompson D.T.	ḋa
18b		come on/see there		those	right	Then	Fort Thompson D.T.	and
18c		Well, those are true.				Then, today a letter came		

19a	Héciyataŋhaŋ	nakaka	Wówapi	hi	óŋkaŋ	Ate	Tahoĥpin wakaŋ	ta
19b	from that place	now/today	paper/letter	come/came	and	Father	His Sacred Nest	died
19c	from Fort Thompson, Dakota Territory [Crow Creek], and they said Father His Sacred Nest died,							

20a	kéyapi	nawaĥoŋ	Hécen	nína	Caŋte maŝice	do.
20b	they said	I heard	Therefore	very	sad I am	it is so.
20c	I just heard this.		Therefore, I am very sad—it is so.			

21a	Mitakuye	micaŋte	oŋ	nape	ciyuze	do
21b	my relative	my heart	with	hand	I hold	it is so
21c	My relative, with my heart I shake your hand—it is so.					

22a		Elias Reuben

23a		Óĥaŋwayakapi
23b		They See His Ways

24a		miye
24b		it is me

Hecen Wetukinhan token Oyakihi Omayakiye ça mitawinaħtin kin hena Wicaduha
waon kta wacin do Eya hena dehan tuwedan Wicayuha onxni kin hena niś Sdonyaye
    Iho Hena hecetu Hehan Fort Thompson D.T. qa Heciya tanhan nakaka Wowapi hi onkan
Ate Tahoħpin wakan ṭa keyapi nawaħon Hecen nina Cante maśice do
Mitakuye micante on nape ciyuze do.

    Elias Reuben
    Oħanwayakapi
        miye

· · · ·

    So this spring if you are able to help me, I want you to take care of my very dear wife and
family—it is so. Also, you know that no one is caring for my family right now.
    Well, those are true. Then, today a letter came from Fort Thompson, Dakota Territory
[Crow Creek], and they said Father His Sacred Nest died, I just heard this. Therefore, I am very
sad—it is so.
My relative, with my heart I shake your hand—it is so.

    Elias Reuben
    They See His Ways
        it is me

MS/AC

1   Camp McClellan
2a   Davenport Iowa

3a   Tamakoce   Mitakoda aŋpetu kiŋ dehan Wakaŋtaŋka waŝake ca iyokipiya
3b   His country my friend day   the   now   God   strong so joyfully
3c   My friend, His Country, today I write this letter to you, we are joyful, God is strong,

4a   waoŋkiciyakapi   ateyapi iyecen waoŋ   nihdakapi hėoŋ   etaŋhaŋ nína
4b   we see each other father   like   you are see you   therefore from   very
4c   We see each other, we look to you like a father.   For this reason, we are very

5a   táku Wakaŋ oŋkiyuŝkiŋpi Wakaŋtaŋka oie   kiŋ etaŋhaŋ táku   waŝte
5b   thing Sacred we are joyfully God   word the from   something good
5c   joyful in the Holy Spirit, we get something good from God's Word.

6a   Sdonyaŋpi kta eciŋ   oŋyakuŋpi óŋkaŋ ake   táku wakaŋ oie
6b   They know will think we are   and   again holy spirit word
6c   We are thinking they will learn God's Words again from the Holy Spirit.

7a   oŋyakayahi   he waŝte ḣa caŋte Waŝte oŋyeyapi mitakoda hehaŋ
7b   you brought us this good and heart good made us my friend then
7c   You brought good news and comforted us.   My friend,

8a   ito táku waŋżi tókca   epe   kta tka Wicawake   ḣa   wicawake ŝni
8b   well thing one   different I say will but I am truthful and I am truthful not
8c   there is one thing different I want to say, but whether I tell you the truth or not,

9a   kiŋhaŋ Sdonyaye kta eciŋ   en yaoŋ   ḣa sdonyaye do   eya
9b   if   you know will because   at you are and you know it is so to say
9c   you will know, because you are there.   My friend you know the truth,

10a   mitakoda wicoḣaŋ ŝíca icaġa óŋkaŋ   Wópetoŋhaŋska ḣa   miye
10b   my friend work   bad grow and here Buyer Long   and me
10c   things got bad, and grew worse, Long Buyer [Henry Sibley] and I

11a   kici wicoḣaŋ waŝte yaciŋpi   ḣa   toŋkaŋŝidaŋ econ uŋŝipi ḣa
11b   with work   good you all want and Grandfather ask us to do and
11c   worked good, and did all you want, and all the President asked us to do, and

12a   tóna nipi kta ciŋpi   kiŋ owasiŋ wipe eḣpeyapi ḣa   mniḣuha ska
12b   some live will they want the all   their staff   and cloth   white
12c   some will live, they want to live, they all offered their staff and white cloth of truce

13a   icupi ḣa toŋkaŋŝidaŋ étkiya kúpi   tka toŋkaŋŝidaŋ Waŋna ta
13b   they take and grandfather towards they give but Grandfather now died
13c   toward the President, and gave it to him, but now the President has died.

14a   hécen tóken ouŋpi   kta hwo   once   cíŋpi
14b   thus how   they live will question wondering they want
14c   Thus, we wonder how we are going to live, they want to live.

>

44. Simon Wakaŋhdióta, [1865]

Camp McClellan
Davenport Iowa

Tamakoce Mitakoda anpetu kin dehan Wakantanka waxake ça iyokipiya waonkiciyaka ateyapi iyecen waon nihdakapi heon etanhan nina taku Wakan onkiyuxkinpi Wakantanka oie kin etanhan taku waxte Sdonyanpi kta ecin onkanpi onkan ake taku wakan oie oyagyahi he waxte qa cante Waxte onyayapi mitakoda hehan ito taku wanjin tokca epe kta tka Wicawake qa wicawake xni kinhan Sdoyaye kta ecin en yaon qa sdodyaye do eya mitakoda wicoran xica icaza onkan Wopetonhanska qa miye kici wicoran waxte yacinpi qa tonkanxidan econunxipi qa tona nipi kta cinpi kin owasin wipeerpeyapi qa mniruha ska icupi qa tonkanxidan entkiya kupi tka tonkanxidan Wanna ṭa hecen token ounpi kta hwo onke cinpi

>

• • • •

44. Simon Many Lightning, [1865]

Camp McClellan
Davenport Iowa

My friend, His Country, today I write this letter to you, we are joyful, God is strong, We see each other, we look to you like a father. For this reason, we are very joyful in the Holy Spirit, we get something good from God's Word. We are thinking they will learn God's Words again from the Holy Spirit. You brought good news and comforted us. My friend, there is one thing different I want to say, but whether I tell you the truth or not, you will know, because you are there. My friend you know the truth, things got bad, and grew worse, Long Buyer [Henry Sibley] and I worked good, and did all you want, and all the President asked us to do, and some will live, they want to live, they all offered their staff and white cloth of truce toward the President, and gave it to him, but now the President has died. Thus, we wonder how we are going to live, they want to live.

>

15a Mitakoda héceca šta toŋkaŋšidaŋ ta ešta tóken caŋte oŋkiyuzapi
15b my friend even if Grandfather died even how heart we hold him
15c My friend, even if the President died, we hold him in our hearts,

16a ǫa táku oŋkekiciyapi kiŋ hena ee owihaŋke šni eciŋ oŋkoŋpi
16b and something they say to us the these they are end times not we are thinking
16c and some things they have told us we are thinking about end times,

17a do mitakoda hécen hena awaciŋ waoŋ ǫa wicoȟaŋ šíca mduhe
17b it is so my friend thus these think I am and work bad I have
17c it's true, my friend. I think I will

18a ciŋ owasiŋ abduštaŋ ǫa wakaŋtaŋka ecedaŋ en
18b the all I quit and God alone at
18c quit all sins, and promise to follow God alone.

19a owotaŋna miciconza
19b right/straight I promise to do
19c I promise to go straight.

20a henana epe kta
20b that's all I say will
20c That is all I have to say.

21a Anawagmani Ciŋhiŋtku
21b Galloping Walker son
21c I am Galloping Walker's son.

22a Simon Wakaŋhdiota
22b Simon Many Lightning

23q Miyedo
23b it is me—it is so

Mitakoda hececa xta tonkanxidan ṭa exta token cante onkiyuzapi qa taku onkekiciyapi kin hena ee owihanke xni ecinonkanpi do mitakoda hecen hena awacin waon qa wicoran xica mduhe cin owasin amduxtan qa wakantanka ecedan en owotana miçiconza

      Henana epe kta

Anawagmani Cinhintku
     Simon Wakanhdiota
        Miyedo

• • • •

My friend, even if the President died, we hold him in our hearts, and some things they have told us we are thinking about end times, it's true, my friend. I think I will quit all sins, and promise to follow God alone. I promise to go straight.

      That is all I have to say.

I am Galloping Walker's son.
     Simon Many Lightning
        it is me—it is so

                              CC/MW

1   Febr 1, 1866

2a   Mihuŋka   waŋżi   Tamakoce
2b   My brother one   His Country
2c   My brother   Rev. Stephen R. Riggs

3a   Ito   táku   waŋżi owotaŋna Ecuŋpi wacin he   aŋpetu kiŋ niś
3b   Well something one   straight/right do they want that day   the   you
3c   Well, there is one thing I want them to do right and today I want you to

4a   ito   nayahoŋ kta   wacin ąa héoŋ   wówapi ciĉu
4b   well you hear shall/will I want and so/therefore letter   I give you
4c   hear about it, and so I'm writing this letter.

5a   Cóŋkaśke kiŋ de   wicaśta tóna   winohiŋca yuhapi   tuka owotaŋna
5b   prison/fort the this men   how many women   they have but   straight
5c   There are some men here in this prison-fort that have their women

6a   ecuŋpi śni kiŋ hena Ito owotaŋna ecuŋ wicayaśi   kta   wacin
6b   do they not the those well straight   do   you cause them shall I want
6c   with them but they're not living right, I want you to tell them they must have only one wife.

7a   uŋkiye táku uŋkeyapi kiŋ nauŋhuŋpi śni ókini niye nanihuŋpi kiŋhaŋ
7b   we   what us   the they listen not maybe you they listen if
7c   They do not listen to anything we say, maybe they might listen to you,

8a   hécen waŝte kta   epca hena owotaŋna ecuŋpi śni eciŋ   makoce
8b   therefore good shall/will I think those straight   do they not to think country
8c   I think that will be the best way.   Those that are not doing the right thing, if they

9a   tókeca ekta yápi   kiŋhaŋ Hehan iyotaŋ nína śkáŋpi   kiŋhaŋ hécen
9b   different at they go if   then greater very do/move about if   so/thus
9c   go to a different place, their behavior will become worse.   I think

10a   kośka   owasiŋ Iyutaŋ wicayapi   kta   epca   detaŋhaŋ
10b   young men all   tempt bad influence shall I think   from now on
10c   they will not only tempt all the young men but will be a bad influence on them. From now on,

11a   tokata tuwe winohiŋca waŋżi yuha kte   ciŋhan wakaŋyuze kta epca waun
11b   future who woman   one   has shall/will if/when marry   shall I think I am
11c   whoever is going to have a woman, I think, they should marry them.

12a   wicohaŋ tóna   śíca yuha uŋkicaġapi kiŋ hena owasiŋ owotaŋna
12b   work   how many bad has/have we grew up the those all   straight
12c   I want all of us who grew up with bad behavior to straighten

13a   uŋhduŝtaŋpi kta   wacin Iho waŋna owasiŋ ociciyake kte   do
13b   we finish   shall/will I want Yes now   all   tell you   shall it is so
13c   out our bad habits.   So now I will tell you everything—it is so.

>

45. Joseph Wicaȟiŋca Máza, February 1, 1866

Febr 1, 1866

Mihunka wanji Tamakoce

Ito taku wanji owotanna Ecunpi wacin he anpetu kin niś Ito nayarun kta wacin qa heon wowapi ciçu Cunkaśke kin de wicaśta tona winorinca yuhapi tuka owotanna ecunpi śni kin hena Ito owotanna ecun wicayaśi kta wacin unkiye taku unkeyapi kin naunrunpi śni okini niye nanirunpi kinhan hecen waśte kta epca hena owotanna ecunpi śni ecin makoce tokeca ekta yapi kinhan Hehan iyotan nina śkanpi kinhan hecen kośka owasin Iyutan wicayapi kta epca detanhan tokata tuwe winorinca wanji yuha kte cinhan wakanyuze kta epca waon wicoran tona śica yuha unkicagapi kin hena owasin owotanna unhduśtanpi kta wacin iho wanna owasin ociciyake kte do

>

• • • •

45. Joseph Old Iron Man, February 1, 1866

Febr 1, 1866

My brother Rev. Stephen R. Riggs

Well, there is one thing I want them to do right and today I want you to hear about it, and so I'm writing this letter. There are some men here in this prison-fort that have their women with them but they're not living right, I want you to tell them they must have only one wife. They do not listen to anything we say, maybe they might listen to you, I think that will be the best way. Those that are not doing the right thing, if they go to a different place, their behavior will become worse. I think they will not only tempt all the young men but will be a bad influence on them. From now on, whoever is going to have a woman, I think, they should marry them. I want all of us who grew up with bad behavior to straighten out our bad habits. So now I will tell you everything—it is so.

>

14a	Icaȟape	Tatepiyawiŋ 1
14b	Driver	Woman Fixes the Wind
15a	Wakaŋ dowaŋ	Tatezatawiŋ 2
15b	Sacred Singer	Woman with Forked Wind
16a	Pataŋiŋna	Tamaza 3
16b	Attacks Quietly	Her Iron
17a	Sagyekituŋ	Wíhdeġa ša 4
17b	Uses a Cane	Red Spotted Woman
18a	Tawahiŋkpe	Tipiożaŋżaŋwiŋ 5
18b	His Arrow	Woman Lights Her House
19a	Aŋpetu hokšidaŋ	Tacaŋkutaŋiŋwiŋ 6
19b	Day Boy	Her Way Is Clear Woman
20a	Hepaŋduta	Wabduška tókeca wiŋ 7
20b	Scarlet Second Son	Different Bug Woman

21a	Hena	Éepi	do	hena	Wakaŋkiciyus		wicayaši	kta	Waciŋ	do
21b	Those	that is them	it is so	Those	marriage according to law		tell them	shall	I want	it is so
21c	These are the ones—it is so.			Those are the persons I want you to tell to get married—it is so.						

22a	Iho	mihuŋkawaŋżi	henana	epe	kta
22b	Yes	my brother	only so much	I say	shall/will
22c	Yes, my brother, that is all I will say.				

23a	Joseph Wicaȟiŋca Máza
23b	Joseph Old Iron Man

24a	Miye
24b	That is me

Icarape	Tatepiyawin 1
Wakandowan	Tatejatawin 2
Pataninna	Tamaza 3
Sagyekitunna	Wíhdega ṡa 4
Tawahinkpe	Tipiojanjanwin 5
Anpetuhokṡidan	Tacankutaninwin 6
Hepanduta	Wabduṡkatokecawin 7

Hena Eepi do hena Wakankiciyus wicayaṡi kta wacin do iho mihunkawanji henana epe kta

Joseph Wicarincamaza
    Miye

• • • •

Driver	Woman Fixes the Wind 1
Sacred Singer	Woman with Forked Wind 2
Attacks Quietly	Her Iron 3
Uses a Cane	Red Spotted Woman 4
His Arrow	Woman Lights Her House 5
Day Boy	Her Way Is Clear Woman 6
Scarlet Second Son	Different Bug Woman 7

These are the ones—it is so. Those are the persons I want you to tell to get married—it is so. Yes, my brother, that is all I will say.

Joseph Old Iron Man
    That is me

MS/AC

1a   Wíyawapi   Feb 24th 1866

1b   Month   Feb 24th 1866

2   Mr. S. R. Riggs

3a   Mitakoda   Nakaha   ate   wówapi   yaḳu   e   wanmdake   hécen

3b   My friend now/today father letter   you gave to   I see/have seen so/therefore

3c   My friend, today, I have seen the letter you wrote to the Father.   Therefore

4a   ate   táku   eyakiya   cin   hena   wanmdaka   únkan   wanżi   iyotan

4b   father what   you said/say the   those   I see/have seen   and   one   most

4c   I have seen those things that you said to the Father.   And there is one thing which

5a   waśtewadaka   ake   Wakantanka un   kin   piyaȟin   un   wahokononyakiyapi

5b   I love   again   Great Spirit to be the make anew to be you preached to us

5c   I love that you will preach to us about the Great Spirit, who can make us new, and you

6a   kta   ayakite   kta   kéhe   cinhe   he ake   yedo   hehan miś

6b   Shall/will you search will you said that if/when that again it is so then   I

6c   said that he will search for us if we search for him—it is so.   Then, I

7a   ito   tóken   waun   kinhe   nayaȟon   kta   wacin   yedo

7b   come/well how   I am if/when you hear shall/will I want   it is so

7c   want you to hear about how well I am doing—it is so.

8a   eya   déciya   wahdi   kin he táku   un   tankan   hdicu

8b   also/too here/in this place came home if/when what to be   outside   start to come home

8c   When I came back to this place, I thought about why they released me,

9a   mayayapi   kin he   óhinniyan   tohanyan   ni waun   kin he   ecamon   kta

9b   they sent me if/when always   how long I am alive if/when to do/work shall/will

9c   and as long as I live, I want to do what they asked me

10a   wacin   tuka   nahanȟin   oyate   tókeca   wanżi en   emayahnakapi   śni

10b   I want but   not yet   people different one   at   to place/let rest   not

10c   to do.   You have not yet placed me with a different people, but now with my

11a   tuka   wanna   wayażużu   oyate   tawa   kin   hen   mitakoda   John P. Williamson

11b   but   now   to tear down people his/own the   there   my friend   John P. Williamson

11c   friend The Reverend John P. Williamson, we have gone to the people

12a   kici   wai   tuka wicadapi śni hécen   ake   ekta waki   yedo

12b   with have gone to but refused   therefore again at/to to arrive at home it is so

12c   who tear down others, but they have refused, so once again, I went home—it is so.

13a   tuka ake   tukten   ye mayaśipi   kinhan   mde kta   óhinni   epca   waun   yedo

13b   but again where order me to go if/when I go shall always I think I/to be it is so

13c   But whenever they tell me to go somewhere, I am always willing to go, I think—it is so.

>

46. Robert Hopkins, February 24, 1866

Wiyawapi Feb 24th 1866

Mr. S. R. Rigags

Mitakoda Nakaha ate wowapi yaqu e wanmdake hecen ate taku eyakiya cin hena wanmdaka
onkan wanji iyotan waśtewadake ake Wakantanka on kin piyarin on wahokononyakiyapi kta
ayakite kta ki he cinhe heake yedo hehan miś ito token waon kinhe nayaron kta wacin yedo eya
deciya wahdi kinhe taku on tankan hdicu mayayapi kinhe ohinniyan tohanyan niwaon kinhe
ecamon kta wacin tuka nahanrin oyate tokeca wanji en emayahnakapi śni tuka wanna wayajuju
oyate tawa kin hen mitakoda John P. Williamson kici wai tuka wicadapiśni hecen ake ekta waki
yedo tuka ake tukten yemayaśipi kinhan mde kta ohinni epca waon yedo

\>

• • • •

46. Robert Hopkins, February 24, 1866

Month Feb 24th 1866

Mr. S. R. Riggs

My friend, today, I have seen the letter you wrote to the Father. Therefore I have seen those
things that you said to the Father. And there is one thing which I love that you will preach to
us about the Great Spirit, who can make us new, and you said that he will search for us if we
search for him—it is so. Then, I want you to hear about how well I am doing—it is so. When I
came back to this place, I thought about why they released me, and as long as I live, I want to
do what they asked me to do. You have not yet placed me with a different people, but now with
my friend The Reverend John P. Williamson, we have gone to the people who tear down others,
but they have refused, so once again, I went home—it is so. But whenever they tell me to go
somewhere, I am always willing to go, I think—it is so.

\>

14a hehan ake wétu kiŋhaŋ ake cóŋkicakse en wóžupi kte yedo
14b then again spring if/when again Fort Thompson at they plant will it is so
14c This spring, they will again plant crops at Fort Thompson—it is so.

15a hehan nakaha isaŋyati típi kiŋ en oyate tókeca wicota
15b then now/today Isantis home/tent the at people different many persons
15c Today, where the Isantis live at, a group made up of many different persons came and

16a ahitipi úŋkaŋ héyapi kéyapi wašicoŋ dena
16b to pitch one's tent and they said that they say that white people these
16c camped there. And then, it was told to us, that this is what they said: we will

17a wicoŋkasotapi ḳa aǵuyapi hena yuha waziyata uŋhdapi kta
17b make an end to them/expel and flour those with north we go home shall
17c chase all these white people out of here and we will take all the flour, then we will go home up north,

18a ce eyapi kéyapi hécen cóŋkaške kiŋ natakapi yedo
18b when they said they say that therefore a fence the they locked door it is so
18c after that, we were told, they locked the fence—it is so.

19a hehan déciya nína wašbe yedo ḳa ihaŋktoŋwaŋ nína wicakihaŋ
19b then here very deep snow it is so and Yanktons very starving/starvation
19c Then over here the snow is very deep—it is so. And the Yanktons are really starving to death and

20a yedo teȟike yedo isaŋyati e kítaŋna taŋyaŋ yukaŋpi yedo
20b it is so difficult it is so Isantis to/at a little well to be/there is it is so
20c it is very difficult—it is so. At the Isantis' place they're doing very well—it is so.

21a henana epe kte yedo
21b None/only so much I say shall/will it is so
21c That is all I will say—it is so.

22a Nape Ciyuze do
22b Hand hold your it is so
22c I shake your hand—it is so.

23a mitakuye
23b My relative

24 Robert Hopkins

25a he miyedo
25b that is me

hehan ake wetu kinhan ake conkicakse en wojupi kte yedo hehan nakaha isanyati tipi kin en oyate tokeca wicota ahitipi onkan heyapi keyapi wašicon dena wiconkasotapi qa aguyapi hena yuha waziyata onhdapi kta ce eyapi kiyapi hecen conkaške kin natakapi yedo hehan deciya nina wašbe yedo qa ihanktonwan nina wicaakiran yedo terinke yedo isanyati e kitanna tanyan yukanpi yedo
henana epe kte yedo
Nape Ciyuze do
         mitakuye

    Robert Hopkins
         hemiyedo

· · · ·

This spring, they will again plant crops at Fort Thompson—it is so. Today, where the Isantees live at, a group made up of many different persons came and camped there. And then, it was told to us, that this is what they said: we will chase all these white people out of here and we will take all the flour, then we will go home up north, after that, we were told, they locked the fence—it is so. Then over here the snow is very deep—it is so. And the Yanktons are really starving to death and it is very difficult—it is so. At the Isantis' place they're doing very well—it is so.
That is all I will say—it is so.
I shake your hand—it is so.
    My relative

    Robert Hopkins
         that is me

MS/AC

1   April 8th 1866

2   [S.]R. Riggs

3a   Mitakoda   aŋpetu   kiŋ de   Wakaŋtaŋka   waśake
3b   My friend   day   this   Great Spirit powerful/strong
3c   My friend, the Great Spirit is powerful, therefore, on this day,

4a   hécen   uŋ   nínahiŋ   inawape   kta   waciŋ
4b   therefore/so to be very/especially refuge/trust in shall/will I want
4c   I will go to Him and take refuge in Him, is what I want.

5a   miniwakaŋ mdatke ciŋ he amduśtaŋ kta   waciŋ uŋ   wówapi
5b   liquor   I drink the that I quit   shall/will I want to be letter
5c   I want to quit drinking liquor, that is why I will sign the pledge letter attesting

6a   mdutaŋ   kta   waciŋ hécen   mitakoda wítaya   nayahoŋpi
6b   I sign/to honor shall/will I want therefore my friend together they hear
6c   to my desire to quit drinking.   Therefore, my friend, I want everyone together

7a   kta   waciŋ   tamakoce   mitakoda hécen   yaciŋ   uŋ
7b   shall/will I want His Country my friend so/therefore you want to be
7c   to hear this.   Rev. Stephen R. Riggs, my friend, that is what you want me

8a   ecen   ecamoŋ   kta   waciŋ wi yamni   hehaŋyaŋ wówapi
8b   so/as it was to do/work shall/will I want three moons so long letter
8c   to do, so I am going to do this.   I want to sign the letter pledging

9a   mdutaŋ kta   waciŋ
9b   I sign shall/will I want
9c   myself not to touch liquor for three months.

10   Simon Thomas

11a   Wakaŋhdióta   miye   do
11b   Lightning Face it is me—it is so

47. Simon Thomas Wakaŋhdióta, April 8, 1866

April 8th 1866

[S.]R. Riggs

Mitakoda anpetu kinde Wakantanka waśake hecen on ninarin inawape kta wacin miniwakan mdatke cin he amduśtan kta wacin on wowapi mduta kta wacin hecen mitakoda witaya nayaronpi kta wacin tamakoce mitakoda hecen yacin on ecen ecamon kta wacin wiyamni hehanyan wowapi mduta kta wacin

Simon Thomas
Wakanhdiota miyedo

• • • •

47. Simon Thomas Many Lightning, April 8, 1866

April 8th 1866

[S.]R. Riggs

My friend, the Great Spirit is powerful, therefore, on this day, I will go to Him and take refuge in Him, is what I want. I want to quit drinking liquor, that is why I will sign the pledge letter attesting to my desire to quit drinking. Therefore, my friend, I want everyone together to hear this. Rev. Stephen R. Riggs, my friend, that is what you want me to do, so I am going to do this. I want to sign the letter pledging myself not to touch liquor for three months.

Simon Thomas
Many Lightning it is me—it is so

MS/AC

1   Davenport Iowa The 1866

2   April 8th

3   Rev. S. R. Riggs

4a   Mihuŋkawaŋżi

4b   My brother

5a	Ito	táku	waŋżi	eciciye	kte	do	Maka	akan	mitakuye
5b	Well	what	one	say to you	shall/will	it is so	Earth	upon	my relatives

5c   Well, there is something I will say to you—it is so.   You said, I will be able

6a	wawicawahdake	kta	kéha	úŋkaŋ	hécen	Waŝtewadake
6b	I see my own	shall/will	you said	and	therefore	to love

6c   to see my earthly relatives, and so I loved that.

7a	tuka	winohca	mitawa	tóken	uŋ	kta	hwo	Epca	úŋkaŋ	hécen
7b	but	woman	my/mine	how	to be	will	taken care	I think	and	therefore

7c   I think about the uncertain condition my wife will be in and therefore

8a	Ninaĥin	Ŝíce Wadake	Eya	om	Waŋcake	Wítaya	Wawicawahdaka
8b	especially/very	hate that	Also	with	at once	together	I see my own

8c   I dislike that very much.   Also, it would be good if I could see my own relatives,

9a	uŋkaeŝ	micaŋte	Waŝte	kta	Tka	Epca	Tuka	hécen	hekeŝ
9b	if	my heart	good	shall/will	but	I think	But	so/in this way	that although

9c   immediately, that would make me happy, I think.   I would love that very much,

10a	Ekta	wahdiyahde	kta	owakihi	kehe	ciŋ	héoŋ	Waŝtewadake
10b	at	bring home	shall	I can do	you said that	the	therefore	to love

10c   if I could bring home my wife and my relatives.

11a	ho	hécen	he	winohca	Kiŋ	ate	tóked	uŋpi	héciŋhaŋ	He	ekta
11b	yes	therefore	that	my woman	the	father	how	they are	if it is so	that	at

11c   Yes, therefore, I think of how my wife and father are, and how it would be

12a	kci	wauŋ	Ekeŝ	epca	Eciŋ	Tuŋkaŋwicaŝta	hena	om	uŋ
12b	with	to be	well/although	I think	to think	fathers-in-law	those	with	to be

12c   to be with them, I would love that.   The fathers-in-law the women are

13a	tuka	hécen	Taŋyaŋ	Wicayuha	ŝni	kéya	ohdakapi
13b	but	therefore	well	to have/keep	not	to say that	they told of their own

13c   living with are not treating them very well, the women have said this themselves.

>

48. Maȟpiyacokayamani, April 8, 1866

Davenport Iowa The 1866
April 8th

Rev. S. R. Riggs

Mihuŋkawaŋji

Ito taku wanji eciciye kte do Maka akan mitakuye wawicawahdake kta keha unkan hecen Waśtewadake tuka winurca mitawa token un kta hwo Epca unkan hecen Ninarin Śice Wadake Eya om Wancake Witaya Wawicawahdaka unkaeś micante Waśte kta Tka Epca Tuka hecen heqeś Ekta wahdiyahde kta owakihi he hecin heun Waśtewadake ho hecen he winorca Kin ate toke unpi hecinhan He ekta kci waun Eqeś epca Ecin Tunkanwicaśta hena om un tuka hecen Tanyan Wicayuha śni keya ohdakapi

\>

• • • •

48. Walks Among the Clouds, April 8, 1866

Davenport Iowa The 1866
April 8th

Rev. S. R. Riggs

My brother

Well, there is something I will say to you—it is so. You said, I will be able to see my earthly relatives, and so I loved that. I think about the uncertain condition my wife will be in and therefore I dislike that very much. Also, it would be good if I could see my own relatives, immediately, that would make me happy, I think. I would love that very much, if I could bring home my wife and my relatives. Yes, therefore, I think of how my wife and father are, and how it would be to be with them, I would love that. The fathers-in-law the women are living with are not treating them very well, the women have said this themselves.

\>

14a   Eya   he   taku waŝtewadaka Waŋżi Tuŋkaŋŝidaŋ Ecaŋnicuŋ   kta

14b   also/too that what I love/like that one   grandfather   to do for one   shall/will

14c   What you said about what the President said he would do something for you,

15a   kéha   tuka hécen   Dehaŋyaŋ Décen   wauŋ

15b   you said that but   therefore so long   so/after this manner to be

15c   I like, but so far things remain the same for me.

16a   Ho mihuŋkawaŋżi hécen   waciŋ   uŋ   Nínaĥin ómayakiye kta   Waciŋ

16b   yes my one brother so/therefore I want to be greatly   to help me shall/will   I want

16c   Yes, my brother, I want you to help me, so if you will help me, that would be great.

17a   Henana   Epe   kte   Do

17b   only so much I say shall/will it is so

17c   That is all I will say—it is so.

18a   Maĥpiyacokayamani

18b   Walks Among the Clouds

Eya he taku waśtewadaka Wanji Tunkanśidan Ecannicun kta keha tuka hecen Dehanyan Decen waun Ho mihunkawanji hecen wacin un Ninarin omayakiye kta Wacin Henana Epe kte Do

    Maḣpiyacokayamani

• • • •

What you said about what the President said he would do something for you, I like, but so far things remain the same for me. Yes, my brother, I want you to help me, so if you will help me, that would be great. That is all I will say—it is so.

    Walks Among the Clouds

MS/AC

1a   tamakoce   mihuŋkawaŋźi
1b   His Country   my one brother
1c   Rev. Stephen R. Riggs, my brother

2a	Nakaha	wówapi	cícaġe	do	tóken	waun	kiŋ	ociciyake	kte	do
2b	Now	letter	I make you	it is so	how	I am	the	I tell you	shall	it is so

2c   I now write you this letter—it is so.   I will tell you how I am doing—it is so.

3a	iŝtamaġoŋġa	ca	iyotaŋhaŋiyewakiye	do	tuka	táku	waŋźi	kiksuya
3b	I am blind	and	experiencing difficulty	it is so	but	what	one	remember

3c   I am blind and experiencing great difficulty—it is so.   But there is one thing I

4a	waun	do		niye	eya a	waŋźi	he	wake	do
4b	I am	it is so		you	you said	one	that	I mean	it is so

4c   continue to remember—it is so.   I am referring to one of the things you said—it is so.

5a	ŝuŋkawakaŋ	2	imakicupi	úŋkaŋ	héoŋ	niŝ	táku	iyecen	wadake
5b	horses	two	they took	and	therefore	you	what	like	you will

5c   When they took two of my horses, you said you will

6a	kta	ce	ehe cikoŋ	Dehaŋ	iŝtamaġoŋġa	tuka	tókenken	mawani
6b	shall	when	you said	Now	I am blind	but	in what way	I walk

6c   get back the same at the right time.   But now I am blind and wherever I walk

7a	ka	maĥicahaŋ	ca	eya a ciŋ	he e	weksuya	ece	do	eciŋ
7b	and	I stumble	and	you said	that is it	I remember	always	it is so	then indeed

7c   I stumble and it always causes me to remember what you said—it is so.   Indeed,

8a	Wicaŝta	ksápa	henica	nakaŝ	táku waŝte	ehe cikoŋ	hena	kiksuya	waun	do
8b	man	wise	you are	indeed	what good	you said	those	remember	to be	it is so

8c   you are a wise man, and it causes me to remember the good things you said—it is so.

9a	ḳa	hehan	wópetoŋ	háŋska	aġuyapi	wikcemna	tom	uŋḳupi	kéya
9b	and	then	Long Buyer		flour	ten	four	gave us	he said

9c   And then General Sibley said they gave us forty sacks of flour

10a	úŋkaŋ	ake	ŝakowiŋ	uŋḳupi	do	ḳa	etaŋhan	Wikcemna	núŋpa	ḳa	sáŋpa	3
10b	and	again	seven	gave us	it is so	and	from	ten	two	and	plus	3

10c   and again they gave seven more—it is so.   And from that twenty-three of those

11a	hena	tokaĥoŋ	kiŋ	sdonuŋyapi	ŝni	do		hécen	ŝica
11b	those	lost	the	we know	not	it is so		therefore	bad

11c   are missing and we don't know where they disappeared to—it is so.   So we consider that bad

12a	uŋdakapi	do	ihaŋktuŋwaŋna	wicaḳupi	naceca	uŋkeciŋpi	do
12b	we think badly	it is so	The Yanktonnais	have given	may	we think	it is so

12c and don't like it—it is so.   We think that maybe they may have given it to the Yanktonai—it is so.

13a	hehan	táku	waŋźi	iyomakipi	ŝni	he	ociciyake	kta
13b	then	what	one	I like	not	that	I tell you	shall

13c There is one thing I don't like, I want to tell you about it.

>

49. Wiŋyuha Noŋpakiŋyaŋ, [1866]

tamakoce mihunkawanzi

Nakaha wowapi cicage do itoken waun kin ociciyake kte do ixtamaguga ça iyotanhaniyewakiye do tuka taku wanji kiksuya waun do niye iya a wanji he wake do xunkawakan 2 imakicupi unkan heun nix taku iyecen wadake kta ce ehe ciqu Dehan ixtamaguga tuka taku qin mawani qa maricahan ca iya a cin he e weksuya ece do ecin Wicaxta ksapa henica nakax taku waxte ehe cin hena kiksuya waun do qa hehan wopeton hanska aguyapi wikcemna tom unqupi keya unkan ake xakowina unqupi do qa etanhan Wikcemna nupa qa sapa 3 hena tokaran kin sdonunyapi xni do hecen xice undakapi do ihanktunwana wicaqupi naceca unkecinpi do hehan taku wanji iyomakipi xni e ociciyake kta

>

• • • •

49. Has A Woman Two Places, [1866]

Rev. Stephen R. Riggs, my brother

I now write you this letter—it is so. I will tell you how I am doing—it is so. I am blind and experiencing great difficulty—it is so. But there is one thing I continue to remember—it is so. I am referring to one of the things you said—it is so. When they took two of my horses, you said you will get back the same at the right time. But now I am blind and wherever I walk I stumble and it always causes me to remember what you said—it is so. Indeed, you are a wise man, and it causes me to remember the good things you said—it is so. And then General Sibley said they gave us forty sacks of flour and again they gave seven more—it is so. And from that twenty-three of those are missing and we don't know where they disappeared to—it is so. So we consider that bad and don't like it—it is so. We think that maybe they may have given it to the Yanktonna—it is so. There is one thing I don't like, I want to tell you about it.

>

14a Wicaśta óta nína wicaśtayatapi akitapi he e Wake do wicaśtayatapi óta
14b Men many very chief/leader look for that is I mean it is so chief/leader many
14c Many men are looking to become a chief, that's what I mean—it is so. And there are many

15a úŋkaŋ makoce kiŋ owaŋcaya śíca he sdonwaye do. Qa wanakaźa
15b and country the everywhere bad that I know it is so And long ago
15c chiefs all over the country and many are bad, I know that—it is so. And a long time ago

16a Wicaśtayatapi waŋźigźidaŋ úŋkaŋ waśte he sdonwaye do. Hena idukcan
16b chief/ruler some and good that I know it is so Those to think/decide
16c there were some good chiefs I know that—it is so. I want you to think

17a kta waciŋ ye do. Qa tuwe kośka wicaśtayatapi ca waśaka śni
17b shall I want it is so And who a young man a chief/ruler and strong not
17c about that—it is so. And when a young man is the chief usually he would not be strong,

18a ce ece hena Sdonyaye do. Kośka kiŋ waĥaŋičidapi nakaś
18b when usually those you know it is so a young man the they are arrogant truly
18c those things I know—it is so. Young men are truly arrogant,

19a Héoŋ hécece do. Tuwe wicaĥca waŋźi Wicaśtayatapi
19b therefore always so it is so who older man one a chief/ruler
19c that is why they're always like that—it is so. If an older man was chief

20a kinhan he e waśte kte do. He e Táku waśte ece caźeyad
20b if it is he good shall it is so. It is he what good usually in the name of
20c he would be good—it is so. Usually, people mention their names

21a yaḳoŋpi do. He caźedate Waciŋ uŋ etaŋhaŋ ociciyake do.
21b they are it is so That mention I want to be from I tell you it is so.
21c if things are good—it is so. I want you to mention this, that is why I'm telling you—it is so.

22a Peźihutazizi Oyate kiŋ hen nom héca akinicapi he iyomakipi śni
22b Yellow Medicine people the there two such they argue that I like not
22c There are two men at Yellow Medicine having an argument over this, I don't like it—

23a do. Hécen Cotaŋka inape he e oie oĥaŋ ko waśte Do.
23b it is so Then Flute Appears it is he a word action also good it is so.
23c it is so. Accordingly, there is one, Appearing Flute, his word and action are both good—it is so.

24a Hehan iś nakuŋ qa Napeśa nína ciŋ do. Hehan nakuŋ
24b Then he/she/it also and Red Hand very want it is so Then also
24c Then, Red Hand also really wants to be chief—it is so. Then Left Hand

25a Wakiŋyaŋ catka he nína ciŋ do Qa Napeśa Wakiŋyaŋ catka he
25b Thunder Left that very want it is so And Red Hand Thunder Left that
25c Thunder really wants to be chief—it is so. Neither Red Hand or Left Hand Thunder are

26a uŋmana héca pi kta iyececa śni se ecece do.
26b Neither such they shall such as not as if it was it is so
26c not good choices and should not be considered for leadership—it is so.

>

Wicaxta ota nina wicaxtayatapi akitapi he e Wake do. wicaxtayatapi ota unkan makoce kin owancaya śica e sdonwaye do. Qa wanakaja Wicaśtayatapi wanjigjidan unkan waśte e sdonwaye Do. Hena idukcan kta wacin ye do. Qa tuwe kośka wicaśtayatapi ca waśaka śni ce ece hena Sdonyaye do. Kośka kin waraniçidapi nakaś Heon hecece do. Tuwe wicarinca wanji Wicaśtayapi kinhan he e waśte kte do. He e Taku waśte ece cajeyad yakonpi do. He cajedate Wacin on etanhan ociciyake do. Pejihutazizi Oyate kin hen nom heca Akinicapi he iyomakipi śni do. Hecen Cotanka inape he e oie oran ko waśte Do. Hehan iś nakun ka Napeśa nina cin do. Hehan nakun Wakinyan catka he nina cin do. Qa Napeśa Wakinyan catka he onmana heca pi kta iyececa xni se ecece do.

>

• • • •

Many men are looking to become a chief that's what I mean—it is so. And there are many chiefs all over the country and many are bad, I know that—it is so. And a long time ago there were some good chiefs I know that—it is so. I want you to think about that—it is so. And when a young man is the chief usually he would not be strong, those things I know—it is so. Young men are truly arrogant, that is why they're always like that—it is so. If an older man was chief he would be good—it is so. Usually, people mention their names if things are good—it is so. I want you to mention this, that is why I'm telling you—it is so. There are two men at Yellow Medicine having an argument over this, I don't like it—it is so. Accordingly, there is one, Appearing Flute, his word and action are both good—it is so. Then, Red Hand also really wants to be chief—it is so. Then Left Hand Thunder really wants to be chief—it is so. Neither Red Hand or Left Hand Thunder are not good choices and should not be considered for leadership—it is so.

>

27a   Ecin   hena   Táku wakan   awaciŋpi   śni   kiŋ   hécapi   do.
27b   Then indeed   those   Great Spirit   to believe in   not   the   they're such   it is so
27c   Then indeed, both are non-believers in the Great Spirit, they're that type of person—it is so.

28a   qa   uŋkiye   qa   Tapetataŋka   kici   den   Wauŋ   tka   héca   uŋkakitapi   śni
28b   And   we   and   His Big Fire   with   here   to be   but   such   to make effort to get   not
28c   We together with His Big Fire will remain here but we are not enthused about it—

29a   do.   Uŋkiye   hena   es   Wicaśtayatapi   etaŋhan   uŋkicaǵapi   tka uŋkiye   qa
29b   it is so   We   those   are chief/ruler   from   we grew up   but we   and
29c   it is so.   We are descendants who come from chiefs but we grew up afraid of

30a   héca   kouŋkipapi   do.   Hehan   eya   teĥiya   wauŋ   e
30b   such   we are afraid   it is so   Then   also/too   with difficulty   to be   at
30c   such responsibility—it is so.   Then I want to tell you I am

31a   ociciyake   Tókiyataŋhan   táku   wókamna   owasiŋ   owakihi   śni   qa
31b   I tell you   from where   what   wages/to get   all   I am able to   not   and
31c   having a difficult time, I can't find any work anywhere and I don't have

32a   Śúŋkanwakaŋ   manica   tka   óhinni   uŋhdaka   wauŋ   e cée   do.
32b   horses   I have none   but   always   move about   to be   usually   it is so
32c   any horses, but usually I am able to move about from place to place—it is so.

33a   qa   tókiyataŋhan   táku   bduhe   kta   oyakihi   úŋkaŋŝ   Táku wakaŋ
33b   and   from what place   what   I have   shall   I am able to   if   Great Spirit
33c   If you will get some things for me from somewhere, the Great Spirit

34a   waśtedake   kta   tka   héoŋ   táku Wakaŋ   tóken   waciŋwaye   hécihaŋ
34b   to love   shall   but   therefore   Great Spirit   how   I depend on him   if it is so
34c   will love that.   Therefore, in the same way that I depend upon the Great Spirit,

35a   he   Iyecen   waciŋciye   do.   Qa   nína   ómayakiye   waciŋ   do
35b   that   like   I depend on him   it is so   And   very   to help me   I want   it is so
35c   I likewise depend upon you—it is so.   And I really want you to help me—it is so.

36a   Hehan   Oyate   kiŋ   de   táku Wakaŋ   tóken   waciŋunyaŋpi   hécihaŋ   ociciyake
36b   Then   people   the   this   Great Spirit   how   to depend upon   if it is   so I tell you
36c   Then, I will tell you how these people depend upon the

37a   kte   do.   Qa   táku wakan   cékiyapi   ca   Típi   kiŋ   tóna
37b   shall   it is so   And   Great Spirit   they pray   when   house   the   those
37c   Great Spirit—it is so.   And when those persons who made it home pray to the Great Spirit

38a   kípi   henakca   ożudaŋ   ce e   do.   Tka   nahahiŋ   waŋżigżi
38b   arrive at one's house   so many   full   usually   it is so   But   yet   some
38c   the church is usually full—it is so.   But there are some

39a   ópapi   śni   do.   Héoŋ   óhiŋni   icaŋtemaśica   waoŋ   do.
39b   they join   not   it is so   Therefore   always   I am worried   to be   it is so
39c   who have not joined—it is so.   Therefore, I am always worried—it is so.

Ecin hena Taku wakan awacinpi śni kin hecapi do. qa unkiye qa Tapetatanka kici den Waon tka
heca onkakitapi śni do. Unkiye hena es Wicaśtayatapi etanhan onkicagapi tka onkiye qe heca
koonkipapi do. Hehan eya teriya waon e ociciyake Tokiyatanhan taku wokamna owasin owakihi
śni qa Śunkawakan manica tka ohni onhdaka waon e cee do. qa tokiyatanhan taku bduhe kta
oyakihi unkanś Taku wakan waśtedake kta tka heon taku Wakan token wacinwaye hecinhan
he Iyecen wacinciye do. Qa nina omayakiya wacin do. Hehan Oyate kin de taku Wakan token
wacinonyanpi hecinhan ociciyake kte do. Qa taku wakan cekiyapi ca Tipi kin tona kipi henakca
ojudan ce e do. Tka naharin wanjigji opapi śni do. Heon ohni icantemaśica waon do.

>

• • • •

Then indeed, both are non-believers in the Great Spirit, they're that type of person—it is so.
We together with His Big Fire will remain here but we are not enthused about it—it is so. We
are descendants who come from chiefs but we grew up afraid of such responsibility—it is so.
Then I want to tell you I am having a difficult time, I can't find any work anywhere and I don't
have any horses, but usually I am able to move about from place to place—it is so. If you will
get some things for me from somewhere, the Great Spirit will love that. Therefore, in the same
way that I depend upon the Great Spirit, I likewise depend upon you—it is so. And I really
want you to help me—it is so. Then, I will tell you how these people depend upon the Great
Spirit—it is so. And when those persons who made it home pray to the Great Spirit the church
is usually full—it is so. But there are some who have not joined—it is so. Therefore, I am always
worried—it is so.

>

40a   Owasiŋ ópapi   úŋkaŋŝ waŝtewadake kta   tka   do.   Hehan   Waŝicuŋ wakaŋ
40b   All   they join if   I love that   shall but it is so Then   white ministers
40c   But if all of them joined I would love that very much—it is so.   Then, you white ministers that are

41a   yauŋpi   kiŋ Táku wakaŋ kiŋ he   iyecen Maka akaŋ Waciŋuŋniyaŋpi do.
41b   they are the Great Spirit the that like   earth upon we depend upon it is so
41c   here upon this earth, we depend upon you just like the way we depend upon the Great Spirit—it is so.

42a   hécen   óhiŋni táku Wakaŋ Céuŋkiyapi ca   uŋniksuyapi   ce e   do
42b   therefore always Great Spirit we pray to and   we remember you when it is so
42c   Therefore, each time when we pray to the Great Spirit we remember you—it is so.

43a   Nis he   iyecen Maka Akaŋ uŋyeksuyapi   kta   waciŋ yedo.   Qa
43b   you that like   earth upon you remember us shall I want it is so And
43c   We want you to remember those of us on this earth—it is so.   And

44a   hehan táku Tókeca   epe   kte   do.   Mr. Wópetoŋ háŋska Den hi
44b   then   what different I say shall it is so Mr. Long Buyer   here came
44c   then I shall say something different—it is so.   When General H. Sibley came here

45a   úŋkaŋ Wakpa ipakŝaŋ kiŋ Hen   uŋkaŋpi kta   kéye   do.   Wakpa ipakŝaŋ
45b   and   Bend in River the there we are to shall he said it is so Bend in River
45c   he said we would be living at Bend in River [Flandreau]—it is so.   I think if

46a   caŋoikpa   kiŋ héci uŋkaŋpi   kiŋhaŋ Waŝte kta Ibdukcaŋ   do.
46b   tip of trees the there we are to be if   good   shall I think/thought it is so
46c   we live at the tip of woods at Bend in River, that would be good—it is so.

47a   qa Mniŝoŝe   Ikiyedaŋ uŋkaŋpi   kiŋhaŋ Hótaŋka   qa Omaha nína uŋktepi
47b   and Missouri River near   we are to be if   Winnebagos and Omahas very kill us
47c   And if we stay near the Missouri River, I think the Winnebagos and Omahas will kill many

48a   kta Ibdukcaŋ   do   Qa hehan wówapi kiŋ De waŋdake ciŋhaŋ tóken
48b   will I think/thought it is so And then   letter the this you see if/when how
48c   of us—it is so.   And when you see this letter, I want you

49a   uŋyakoŋpi kta hécihaŋ omayakidake Kta waciŋ do.   Héoŋ   wówapi mayaku
49b   we are   shall if   to tell me   shall I want it is so Therefore letter   you give me
49c   to tell me where we will be staying at—it is so.   Therefore I want you

50a   Waciŋ yedo.   qa Wicaŝta   ksápa yauŋpi kiŋ Óhinni Cíksuyapi   do.
50b   I want it is so and man/men wise   you are the always we remember you it is so
50c   to write me a letter, it is so.   You are wise men, and I always remember you—it is so.

51a   qa Iŝta taŋka   He tohaŋ weksuya   ca   caŋtemaŝica   wauŋ Do
51b   and Eyes Large/Big that when I remember and to be sorrowful I am   it is so
51c   And when I remember Big Eyes, my heart becomes very sad—it is so.

>

Owasin opapi unkanś waśtewadake kta tka do. Hehan Waśincon wakan yaonpi kin Taku wakan kin he iyecen Maka akan Wacinonniyanpi do. hecen ohni taku Wakan Ceonkiyapi ca onniksuyapi ce e do Niś he iyecen Makan Akan onyeksuyapi kta wacin yedo. Qa hehan taku Tokeca epe kte do. Mr. Wopetonhanska Den hi unkan Wakpa ipakśan kin Hen unkanpi kta keye do. Wakpa ipakśan canoikpa kin heci unkanpi kinhan Waśte kta Ibdukcan do. qa Mniśośe Ikiyedan unkanpi kinhan Hotanke qa Omaha nina onktepi kta Ibdukcan do. Qa hehan wowapi kin De wandake cinhan token onyakonpi kta hecinhan omayakidake Kta wacin do. Heon wowapi mayaqu Wacin yedo. qa Wicaśta ksapa yaonpi kin Ohni Ciksuyapi do. qa Iśta tanka He tohan weksuya ca cantemaśica waon Do

>

. . . .

But if all of them joined I would love that very much—it is so. Then, you white ministers that are here upon this earth, we depend upon you just like the way we depend upon the Great Spirit—it is so. Therefore, each time when we pray to the Great Spirit we remember you—it is so. We want you to remember those of us on this earth—it is so. And then I shall say something different—it is so. When General H. Sibley came here he said we would be living at Bend in River [Flandreau]—it is so. I think if we live at the tip of woods at Bend in River, that would be good—it is so. And if we stay near the Missouri River, I think the Winnebagos and Omahas will kill many of us—it is so. And when you see this letter, I want you to tell me where we will be staying at—it is so. Therefore I want you to write me a letter, it is so. You are wise men, and I always remember you—it is so. And when I remember Big Eyes, my heart becomes very sad—it is so.

>

52a ḱa nakuŋ Iyohahiŋśma maka akaŋ niuŋ óhiŋni wéksuya do.
52b and also Hairy All Over earth upon to be living always remember him it is so
52c And also Hairy One All Over was alive upon this earth, I always remembered him—it is so.

53a Ĥtayetu waŋẓi Caŋuŋpé śni maka ca henaos wicaweksuye ce e do.
53b Evening one smoke not I sit and those two remember them when it is so
53c And on the evenings when I'm sitting and not smoking, I remember the two of them—it is so.

54a Hécen henana epe kte do.
54b Then only so much I say shall it is so
54c That is all I will say—it is so.

55a Mihuŋkawaŋẓi nitawiŋ kici nape ciyuze do And I kiss you
55b My one brother your wife with hand I hold it is so
55c My brother, I shake your and your wife's hands—it is so. And I kiss you.

56a Wiŋyuha Noŋpakiŋyaŋ he miye do
56b Has a Woman Two Places, that is me—it is so

qa nakun Iyorahinśma maka akan nion ohni weksuye do. Rtayetu wanji Cannope śni maka ca
henaos wicaweksuya ce e do.
Hecen henana epe kte do.
Mihunkawanji nitawin kici nape ciyuze do And I kiss you

Winyuha Nopakinyan hemiye do

• • • •

And also Hairy One All Over was alive upon this earth, I always remembered him—it is so.
And on the evenings when I'm sitting and not smoking, I remember the two of them—it is so.
That is all I will say—it is so.
My brother, I shake your and your wife's hands—it is so. And I kiss you.

Has a Woman Two Places, that is me—it is so

MS/AC

1a   Wíyawapi

1b   Month

2   Rev. S. R. Riggs

3a   Mitakuye   eya   wówapi   cícaga   óŋkaŋ   niŝ   wówapi   nakaha

3b   My relative   to say   letter   I make for you   and here   you   letter   now

3c   My relative, I write this letter to you, and now, you wrote me a letter,

4a   mayaḳu   héceŋ   ake   miŝ   wówapi   Cícaǧe   ca   tóken   waoŋ   kiŋ   heŋa

4b   you gave me   thus   again   me   letter   I make   for when   how   I am   the   these

4c   again, in writing this letter to you, I want you to know how I am.   Again,

5a   Ake   nayaȟoŋ   kta   waciŋ   ye do   Eya   taku   wakaŋ   waciŋye

5b   again   you hear   will   I want   it is so   Also   thing   holy   think about

5c   I want you to know how things are here.   Also, you want us to depend on the Holy Spirit,

6a   onyaŝipi   hécen   miŝ   dehaŋyan   iŝta   maǧoŋǧa   tuka   tawaciŋ   kiŋ

6b   you tell us   thus   I   so far   eye   blind   because   my mind   the

6c   so far I am blind, because, my relative, I am thinking

7a   eqeŝ   tóken   owakihi   hécen   waciŋyaŋ   waoŋ   do   eya   mihunkawaŋżi

7b   even so   how   I can   thus   thinking   I am   it is so   to say   one of my relatives

7c   about this.   I am thinking how I can do this.   Also, one of my relatives,

8a   iapi   waŋ   emayakiye   ciŋ   iyukcaŋ   waoŋ   kte   ye do   tapetataŋka   kici

8b   words   a   you told me   the   think   I am   will   it is so   His Big Fire   with

8c   I am thinking of what you said to me—it is so.   You told His Big Fire

9a   wahokuŋ   wicakiye   mayaŝi   kiŋ   he   ito   wani   ociciyake   kta   eya

9b   preach to them   you ask me to   the   this   well   now   I tell you   will   to say

9c   and me to preach, I will tell you this now.

10a   iŋhaŋktoŋwaŋ   oyate   kiŋ   he   taku   wakaŋ   oie   oŋ   wahokoŋ   wicakiyapi

10b   Yankton   people   the   this   thing   holy   word   to   preach to them

10c   I am preaching to the Yankton people about the Holy Spirit, it is hard to preach to the

11a   teȟike   ye do   tapetataŋka   Robert Hopkins   heŋaos   ekta   ípi

11b   hard   it is so   His Big Fire   Robert Hopkins   these two   at   arrive

11c   Yankton people—it is so.   His Big Fire and Robert Hopkins have come and preached to them,

12a   tuka   wicadapi   ŝni   ye do   hehaŋ   iapi   tókeca   eciciye   kta

12b   but   believe   not   it is so   then   speaking   different   speak to you   will

12c   but they don't believe—it is so.   I will tell you about another issue, I will tell you about

13a   makoce   en   tóken   oŋkaŋpi   kiŋ   he   ociciyake   kta   eya

13b   country   at   how   we are   the   this   I tell you   will/shall   to say

13c   how we are here, in this country.

>

50. Núŋpakiŋyaŋ, [1866]

Wiyawapi

Rev. S. R. Riggs

Mitakuye eya wowapi cicaga onkan niś wowapi nakaha mayaqu hecen ake miś wowapi Cicage ça token waon kin hena Ake nayaron kta wacin ye do Eya taku wakan wacinye onyaśipi hecen miś dehanyan iśta magonga tuka tawacin kin eqeś token owakihi hecen wacinyan waon do eya mihonkawanji iapi wan emayakiye cin iyukcan waon kte ye do tapetanka kici wahokon wicakiye mayaśi kin he ito wanji ociciyake kta eya inhanktonwan oyate kin he taku wakan oie on wahokon wicakiyapi terike ye do tapetanka Robert Hopkins henaos ekta ipi tuka wicadapi śni ye do hehan iapi tokeca eciciye kta makoce en token onkanpi kin he ociciyake kta eya

>

• • • •

50. Flies Twice, [1866]

Month

Rev. S. R. Riggs

My relative, I write this letter to you, and now, you wrote me a letter, again, in writing this letter to you, I want you to know how I am. Again, I want you to know how things are here. Also, you want us to depend on the Holy Spirit, so far I am blind, because, my relative, I am thinking about this. I am thinking how I can do this. Also, one of my relatives, I am thinking of what you said to me—it is so. You told His Big Fire and me to preach, I will tell you this now. I am preaching to the Yankton people about the Holy Spirit, it is hard to preach to the Yankton people—it is so. His Big Fire and Robert Hopkins have come and preached to them, but they don't believe—it is so. I will tell you about another issue, I will tell you about how we are here, in this country.

>

14a wóyute oŋ taŋyaŋ oŋkaŋpi ce epa tuka ake waŋna teȟiya oŋkaŋpi ye do
14b food is good we are this I say because again now terrible we are it is so
14c I say the food we are given is good, but now things have changed, it is terrible,

15a oyate tókece óta deŋ ahi qa héceŋ tuŋkaŋšidaŋ wóyute uŋqupi
15b people different a lot here arrive and then grandfather food gave us
15c they have brought a lot of different people, and then the President gave us food,

16a kiŋ oŋkišnana oŋtapi šni ye do eyako wacakipapi héoŋ óhiŋniyaŋ
16b the alone eat not it is so also they called thus always
16c we are sharing with these people—it is so.   Also, they called a lot of different people,

17a wówicaquipi ye do hehan ake taku waŋži caže mdata oŋkaŋ waŋna
17b feed them it is so then again thing one name I say and here now
17c they feed them—it is so. Again, I mentioned something, but you said this

18a okihipica šni kéha he niye he héceŋ epa héoŋ óhiŋni wakta waoŋ
18b can do not you said this you this thus I said thus always watchful I am
18c cannot be done. You said this.   I am always watchful, and saddened.

19a tuka waŋna tohaŋ qa okihipica šni kéha héceŋ nína Caŋte masice ye do
19b because now when and can be done not you said thus very heart bad it is so
19c Because now you said this cannot be done, thus, I am very heartbroken—it is so.

20a hehan mdowakatowan om oŋyakoŋpi om kiŋ he kinokaŋkiyaŋ
20b then Spirit Lake people with we are living with the this both sides
20c They have brought some Mdewakantonwan people, we are living together, so,

21a oŋyakoŋpi óŋkanš héceŋ waštewadake kta tuka wašicuŋ wakaŋ
21b we are living if then I like will because white man holy
21c we are living on both sides, and I like it.   And you white people

22a eceyedaŋ wanišakapi he ito yakuwapi qa oŋyakihipi óŋkanš pida
22b alone you are strong this well try/ attempt and you can if thank
22c are powerful, you can do something about this.   And because

23a onyayapi kta tuka ye do eciŋ mdowakaŋwaŋ hena tóhiŋni om
23b we be will because it is so suppose Spirit Lake people these never among
23c you will make us thankful—it is so. Because the Mdewakanton people, these we

24a onyaŋkoŋpi šni e sdoŋyaye heŋa teriya econpi qa dehan teriya
24b we live not this you know these terrible they did and now terrible
24c have not lived with, they have done some terrible things, now we are suffering

25a om oŋyakoŋpi tuka taku waŋži iyotaŋoŋ teȟiya
25b among we live because thing one more terrible
25c amongst them, because of one more terrible event.

26a oŋyaŋkoŋpi wapamŋipi eca pežihutazizi oyate kiŋ he ciŋstiŋna wicayaqupi
26b we are living at annuities truly Yellow Medicine people the this small/few getting
26c At annuities, we Yellow Medicine people are getting smaller portions.

>

woyute on tanyan onkanpi ce epa tuka ake wanna terinya onkanpi ye do oyate totokeca ota den
ahi qa hecen tonkanśidan woyute onqupi kin onkiśnana ontapi śni ye do eyako wacakipapi
heon ohinniyan wowicaqupi ye do hehan ake taku wanji caje mdata onkan wanna okihipica śni
keha he niye he hecen epa heon ohinni wakta waon tuka wanna tohan qa okihipica śni keha
hecen nina Cante maśice ye do hehan mdowakatowan om onyakonpi om kin he kinokankiyan
onyakonpi onkans hecen waśtewadake kta tuka waśicun wakan eceyedan waniśakapi he ito
yakuwapi qa oyakihipi onkanś pida onyayapi kta tuka ye do ecin mdowakanwan hena tohinna
om onyankonpi śni e sdonyaye hena teriya econpi qa dehan teriya om onyakonpi tuka taku
wanji iyotanon teriya onyankonpi wapamnipi eca pejihutazizi oyate kin he cinstinna wicayaqupi

>

• • • •

I say the food we are given is good, but now things have changed, it is terrible, they have
brought a lot of different people, and then the President gave us food, we are sharing with these
people—it is so. Also, they called a lot of different people, they feed them—it is so. Again, I
mentioned something, but you said this cannot be done. You said this. I am always watchful,
and saddened. Because now you said this cannot be done, thus, I am very heartbroken—it is
so. They have brought some Mdewakantonwan people, we are living together, so, we are living
on both sides, and I like it. And you white people are powerful, you can do something about
this. And because you will make us thankful—it is so. Because the Mdewakanton people, these
we have not lived with, they have done some terrible things, now we are suffering amongst
them, because of one more terrible event. At annuities, we Yellow Medicine people are getting
smaller portions.

>

27a	kta	ce	eya	oŋpi	kiŋ	he	iyotaŋ	wicoie	he	śíce	wadake	ye do
27b	will	so	I say	they live	the	this	more	word	is	bad	I think	it is so

27c So I say, I am not happy about this.

28a	oŋkiye	tuwedaŋ	wicaśta	yatapi	oŋhaŋpi	śni	ǫa	tuwedaŋ	óheŋa	caże
28b	us	no one	man	chief	have	not	and	no one	always	name

28c We are living here without a headman, we have no one

29a	oŋkiciyatapi	śni	ye do	héoŋ	he	Wópetoŋ	háŋska	oyakidaka	waciŋ	ye do
29b	speak for us	not	it is so	thus	this	Buyer	Long	tell him	I want	it is so

29c to speak for us here—it is so. I want you to tell Sibley.

30a	wana	każa	wicaśtayatapi	codaŋ	nóŋpapi	tuka	oŋkiye	hena	dehaŋ
30b	long	ago	man/chiefs	none	they two	because	speak for us	these	now

30c Long ago, we had two chiefs who spoke for us, now

31a	tuwedaŋ	wicakikśuye	śni	ǫa	wicaśtayatapi	codan	onyakonpi
31b	no one	remembers	not	and	man/chief	none	we live

31c no one remembers us, we are forgotten here, and we have no leader,

32a	ǫa	teȟiya	onyakonpi	ye do	Ínyaŋmani	ǫa	Núŋpakiŋyaŋ	henaoś
32b	and	terrible	we are living	it is so	Running Walker	and	Flies Twice	both

32c and we are living terribly—it is so. Running Walker and Flies Twice, these two

33a	naŋa	wicaśtayatapi	hécapi	tuka	ohakam	wicaśtayatapi	ota	áya	oŋkaŋ
33b	alone	man/chief	they are	because	later	man/chief	lots	say	and so

33c alone are chiefs of later times. Previously, there were a lot of chiefs,

34a	ociŋ	śíca	áye	ca	ecen	táku	teȟika	sdoŋoŋyaŋpi	hécen	dehaŋ	heŋa
34b	action	bad	say	so	thus	thing	terrible	we know	thus	now	these

34c some did bad actions, as you know, so I want you to call

35a	waśicuŋ	ekta	hena	nína	caże datapi	kta	waciŋ	ye do
35b	white man	at	these	very	call them	will/shall	I want	it is so

35c those white men, and let them know this—it is so.

36a	iho	hécen	mitakuye	henaŋa	epe	kte	ye do
36b	so then	thus	my relative	all	I say	will	it is so

36c So, my relative, that is all I have to say—it is so.

37a	Micaŋte	on	Nape	Ciyuze	ye do	Mitakuye
37b	my heart	use	hand	shake	it is so	my relative

37c I shake your hand with my heart, my relative—it is so.

38a	Mr. Hopkins	Núŋpakiŋyaŋ
38b	Mr. Hopkins	Flies Twice

39a	He miye	do
39b	It is me—it is so

kta ce eya onpi kin he iyotan wicoie he śice wadake ye do onkiye tuwedan wicaśta yatapi
onhanpi śni qa tuwedan ohena caje onkiciyatapi śni ye do heon he Wopeton hanska oyakidaka
wacin ye do wana kaja wicaśtayatapi nonpapi tuka onkiye hena dehan tuwedan wicakiksuye śni
qa wicaśtayatapi codan onyankonpi qa teriya onyakonpi ye do Inyangmani qa Nopakiya hena
osnana wicaśtayatapi hecapi tuka ohakam wicaśtayatapi ota aya onkan ocin śica aye ça ecen
taku terika sdononyanpi hecen dehan hena waśicon ekta hena nina caje datapi kta wacin ye do
iho hecen mitakuye henana epe kte ye do Micante on Nape Ciyuze ye do Nitakuye

    Mr. Hopkins   Nopakinyan
         He miye do

• • • •

So I say, I am not happy about this. We are living here without a headman, we have no one to
speak for us here—it is so. I want you to tell Sibley. Long ago, we had two chiefs who spoke for
us, now no one remembers us, we are forgotten here, and we have no leader, and we are living
terribly—it is so. Running Walker and Flies Twice, these two alone are chiefs of later times.
Previously, there were a lot of chiefs, some did bad actions, as you know, so I want you to call
those white men, and let them know this—it is so. So, my relative, that is all I have to say—it is
so. I shake your hand with my heart, my relative—it is so.

    Mr. Hopkins   Flies Twice
        It is me—it is so

MS/AC

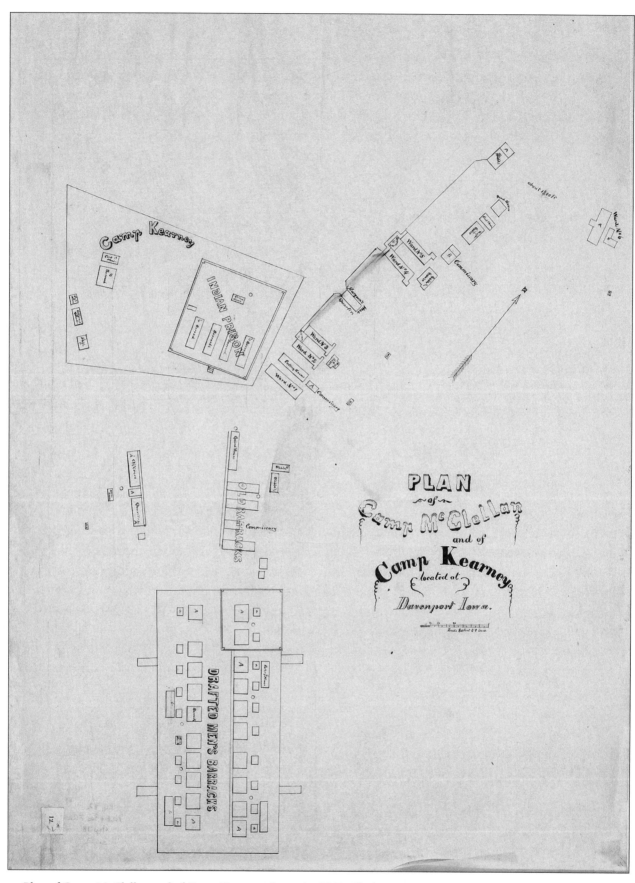

Plan of Camp McClellan and of Camp Kearney, drawn by W. D. Clark, Davenport City Engineer, late in 1865. The Indian Prison includes four barracks and a cook house. Other Camp Kearney buildings on this map are labeled, from top, cook house, barracks, cook house, officers' quarters, and stable.

Afterword

John Peacock

The Dakota–U.S. War of 1862 has long been a part of Dakota oral tradition, which, because unwritten, has never been given as much credence by historians as documents written by non-Natives at the time. In mainstream American culture, both popular and academic, writing trumps oral tradition every time as a putative source of historical truth. These translated letters now make available to everybody a primary documentary source of Dakota history not only through Dakota eyes but written by some of the same Dakota hands that brought life or death to their fellow human beings on the battlefield.

The translated letters are also a valuable tool for learning the once-suppressed and still endangered Dakota language. Perhaps most important, the Dakota letters are a resource for many of the writers' twenty-first-century descendants; until now, some of them have known no more about what happened to the writers than the writers themselves knew about their own displaced relatives, lost in the diaspora and so eagerly sought in these letters to missionary Riggs.

Every other year since 2002, descendants return to Minnesota from all over the United States and Canada to march along the same 150-mile route from Lower Sioux to Fort Snelling that 1,700 Dakota women and children had been forced to march in 1862. Some of these twenty-first-century descendants' reflections have been collected in *In the Footsteps of Our Ancestors: The Dakota Commemorative Marches of the 21st Century,* a book edited by Waziyatawin Angela Wilson. This book makes for poignant reading alongside the nineteenth-century Dakota letters. One twenty-first-century marcher, Edward Valandra from Rosebud, was made keenly aware on a commemorative march that able-bodied adult Dakota men like himself had been separated from the women, children, and old men on the original march in 1862. He wrote "it was excruciating for me to imagine that our men during that initial march could not perform their fundamental responsibilities of kinship for the most vulnerable of our nation."[1] As twenty-four leaders wrote in their petition to Sibley, one of the earliest letters from the Davenport prison, "Since last summer we have not seen our children and wives."[2] That had not changed almost three years later, on April 8, 1866, according to another letter to Reverend Riggs:

> My brother, Well, there is something I will say to you—it is so. You said, I will be able to see my earthly relatives, and so I loved that. I think about the uncertain condition my wife will be in and therefore I dislike that very much. Also, it would be good if I could see my own relatives, immediately, that would make me happy, I think. I would love that very much, if I could bring home my wife and my relatives. Yes, therefore, I think of how my wife and father are, and how it would be to be with them, I would love that. The fathers-in-law the women are living with are not treating them very well, the women have said this themselves.[3]

Not knowing if your family is alive is a relatively straightforward agony compared to the recriminations that have plagued Dakota people from 1862 to the present about what, if anything, they could or should have done differently—recriminations complicating and thus extending the grieving process for many Dakota descendants for whom the wounds from this war still run deep. What are some of these complicating factors? Some Dakota families, indeed some Dakota individuals within their own minds, were (and continue to be) split between allegiances to full-blood relatives versus to the whites they married and with whom they had mixed-blood children. Dakota did not generally trade with non-relatives, and they did not make war on relatives. Intermarriage with non-Dakota was traditionally the way Dakota made alliances for peace and trade with other groups; they had done this for generations with other tribal peoples, and, for over a hundred years before the Dakota War of 1862, traditional Dakota women formed what were at first known as "country marriages" with white fur traders, marriages not generally sanctified by Christian authorities, as they later would be after missionaries entered Dakota territory.

Dakota who, like many of the letter writers, refused to fight against whites to whom they were related by marriage were not "traitors of Dakota people"—the words are those of contemporary Dakota activist Waziyatawin Angela Wilson.[4] These Dakota protected their white relatives in accordance with customary Dakota obligations to relatives by marriage. The Dakota letter writers were preoccupied far more by family considerations than by either of the motives—insolence to whites, unequivocal loyalty to the Dakota war party—that their critics and champions, respectively, sometimes impute to them. Scholars and activists who want to determine which "side" the writers were on will be missing the point of those writers who, even if they did fight on the Dakota side, focused on the *noncombatant* status of the relatives they were often writing to missionary Riggs for help finding, some of whom, in the chaos of war, had protected or been protected by whites.

Diane Wilson, a 2002 Dakota Commemorative marcher who wrote about her great-great-grandmother, wondered "what it would be like for a Dakota woman married to a white man with mixed-blood children, with family inside the fort and family outside—what that would be like in the middle of the war."[5] Might not such a woman and her mixed-blood children have wanted to be reconciled to their white husband and father even (or especially) if he were fighting against their male Dakota relatives? One such Dakota woman was my own ancestor Nagitopawiŋ, Four Spirit Woman, whose name Dr. Canku showed me on the list of women prisoners at Fort Snelling after the 150-mile march of women and children. Because whites were and still are the spouses and parents of many Dakota children—my own father was white—any healing amongst Dakota people that does not include some sort of coming to terms with their white relatives will simply pass on the legacy of confusion and guilt to yet another generation of mixed-blood children, further deepening their wounds. For those who know little of the war beyond partisan views of it, for those who feel torn between Dakota and white worlds, it may be healing to learn how some of their nineteenth-century ancestors wrote these letters in order to bridge the two worlds that they, in their day, felt torn between.

Commemorative marcher Amy Lonetree wrote, "we as Native People have sought to emphasize only the stories of resistance . . . and have ignored . . . stories of capitulation and assimilation. At the same time, Whites in Minnesota have always honored the stories of Dakota capitulation and assistance to their cause in their remembrances of the war."[6] Commemorative march organizer and spiritual leader Leo Omani, former chief of the Wahpeton Dakota Nation near Prince Albert, Saskatchewan, wrote, "We were torn apart. It was beyond our control . . . And it's hard to talk about . . . because we know our relatives, which side they were on."[7]

Another Davenport prisoner, also one of my ancestors, Wakaŋhditopa, Four Lightning, aka David Faribault, ended up among those whom an 1867 Treaty called

> a portion of the Sissiton and Warpeton [*sic*] bands of Santee Sioux Indians, numbering from twelve hundred to fifteen hundred persons [who] not only preserved their obliga-tions to the Government of the United States, during and since the outbreak of the Mede-wakantons [*sic*] and other bands of Sioux in 1862, but freely periled [*sic*] their lives during that outbreak to . . . obtain possession of white women and children made captives by the hostile bands.

Executive Document 66 of the fifty-first Congress (January 28, 1890) said that these people "remained loyal to the Government and furnished scouts and soldiers to service against their own people."[8] They were given reservations at Sisseton and Fort Totten, where my grandfather and grandmother, respectively, were enrolled. After Grandmother's own mother died of smallpox, she was adopted by David Faribault's nephew, the mixed-blood George Faribault, translator of an 1873 Dakota Agreement that violated the 1867 Treaty by greatly reducing Dakota lands. The complicit George Faribault was as much my ancestor as was the victimized Nagitopawiŋ. Without them both, I would not exist.

Just as the Dakota letters shed light on Dakota oral history, some of the less often told Dakota oral stories of the war can bring some of the Dakota letters into sharp perspective. Sisseton elder Ed Red Owl recalls, "One of the chief scouts here tells . . . of encountering his own nephew. When he saw his nephew coming, he said, 'I had tears in my eyes, but yet I had orders of the United States Army to fulfill. And so before my own eyes, I shot him until he died.'"[9] Chris Mato Nunpa, retired associate professor at Southwest State University, noted that "our people had to make horrible, horrible choices" and wrote, "I was able to see John Other Day [who rescued sixty-two whites and scouted for the United States against other Dakota people] in a different light . . . [A]ll of us . . . descendants of people living back then [have] our own issues to deal with in terms of historical grief and trauma and real anger, real resentment. . . . As Dakota People, we need to do a lot of healing."[10]

Commemoration does not have to idealize our Dakota ancestors as unified in their resistance, and it should not idealize our ancestors in any other way if the purpose of commemorating them is to grieve and heal. Moving forward entails acknowledging the whole truth, not only about our just cause and the historical injustices done to us, but about the full range of our own and our ancestors' human reactions—sometimes heroic, sometimes not. Of our ancestors Chief Leo Omani rightly says, "we honor them. No matter which side they were on, it doesn't matter."[11] After Dr. Canku himself marched, he wrote "when people . . . march to reconcile a part of their history that has never been acknowledged, then they are slowly putting together the pieces of their lives, like a puzzle."[12]

These fifty letters are pieces of an enormous, difficult, and painful puzzle that we must all put together. Having once bridged Dakota oral and American epistolary cultures, the Dakota letters today serve as a bridge between Dakota oral and American historical accounts of the Dakota–U.S. War of 1862. The Dakota letters implode the false dichotomies of Dakota innocence and insolence, loyalty and disloyalty, leaving readers instead with the sentiment with which Dakota ceremonies, orations, and prayers traditionally close—*mitakuye owasiŋ,* we are all related.

Notes

Translator's Preface

1. *Davenport Democrat and News,* April 27, 1863. The letter referring to the men who disappeared is not included in this book.

2. Bonnie Sue Landes, *Creating Christian Indians: Native Clergy in the Presbyterian Church* (Norman: University of Oklahoma Press, 2003), 63.

3. Stephen R. Riggs, *Mary and I: Forty Years with the Sioux* (Boston: Congregational Sunday School and Publishing Society, 1887), 222.

4. As quoted in Nick Coleman, John Camp, and Joe Rossi, *The Great Dakota Conflict* (St. Paul: St. Paul Pioneer Press, 1987), 7, 9.

5. As quoted at http://discovery.mnhs.org/MN150/index.php?title=Nominations:U.S.%E2%80%93Dakota_War.

6. As quoted in Edward C. Valandra, "Decolonizing 'Truth': Restoring More than Justice," in Wanda D. McCaslin, ed., *Justice as Healing: Indigenous Ways. Writings on Community Peacemaking and Restorative Justice from the Native Law Centre* (St. Paul: Living Justice Press, 2005).

Introduction

1. For background on the camp, see Stephen R. Riggs, *Tah-koo Wah-kan, or, The Gospel Among the Dakotas* (Boston: Congressional Sabbath-School and Publishing Society, 1869), 372–91; Seth J. Temple, *Camp McClellan During the Civil War* (Davenport, IA: Contemporary Club and Davenport Public Museum, 1928), 28–41, 47–48; and James E. Jacobsen, "Iowa's Civil War Rendezvous Camps, 1861-1866, A Study" (History Pays! Historic Preservation Firm, February 23, 2011, copy in Davenport Public Library), 377-525.

2. William W. Folwell, *A History of Minnesota,* vol. 2 (St. Paul: Minnesota Historical Society, 1924; reprint ed., 1961), 249, quoting Riggs.

3. Beverly Olson Flanigan, "American Indian English and Error Analysis: The Case of Lakota English," *English World-Wide* 6.2 (1985): 223; Elizabeth S. Grobsmith, "Styles of Speaking: An Analysis of Lakota Communication Alternatives," *Anthropological Linguistics* 21.7 (October 1979): 360; William L. Leap, *American Indian English* (Salt Lake City: University of Utah Press, 1993), 127. Flannigan and Leap write about Lakota, which is a different dialect of the same language spoken by Dakota people.

4. Flanigan, "American Indian English," 218.

5. Flanigan, "American Indian English," 218.

6. Elias Ruban to S. R. Riggs, May 11, 1864 (not included in this book).

7. Elias Ruban to S. R. Riggs, November 14, 1864, Letter 19.

8. Beverly Olson Flanigan, "Language Variation Among Native Americans: Observations on Lakota English," *Journal of English Linguistics* 20.2 (October 1987): 229, 188.

9. Franz Boas and Ella Deloria, *Dakota Grammar, Memoirs of the National Academy of Sciences,* vol. 23 (Washington, DC: U.S. Government Printing Office, 1941), 3.

10. David Faribault and 23 others to Gen. H. H. Sibley, May 18, 1863.

11. Flanigan, "Language Variation," 188. In Dr. Canku and Mr. Simon's translations of the Davenport letters I can find none of the following other typical Dakota English features cited by Flanigan: "lack of subject-verb agreement [*he do that every day*] . . . lack of plural marking and number agreement [*there's two way of talking*] . . . tense shifting [*I came back and I stick with the elementary*] . . . uninflected or deleted verb *to be* [*this room too small*] . . . deletion of function words [prepositions, articles, conjunctions, and auxiliaries] [*we have bacon in morning*]" (Flanigan, "Language Variation," 184). Clearly Dr. Canku and Mr. Simon have used Standard English forms in these cases of grammar and syntax.

12. Leap, *American Indian English,* 243.

13. Flanigan, "Language Variation," 188.

14. R. D. Theisz, *Buckskin Tokens: Contemporary Oral Narratives of the Lakota* (Aberdeen, SD: North Plains Press, 1975), 44, quoted in Flanigan, "Language Variation," 229.

15. Antoine Provençalle to Stephen R. Riggs, August 22, 1864, Letter 14.

16. Cf. Jennifer Graber, "Mighty Upheaval on the Minnesota Frontier: Violence, War, and Death in Dakota and Missionary Christianity," *Church History* 80. 1 (March 2011): 76–108.

17. Flanigan, "American Indian English," 217.

18. Leap, *American Indian English*, 197.

Afterword

1. Waziyatawin Angela Wilson, ed., *In the Footsteps of Our Ancestors: The Dakota Commemorative Marches of the 21st Century* (St. Paul, MN: Living Justice Press, 2006), 189.

2. David Fairbault and 23 others to Gen. H. H. Sibley, May 18, 1863, Letter 2.

3. Walks in Center of Clouds to Stephen R. Riggs, April 8, 1866, Letter 48.

4. Waziyatawin, *What Does Justice Look Like? The Struggle for Liberation in the Dakota Homeland* (St. Paul, MN: Living Justice Press, 2008), 122.

5. Waziyatawin, ed., *In the Footsteps of Our Ancestors*, 127.

6. Waziyatawin, ed., *In the Footsteps of Our Ancestors*, 251.

7. Waziyatawin, ed., *In the Footsteps of Our Ancestors*, 251.

8. Fifty-first Congress Session, Ex. Doc. No. 66, Dept. Interior, Office of Indian Affairs, dated Washington, January 28, 1890, quoted in Waziyatawin, ed., *In the Footsteps of Our Ancestors*, 86.

9. Ed Red Owl, Minnesota Public Radio, September 26, 2002, "Execution and Expulsion" by Mark Steil and Tim Post in the MPR series *Minnesota Uncivil War*; quoted in Waziyatawin, ed., *In the Footsteps of Our Ancestors*, 64n9.

10. Waziyatawin, ed., *In the Footsteps of Our Ancestors*, 289.

11. Waziyatawin, ed., *In the Footsteps of Our Ancestors*, 251.

12. Waziyatawin, ed., *In the Footsteps of Our Ancestors*, 246.

Index

Italicized page numbers indicate an image.

Fischer Portrait Studio, Sisseton, SD   Nicolette Simon

Dr. Clifford Canku *(left)* is an assistant professor of Dakota Studies at North Dakota State University. Michael Simon *(right)* is an instructor of Dakota language for the Moorhead (Minnesota) Public Schools. Both are enrolled members of the Sisseton Wahpeton Oyate.